CIA
The Pike Report

CIA

The Pike Report

*With an introduction
by Philip Agee*

Spokesman Books
1977

Introduction © Spokesman Books 1977.

The publishers acknowledge their gratitude to the New York *Village Voice*, which first published Parts I and II of the Pike Report in newspaper format in February 1976.

Hardback edition: ISBN 0 85124 172 7
Paperback edition: ISBN 0 85124 173 5

Published by Spokesman Books for the Bertrand Russell Peace Foundation, Bertrand Russell House, Gamble Street, Nottingham.

Printed by the Russell Press Ltd., 45 Gamble Street, Nottingham NG7 4ET. Tel: (0602) 74505

Contents

Introduction by Philip Agee   7

Section One:

  The Select Committee's
  Oversight Experience   25

Section Two:

  The Select Committee's
  Investigative Record   96

Section Three:

  Committee Recommendations   257

Introduction

by Philip Agee

> "Pike will pay for this, you wait and see . . . We will destroy him for this."[1]

Strong words, quoted on the floor of the US House of Representatives by Congressman Otis Pike himself. He was quoting from an alleged threat made by Mitchell Rogovin, the CIA's Special Counsel for legal affairs, to Searle Field, staff director of the House Select Committee on Intelligence headed by Pike. According to Pike, the CIA's Counsel went on:

> "I'm serious. There will be political retaliation. Any political ambitions in New York that Pike had are through. We will destroy him for this."[2]

Pike's revelation of the threats, which were immediately denied by the CIA's Counsel, came on March 9, 1976, a month after his committee for investigating the CIA had submitted its recommendations and gone out of existence. Even if the threats were never made, or if they were in fact expressed in a milder, more suggestive fashion, they were consistent with the controversy within the committee and its stormy relations with the executive branch that had prevailed from the time the committee was established thirteen months earlier.

In his denunciation of the threats, Pike was reacting to a series of events that culminated only days earlier when New York's weekly *Village Voice*, in special supplements on February 16 and 23, 1976, published most of the secret report based on the work of Pike's investigating committee. Publication of the report, highlights of which had already leaked into the press from January 20 onwards, provoked an emotional and angry outburst from Secretary of State Henry Kissinger who was criticized severely in the report for his "passion for secrecy" and for making false statements to the Congress. At a news conference Kissinger denounced the committee's "totally irresponsible behaviour . . . the misuse of highly classified information in a tendentious and misleading manner [that] must do damage to the foreign policy of the United States . . . the use of classified information in a manner that is so distorted that the total impact is to produce a malicious lie . . . a new version of McCarthyism."[3]

Meanwhile a spokesman for the White House said President Ford believed the report published in the *Village Voice* was leaked by someone in the Congress, while Congressman Pike suggested that it was leaked by the Executive Branch to help the CIA by making the committee look bad. Only days later, in early March, the CIA claimed that the committee had failed to return, and couldn't find, some 230 documents, at least some of which were classified secret, that the Agency had given the committee in the course of its investigation.

Pike had problems with his own House of Representatives as well. As significant leaks of the report began to appear in the *New York Times* and other publications during the last two weeks of January 1976, then-CIA Director William Colby pleaded with the House not to publish the report because to do so would damage the country's intelligence activities and endanger Agency operations. Then on January 29 the full House voted to suppress publication until the White House had been able to censor it — an action tantamount to a rebuke by the House to its own investigating committee. After the vote against him, Pike described his committee's work as "an exercise in futility" and lamented that the House "probably will not ever have a strong oversight committee."[4]

Nevertheless, despite the House's submission to the executive, and despite renewed public sympathy towards the CIA with the executive's adroit manipulation of the killing of Richard Welch, the CIA Station Chief in Athens, in December, and despite the backlash against the continued leaks — not just from the House Report, it should be noted — despite all these factors militating against disclosure of the report, it got out.

In late January, someone still unidentified gave a copy of the report to Daniel Schorr, the CBS television news reporter based in Washington, who began using parts of the report in his broadcasting when its full publication was expected shortly — before the House voted to allow executive censorship. After the House vote, Schorr tried first to get the report published in book form, but in the anti-release-of-secrets atmosphere prevailing in February his only sure outlet was the *Village Voice*. After the *Voice* published, Schorr explained,

> "I found myself unexpectedly, because of a surprise action by the House, in possession of possibly the only available copy of a report, bearing no classification on its face, its principal sensations already divulged . . . My problem was that doing nothing would mean that I would be suppressing a report that might be interesting as a matter of public record."[5]

Schorr's admission brought calls in the House for revocation of his Congressional press credentials while at the same time the Department of Justice pondered whether he should be prosecuted under the espionage laws — thus reviving First Amendment issues left unresolved when the "Pentagon Papers" trial of Daniel

9

Ellsberg and Anthony Russo was aborted during the Watergate scandals. The House voted to have its ethics committee (House Committee on Standards of Official Conduct) investigate the leak, later appropriating $150,000 for the effort. CBS, for its part, suspended Schorr from all reporting duties pending the outcome of the Congressional investigation. Schorr was clearly, and surprisingly, on the defensive.

What had happened in the United States during the two months since Welch's death? It seemed that the American public had had enough. Almost two years had passed, beginning with publication in May 1974 after a long court battle of *The CIA and the Cult of Intelligence*,[6] during which one scandal and "abuse" after another were charged to the CIA, FBI and other security agencies. After an initial overlap with the Watergate episode and the end of the Nixon presidency, the scandals had grown dramatically with revelations of the CIA's subversion of the Allende government in Chile (September 1974) and of the CIA's massive, illegal domestic operations (December 1974). My own book on the CIA[7] appeared first in January 1975, the same month President Ford appointed the Rockefeller Commission to investigate the CIA's domestic activities, and the same month the Senate established its investigating committee under Senator Frank Church. By February 1976 when the Pike Report was published, a large sector of the American public seemed not to want to hear it — some, no doubt, having no more stomach for scandal, disillusion and moral conflict; others, surely, because they were beginning to realize just how damaging the revelations had become.

In the midst of the controversy, on February 17, President Ford seized more initiative by announcing his "reform" plan for the CIA and other security services. With media coverage that only an American

President can command, Ford described his executive order to strengthen the intelligence agencies, and he recommended to Congress a new law providing fines and prison terms for persons who disclose classified information. In his appeal for new legislation, Ford said,

"It is essential that the irresponsible and dangerous exposure of our nation's intelligence secrets be stopped. Openness is a hallmark of our democratic society but the American people have never believed that it was necessary to reveal secret war plans of the Department of Defense, and I do not think they wish to have true intelligence secrets revealed either."[8]

Nevertheless the world already had the Pike Report, a truly extraordinary and revealing document, thanks to the persistence and courage of Otis Pike and the members of his committee, of Daniel Schorr, and of the *Village Voice*. When reading the report one should keep in mind not only the conflicting circumstances surrounding its original publication, but also the quite real possibilities that existed during the committee's early months, first that the committee would make no real investigation, or, second, that the committee would be abolished before even beginning its work.

Established by a House resolution in February 1975, the Select Committee on Intelligence was first placed under the chairmanship of Representative Lucien Nedzi of Michigan who was also the chairman of the House Armed Services Intelligence Subcommittee. Since this Subcommittee had for many years exercised the House's watchdog responsibility over the CIA, Nedzi, as Chairman of the Select Committee, would in a very real sense be investigating his own performance. Fortunately he was subject to some strong and effective pushing from two Select Committee members whose opposition to the CIA's clan-

11

destine interventions abroad was well known: Michael Harrington of Massachussetts and Ronald Dellums of California.

Even so, by June 1975 the committee had hardly turned a stone when the *New York Times* dropped a blockbuster on them. On June 5 the *Times* revealed that two years earlier Nedzi had been briefed by the new CIA Director, William Colby, on the results of a recent CIA "in-house" investigation of assassinations, illegal operations, and other abuses. Nedzi had taken no action and had not even informed the other members of his House Armed Services Intelligence Sub-committee. Harrington, Dellums and liberals on the Select Committee demanded Nedzi's resignation, which he gave, but which was refused by the full House in a vote on June 16. Thereafter Nedzi refused to function as Chairman of the Select Committee, and a move began to abolish it.

Complicating the impasse was Nedzi's refusal to make classified information available to Harrington from Nedzi's Armed Services Intelligence Subcommittee because Harrington had been partly responsible for the leaking in September 1974 of details of the CIA's subversion of the Allende government. Harrington's information had come from the subcommittee documents of Nedzi, who was determined not to give Harrington any more ammunition.

Finally, on July 17, the House abolished the Select Committee under Nedzi and established a new Select Committee under the chairmanship of Otis Pike. Both Nedzi and Harrington were left off the new committee which set about the investigation that eventually produced the Pike Report. In one of those apparent contradictions not uncommon in American politics, Pike, 54, son of a Republican Long Island banker and representative of a conservative Long Island district, a Democratic Party member since he was 21 and foe of expensive Pentagon weapons projects, was responsible for some of the most important and enlightening revelations on CIA operations to date.

Part I of the Select Committee's report, published in the February 23 issue of the *Voice,* details the delays, obstructions and refusals by members of the executive, mainly Director Colby, Secretary Kissinger, and President Ford, to provide the documents needed by the committee for its investigation. The main administration tactic was to delay turning over documents, in spite of the President's public assurances that he would cooperate in making available all material in the executive branch. This tactic eventually provoked a number of subpoenas by the Pike committee, some of which at length brought forth the documents. Yet the administration, knowing that the committee had a short lifetime and was working against an approaching deadline, stalled on issue after issue in order to conceal a maximum amount of material over the investigative period. Thus the committee, which wasted the February-July period in internal disputes, really only had about five months — from August to December 1975 — to do its investigation and get a report written and submitted to the House by its January 31, 1976 deadline.

Besides delay, the executive agencies also at times rendered important documents useless by excising significant content and even by flatly refusing to turn over documents requested by the committee. Finally, fierce battles were fought over the public release of information obtained by the committee: both over the specific information and the manner of release. Usually the reason given was some questionable allegation that revelation would endanger the "sources and methods" of the CIA or one of the other agencies. Yet another tactic was to prevent testimony by certain witnesses, as in the case of the State Department officer in charge of the Cyprus desk at the time of the coup against Makarios. This officer had written a dissenting report on the handling of intelligence in the State Department at the time of the Cyprus crisis, but he was prevented by Kissinger from testifying on what had happened and why he dissented. In another instance a witness who had revealed financial improprieties in FBI purchasing of wiretapping equipment was afterwards subjected to a six-hour "interview" by two FBI agents who convinced him to sign a statement recanting insignificant details of his testimony. The witness later repudiated the statement, claiming intimidation by the two FBI agents.

With all the administration's delays, refusals of documents, interference with testimony and deletions of content, there can be no doubt that President Ford, Secretary Kissinger and Director Colby, to name only the major administration figures, were determined to prevent the Pike Committee from making a thorough and effective investigation. In this respect the charge can validly be made that the administration tried a cover-up operation with the Pike Committee, and to a certain degree probably succeeded.

Yet, the content of Part II of the committee's report is most extraordinary and revealing. The major sections deal with costs, failures to anticipate important events, and an analysis of covert action operations between 1965 and 1975. We find that the total US intelligence budget exceeds $10 billion. The Congress, however, which appropriates the money, has been told consistently that intelligence costs much less because intelligence activities have been placed in non-intelligence categories in the budget exercises. On analysis the foreign intelligence budget was found to total between three and four times more than Congress was told, while the domestic budget was more than five times the reported amount. The committee found accountability for secret funds lacking and the consequent spending abuses considerable. One CIA Station, for example, spent $41,000 on whisky and other alcoholic beverages during 1971, after which the Station Chief was placed in charge of Agency operations in Angola.

Failure to anticipate major events in recent years reflects, in the Select Committee's view, serious shortcomings of the entire US intelligence apparatus. The Tet offensive of 1968, for example, wasn't foreseen, partly, at least, because of the American prejudiced, degraded view of the Vietcong. Because the technical monitoring system lost track of the Russian army in Poland during the first two weeks in August 1968, American intelligence failed to detect the first Warsaw Pact invasion move against Czechoslovakia. President Johnson's first news of the invasion came from Soviet Ambassador Dobrynin in Washington. Similarly the Egyptian and Syrian attacks that launched the Yom Kippur war in 1973 caught the intelligence community by surprise, as did the coup in Portugal in April 1974, the Indian nuclear explosion in May 1974, and the coup against the Makarios government in Cyprus in July 1974.

The Select Committee's review of CIA covert action operations is perhaps the most interesting section of the report. Unfortunately the committee's attention was limited to the covert action projects approved by the Forty Committee during the 1965-1975 period. As only the most sensitive and costly projects required approval by Forty Committee, composed of the Assistant to the President for National Security Affairs, the Deputy Secretary of Defense, the Undersecretary of State for Political Affairs, the Chairman of the Joint Chiefs of Staff, and the Director of Central Intelligence, the Select Committee's investigation missed the vast majority of these kinds of operations which would have been approved internally in the CIA. Nevertheless the revelations on covert action in the report are quite significant.

We find, for example, that interference in the revered "free electoral processes" of other countries was the largest covert action category, comprising 32 per cent of the Forty Committee approvals. Twenty-nine per cent of approvals were for media and propaganda operations in which American government sponsorship was to be hidden. Twenty-three per cent of approvals were for paramilitary operations involving secret support to foreign armies and irregular military groups in the form of finance, training and weapons supplies. Still other CIA covert action operations involved CIA funding of a "plethora" of civic, religious, professional and trade union organizations.

In-depth analyses appear in the Select Committee's report of three major covert action projects, each of great interest. Intervention in Italian elections since 1948 cost the CIA $75 million, including $10 million spent in 1972 alone. Most of this money went to the Christian Democrats, although Ambassador Graham Martin obtained, over the CIA's objection, a donation of $800,000 in 1972 for political forces of the Italian neo-fascist movement. The Ambassador insisted on the donation in order "to demonstrate solidarity for the long pull". Underlining the CIA's intervention in Italy was the revelation, in early 1976, from government sources other than the Select Committee, that President Ford had approved in December 1975 the spending by the CIA of an additional $6 million in the Italian electoral process during the months preceding the next Italian elections. (At the time of approval it was not known that elections would be held as soon as June 1976.)

Paramilitary support by the CIA to the Kurdish rebellion against the Iraqi government from 1972 to

1975, which cost some $16 million, was initiated at the request of the Shah of Iran, then engaged in a border dispute with Iraq. Once the Iraqis agreed to a settlement favourable to Iran, the Shah had the support to the Kurds cut off. The rebellion collapsed, over 200,000 Kurds became refugees, and neither Iran nor the US set up adequate refugee assistance. As one high-ranking but unidentified witness told the Select Committee, "covert action should not be confused with missionary work".

The third major covert action operation examined by the Pike Committee was the CIA's intervention in Angola in support of the Holden Roberto and Jonas Savimbi forces. Here we find the conclusion that the massive Soviet and Cuban intervention was in large part a reaction to the CIA's prior intervention that threatened to upset the three-way stalemate existing before the CIA got going.

As a final observation on covert action operations, and one that is perhaps the most important of all, the Pike Committee destroyed the old doctrine of "plausible denial" whereby a President or Secretary of State could plead ignorance if operations went awry. In public testimony Secretary Kissinger admitted that every CIA operation of consequence was approved by the President, under the Ford as well as previous administrations. And in its report, the committee concludes, "All evidence in hand suggests that the CIA, far from being out of control, has been utterly responsive to the instructions of the President and the Assistant to the President for National Security Affairs."

For all the valuable information contained in the Pike Committee's report, one most important area of CIA operations was completely overlooked, possibly because the committee considered the matter too hot to handle. These are the relations between the CIA and foreign intelligence and security services — commonly known in the Agency as liaison operations. Through these operations the CIA trains, finances and in varying degrees guides the foreign services into operations that will help the CIA. Over the years the CIA has played a major role in the growth and strengthening of many of the world's most dreaded and cruel security services: the South Korean CIA, the Indonesian KOPKAMTIB, the Thieu security services in South Vietnam, the SAVAK in Iran, the OBAN, CODI, DOPS and SNI in Brazil, the DINA in Chile and the Federal Police in Argentina. These services and others helped by the CIA happen to be the most notorious practitioners of institutionalized torture and murder in the "free" world today. They also happen to be the main sustaining force for the gross social and economic injustices prevailing in their countries.

Nowhere in the Pike Report can one find an indication that the Select Committee even considered the CIA's role in promoting and supporting such repressive security services. On the contrary, the committee laments the termination of the AID Public Safety programmes of assistance to foreign police services (a "legitimate foreign aid programme") because of the CIA's involvement in it and bad publicity such as the film *State of Siege*. If the committee had wanted to get the truth, it could have discovered that the Public Safety programmes were an extension of operations already initiated by the CIA to establish better "internal security" in foreign countries — and that the CIA has continued police assistance work even though the Public Safety programmes were abolished.

If the Select Committee had investigated the CIA's liaison operations, they would also have discovered that these operations, while considered within

18

the CIA to be primarily counter-intelligence in nature, produce results quite similar to most covert action operations, i.e., they strengthen certain political forces and weaken others just as propaganda, labour and election operations do.

Only Congressman Ronald Dellums, in arguing for abolition of all covert action operations in the Recommendations section of the report, is willing to face the political issue:

> "Where have covert operations taken us? Are the nations that we have been involved with free democratic societies where the masses of people have benefits of democracy, or are those nations for the most part, military dictators, right-wing juntas, or régimes with extraordinary wealth and power in the hands of a few elitists? If the latter holds, it totally contradicts stated principles of this country. If we have been involved in covert actions which generated democracy, freedom and justice around the world, maybe we might arrive at some different conclusion. But I don't think anyone can justify continued covert action on grounds that we foster and develop democracy around the world."

Part III of the Pike Report outlines the Select Committee's 32 recommendations together with additional recommendations of individual committee members. This section was not meant to be kept secret and was not published by the *Village Voice* with Parts I and II. At its last session on February 10, the committee approved the recommendations which were then filed with the Clerk of the House for possible future action, and they were simultaneously released to the press. In fact there was little likelihood that the House would take early action on the proposals, partly because of the emerging US electoral campaigns, but mainly because of the general backlash against intelligence community "reformers" following the Welch death and the spate of leaked secrets — including Parts I and II of the Pike Report.

Most of the recommendations relate to increasing

Congressional control over the intelligence community, especially the CIA, and to improving the quality of management and of the intelligence product. The report recommends a permanent House Intelligence Oversight Committee along with closer review of intelligence spending. While the committee would require that the CIA advise the House Intelligence Oversight Committee within 48 hours of the approval of any covert action operation, the main restriction recommended is to limit each operation to 12 months. Assassinations and paramilitary operations would be prohibited except in time of war, and the general approval mechanism for covert action operations would be institutionalized and upgraded. Finally, the Pike Committee recommended that the Director of Central Intelligence become a real manager of the whole intelligence community and that an Inspector General for the community be established to watch out for "abuses".

Many will conclude that the Pike Committee failed because its recommendations were so limited and in any case would serve to strengthen the CIA and the other agencies. To evaluate the committee's work one must examine it along with the other investigative bodies: the Senate investigating committee under Frank Church, and the Rockefeller Commission. Both of these groups, and President Ford as well, in his "reforms" of February 18, 1976, concentrated quite naturally on the same areas as the Pike Committee: increasing Congressional oversight, improving the quality of intelligence and the management of intelligence agencies and their budgets, and preventing future "abuses". To expect more, like the complete abolition of covert action operations or prohibiting CIA support to foreign services that torture and murder, was unrealistic. After all, the CIA and the other services exist to protect both the government of which the investigators are a part and the private interests protected by the government.

Yet, for all the limitations of the reform exercise, the work of the Pike Committee and the other bodies is an exceedingly positive chapter in American history. Who would have dreamed, two years ago, that such a great volume of information on secret American intervention in foreign countries would ever be made public? Who would have dreamed that the vast, illegal domestic operations of the CIA, FBI and NSA would be revealed in great detail? Every bit of this information, together with the general methodology that emerges, can be used by people and organizations to protect themselves now and when the next wave of the same occurs. No doubt wide areas of CIA operations were omitted almost entirely, such as those in the trade union field, but no one can say the world's knowledge of secret intervention hasn't improved thanks to the investigations.

Of equal importance is the continuing strength of the best popular traditions in the United States that the investigations demonstrate: the free flow of information, resistance to oppression by government bureaucracy, resistance to government secrecy and coverups. Through the effective functioning of these traditions Americans have been able to learn how necessary corruption and hypocrisy are to the way the current system operates. Abolition of covert action operations, which corrupt the country's expressed principles, cannot come until fundamental changes are made in other institutions. Meanwhile, the treasure of knowledge gained through the investigations must surely contribute to the understanding that government in a "liberal" society must of necessity function in favour of one class and to the detriment of another.

In July 1976 the chief investigator of the House

Committee on Standards of Official Conduct, who had been trying since March to discover how the copies of Parts I and II of the Pike Report were leaked to Daniel Schorr, reported that nearly 50 copies of the report were in different executive and congressional offices when the leak occurred. None of the 207 government officials questioned, including Secretary Kissinger and the members of the Pike Committee, would admit to being the culprit. Thanks to one of them, at least, the Bertrand Russell Peace Foundation is able to present for the first time in book form Parts I, II and III of the Pike Report, a document of truly historic significance not only for Americans but also for peoples the world over who have suffered from clandestine American intervention.

Cambridge, England
August, 1976

FOOTNOTES

1. As reported in the *International Herald Tribune*, March 11, 1976.
2. Ibid.
3. *International Herald Tribune*, February 13, 1976.
4. *International Herald Tribune*, January 31-February 1, 1976.
5. Daniel Schorr, letter to the *New York Times* dated February 16, 1976, published in the *New York Times* February 22, 1976.
6. *The CIA and the Cult of Intelligence*, by Victor Marchetti and John Marks, Jonathan Cape, London, 1974; Coronet Books, 1976.
7. *Inside the Company: CIA Diary*, Penguin Books, Harmondsworth, 1975.
8. *Los Angeles Times*, February 19, 1976.

Section One:

The Select Committee's Oversight Experience

If this Committee's recent experience is any test, intelligence agencies that are to be controlled by Congressional lawmaking are, today, beyond the lawmaker's scrutiny.

These secret agencies have interests that inherently conflict with the open accountability of a political body, and there are many tools and tactics to block and deceive conventional Congressional checks. Added to this are the unique attributes of intelligence —notably, "national security,"[1] in its cloak of secrecy and mystery—to intimidate Congress and erode fragile support for sensitive inquiries.

Wise and effective legislation cannot proceed in the absence of information respecting conditions to be affected or changed.[2] Nevertheless, under present circumstances, inquiry into intelligence activities faces serious and fundamental shortcomings.

Even limited success in exercising future oversight requires a rethinking of the powers, procedures, and duties of the overseers. This Committee's path and policies, its pluses and minuses, may at least indicate where to begin.

Access to Information

The key to exercising oversight is knowledge. In the case of intelligence agencies, this translates into a need for access to information often held by the agencies themselves, about events in distant places.

It is an uncertain approach to gathering facts, given the best of circumstances. The best of circumstances thereby become a minimum condition.

The Select Committee's most important work may well have been its test of those circumstances, testing perhaps for the first time what happens when Congress unilaterally decides what it wants to know and how it wants to know it.

There were numerous public expressions by intelligences agencies and the Executive that full cooperation would be accorded.[3] The credibility of such assurances was important, since almost all the necessary materials were classified and controlled by the executive branch. Despite these public representations, in practice most document access was preceded by lengthy negotiations. Almost without exception, these negotiations yielded something less than complete or timely access.[4]

In short, the words were always words of cooperation; the reality was delay, refusal, missing information, asserted privileges, and on and on.[5]

The Committee began by asserting that Congress alone must decide who, acting in its behalf, has a right to know secret information. This led to a rejection of Executive "clearances"[6] or the "compartmentation"[7] of our staff. The Committee refused, as a matter of policy, to sign agreements. It refused to allow intelligence officials to read and review our investiga-

26

tors' notes, and avoided canned briefings in favor of primary source material. The Committee maintained that Congress has a right to all information short of direct communications with the President.

Our ability to abide by these policies has been a mixed record.

On the plus side, an aggressive pursuit of facts and a willingness to back up this pursuit with subpoenas produced some unprecedented results. As an example, never before had either the Executive or Congress put together a ten-year review of covert action projects. By subpoena—which, unfortunately, had to be taken to the brink of contempt enforcement—the staff of the Committee analyzed all official covert action approvals since 1965, and reported its results to the Committee in a closed hearing.[9] That presentation was one of the more interesting and accurate pictures of U.S. covert policies yet assembled, and was of no small value to our findings. Other examples appear throughout the remainder of this report.

Nonetheless, if that is the positive side, it was offset by the extraordinary efforts that were required, even in a climate favorable to reviewing past Executive conduct, to identify and obtain documents.

It is a commentary in itself that subpoenas were necessary.

It is a further commentary that much of the time subpoenas were not enough, and only a determined threat of contempt proceedings brought grudging results.

Footnotes:

[1]It is interesting to note that, despite volumes of literature, public utterance, and court cases on the subject, there are no clear definitions of what national

security is. E.q., Note 87 Harv. L. Rev. 976 (1974); Becker, *The Supreme Court's Recent "National Security" Decisions: Which Interests Are Being Protected?* 40 Tenn. L. Rev. 1 (1972).

[2]Justice Van Devanter, speaking for a unanimous Supreme Court, wrote that the Congressional "power of inquiry—with process to enforce it—is essential and appropriate as an auxiliary to the legislative function." *McGrain v. Daugherty* (1972).

Early in the history of our republic, the power was accompanied by "instructions to inquire into the condition of the various executive departments, and the ability and integrity with which they have been conducted." 13 Cong. Deb. 1057, 1067, (1836).

[3]In a letter to the Chairman dated October 14, 1975, Secretary of State Kissinger stated: "I have no desire to keep anything from the Select Committee with regard to the Cyprus crisis or any other subject." Letter to Chairman Pike, from Dr. Kissinger, State Dept., Oct. 14, 1975.

In a second letter to the Chairman, dated November 3, 1975, Dr. Kissinger again pledged his cooperation: "Let me reiterate that my intention is not to withhold any information of use to the Committee . . . I remain as determined as ever to do everything possible to assist the Committee in its difficult and important task." Letter to Chairman Pike, from Dr. Kissinger, State Dept., Nov. 3, 1975.

At a news conference on June 10, 1975, President Ford stated: "I will make available to the Senate and House Select Committees these [Rockefeller Commission] materials, together with other related materials in the executive branch." He went on to say: "So there's not going to be any possibility of any cover-up because we're giving them the material that the Rockefeller Commission developed in their hearings, *plus any other material that is available in the executive branch*." (Emphasis added.) President's News Conference, Wash. D.C., June 10, 1975.

[4]The following statement by the Chairman; on November 14, 1975, with reference to a subpoena of State Department documents, is typical:

"Chairman PIKE. That troubles me, Mr. McClory. The fact is that three days after the subpoena was due, we have nothing. You have had phone calls. Mr. Donner and Mr. Field have had phone calls. The President has not asserted executive privilege, but he hasn't done it."

The Committee also discovered what Chairman Pike described as the "dribble treatment," where one or two documents were delivered each day over the course of several weeks. This was a particularly subtle impediment, as it gave the executive branch an opportunity to deny that it was withholding information, while at the same time delaying the Committee's work.

In the domestic intelligence investigation, Drug Enforcement Administration documents, which had been requested for over three months, were opened for Committee "inspection" 48 hours before a hearing on DEA intelligence. Even then, a subpoena had been necessary to obtain information. The staff was not given access to the 17 so-called Kissinger wiretap materials until 24 hours before Dr. Kissinger appeared before the Committee; and that took place only after lengthy negotiations. (Justice Department memoranda relating to the 17 wiretaps are printed as pp. IX of the Comm. Hearings, Part 3.)

[5]The Chairman's comments on September 29, 1975, in a discussion of proposed agreements with the Executive, illustrate the point:

"Chairman PIKE. . . . You thought we had an agreement with the President two weeks ago—or a week and a half ago—and we adopted your proposals in order to get that agreement.

"Having adopted your proposals, they said, 'Well,

that is the first bite, now we will come back for some more.' They have now come back for some more.

"You want us to adopt these proposals. You keep seeing huge cooperation just around the corner and it is not there, and it has not been there."

At a Committee meeting early in September, the Chairman described the Committee's experience thus far with executive branch cooperation:

"Here is what we run into . . . Nothing is ever refused—things just are not delivered. They very carefully do not refuse, but the language is always the language of cooperation—the fact is the fact of non-production. . . ."

A month later, the degree of cooperation had not noticeably improved. As the Chairman stated:

"I think we all know what is going on here. You asked that we wait another week—and we can wait for another week. You say that we ought to be concerned with the official statements and, as I have indicated from the day I got on the Committee, the official statements always promise cooperation. There has never been an official statement which says, 'In no way are you going to get this information.' But the fact of the matter is that we don't get the information."

[6]The Committee did accept the assistance of the FBI in conducting background investigations of its staff prior to hiring. All decisions, however, concerning the members of the Committee's staff and their work were made by the Committee.

The Director of Central Intelligence requested that the Committee require its staff to sign secrecy oaths comparable to those which the CIA requires of its own employees. The Committee refused. However, each member of the staff was obliged by the Committee to sign an "Employee Agreement."

[7]"Compartmentation" is a system employed by the

intelligence agencies to restrict the distribution of information even among officials with security clearances. The justification for compartmentation is described in the following excerpts from a letter to the Chairman from CIA Director Colby, on July 28, 1975:

"National Security Council Intelligence Directive No. 1 (17 Feb. 1972) instructs the Director of Central Intelligence to '. . . develop and review security standards and practices as they relate to the protection of intelligence and of intelligence sources and methods from unauthorized disclosure.' Since the National Security Act did not provide for an authority corresponding with the DCI's responsibility in this area, the Directive provides that the Members of the U.S. Intelligence Board are responsible for: 'The supervision of the dissemination of security intelligence material.' The Director of Central Intelligence, acting with the advice of the U.S. Intelligence Board, has promulgated a number of directives, regulations, and security manuals, related to the protection of foreign intelligence and foreign intelligence sources and methods." Letter to Chairman Pike, from Mr. Colby, CIA, July 28, 1975.

[9]This report resulted from a subpoena of documents in possession of the "Forty Committee," which is a National Security Council subcommittee that approves covert action.

On November 14, by a vote of 10 to 2, the Committee approved a resolution citing Dr. Kissinger in contempt of Congress for his failure to comply with the Forty Committee subpoena. The report accompanying the resolution (94-693) was filed December 8. On December 10, after negotiations with White House officials, the Chairman informed the House that substantial compliance had been obtained, and the Committee's report was recommitted.

1. Delay

The record of subpoenas is worth reviewing.

It began on August 5, 1975, when an Assistant Secretary of Defense was asked to appear as a witness and bring with him the document by which the National Security Agency (NSA) was set up. It was a simple and logical request. The Defense Department controls NSA; the Comittee was holding hearings on intelligence budgets; NSA has the biggest budget; and the Committee wanted to see the authority by which NSA operates.

The official did not bring the document. He did not have "clearance" to.[10]

For this elementary piece of information, the Select Committee was forced to resort to the first of its many subpoenas. It is worth noting that the subpoena was promptly honored, which raises the question why the document was not delivered in the first place.

By late August, the Committee was preparing for hearings to review what kind of intelligence our money buys. Four events were chosen for hearings: the 1973 Mid-East war, the 1974 Cyprus coup, the 1974 Portuguese coup, and the 1968 Tet offensive in Vietnam. During August and early September there were repeated requests for documents and interviews.[13]

In some cases, we were given heavily "sanitized" pieces of paper. "Sanitized" was merely a euphemism for blank sheets of paper with a few scattered words left in, often illegible, sometimes misleading, and usually inconclusive.[14] In some cases, notably as to the 1974 coup in Portugal, there was an absolute refusal to provide anything, until early October.

As a last ditch effort, with hearings approaching, the Committee turned once again to its subpoena power. On September 10, 1975, it subpoenaed materials from the three major intelligence agencies and the National Security Council.[15]

What were the materials that forced the Committee to resort to the force of law? Were they the names of agents? No. Were they descriptions of secret intelligence techniques? No. They were, simply, copies of intelligence publications that had been circulated in the executive branch during the week preceeding the events that we were examining,[16] documents circulated literally to hundreds, if not thousands, of people.

Were they turned over by the date specified in the subpoena? Not completely.

The three intelligence agencies supplied some of their publications.[17] Dr. Kissinger, as Assistant to the President for National Security Affairs, refused to turn over a single piece of paper from reports provided to the National Security Council during the weeks in question.[18]

By the time hearings on intelligence results began in mid-September, only two agencies had substantially complied with our subpoenas.[19] More than a month would pass before a good faith effort at compliance was forthcoming from the National Security Council.

Footnotes:

[10]On August 5, 1975, the Committee received testimony from Dr. Albert C. Hall, Assistant Secretary of Defense (Intelligence):

"Chairman PIKE. Well, Dr. Hall, we did make a formal request that you bring this piece of paper creating the National Security Agency with you and you tell us that you want us to have everything we need but you didn't bring it. Why?

"Dr. Hall. We have to get clearance for releasing this material to you, sir.

"Chairman PIKE. Here we are representing the legislative branch of Government, asked to appropriate hundreds of millions of dollars to a certain agency and we are having difficulty finding the statutory authority for that agency even to exist. Now, isn't that ridiculous?"

[13] Letters were sent to CIA on Aug. 18, 1975; Aug. 19, 1975; Aug. 27, 1975; and Sept. 5, 1975. State Department requests were sent on Aug. 19, 1975; Sept. 8, 1975; and again on Sept. 8, 1975. Requests were forwarded to the Defense Department on Aug. 15, 1975; Aug. 19, 1975; Sept. 8, 1975; again on Sept. 8, 1975; and Sept. 9, 1975.

[14] The last two pages of one set of documents were typical deletions. The first page was apparently a cable. It was blank, except for the following across the top: 3/ND/DOLL-VNM/T-0144-6SG TRANSLATED DECRYPT VNJAC/VN NR 1 Y 301300G FM IJB TO CQ INFO BBM STOP CNMB 30119 5610M   Tol: 30JA68/1012Z   300"

The second page of the cable was even less informative. It was completely blank, except for a "Top Secret" Stamp.

[15] The subpoenas were directed to the National Security Agency, the Defense Intelligence Agency, the Director of Central Intelligence, and the National Security Council.

[16] The subpoena to the Defense Intelligence Agency on the subject of the Mid-East war illustrates the types of documents called for:

"1. For the period of September 25, 1973, through October 6, 1973, on a daily basis, or as frequently as same were issued, the original documents as follows: all Defense Intelligence Agency estimates. Current Defense Intelligence Summaries, situation Reports, and any and all cables emanating from the Defense Attache Office in Tel Aviv, National Military Intelligence Center daily briefings. . . ."

[17]A staff summary, prepared on September 12, 1975, indicated the following non-compliance:

"DIA Items Not Furnished—Cyprus and Mid-East War

    a. DIA Intelligence Summaries for July 14.

    b. DIA Intelligence Bulletin for July 13, July 14, and July 20.

    c. DIA Daily Current Intelligence Briefings for July 13, July 14, and July 20.

    d. DIA Daily Intelligence Bulletins for September 29, September 30, October 6.

    e. DIA Intelligence Summary for September 30.

"NSA Items Not Furnished—Cyprus

    a. SIGSUM's for July 13, July 14, July 19, July 20.

    b. "Wrap-up messages" for July 13, July 14, July 15, July 16, July 17."

[18]The September 12, 1975, compliance summary for NSC reads as follows:

"NSC Items Not Furnished—Cyprus and Mid-East War

    a. Nothing was furnished, unless NSC maintains that CIA and DCI documents transmitted to HSC via NSC are 'reports provided NSC by U.S. agencies.'

    b. Nothing furnished."

[19]These were the National Security Agency and the CIA.

2. Cut-off

This problem was soon dwarfed by a new tactic—the cut-off.

On September 12, 1975, the President, or someone using his name, cut off the Committee from all classified information. As if that were not enough, his action was accompanied by a demand that we immediately turn over all classified materials from our own internal files.[21]

The reason? The Congress, through this Committee, had passed judgment, after lengthy deliberation of the merits, on whether four words "classified" by the Executive branch could be told to the American people.[22]

The Executive, by its legally questionable reaction,[23] had now set aside any immediate subpoena problems, and the public hearing problems as well.

As background, a hearing on September 11, 1975, had reviewed intelligence performance with respect to the Mid-East war in 1973. The result was shocking. In the words of a CIA document, "the principle conclusions concerning the imminence of hostilities reached and reiterated by those responsible for intelligence analysis were—quite simply, obviously, and starkly—wrong."[24]

That same document had verbatim quotes from two intelligence bulletins that were moderately favorable and from five bulletins demonstrating that intelligence estimates were embarrassingly wrong. The two favorable quotes were declassified and read into the record.[25] The five embarrassing quotes, containing the same type of information, were not declassified by CIA.

The Committee objected.[26]

The CIA returned that afternoon to report that, after all, the five quotes could be declassified.[27] However, in an apparent need not to appear arbitrary in their earlier decision, they insisted that some 13 words still remain classified.

The Committee debated those 13 words for over four hours in a closed session. The CIA Special Counsel was present and in telephone contact with CIA Director Colby; the head of the State Department's Intelligence and Research was there; the head of the Defense Intelligence Agency was there; and a high official of the National Security Agency was there. No agency was without representation, and all had a chance to speak. Nine words were mutually agreed to remain classified,[28] but four words were not.

The four remaining words could not reveal any secret "sources and methods," which is the basis of official classifications,[29] because the information they contained could have come from any number of sources. In addition, the intelligence was so old by the time it was reported that it could not reveal how rapidly our intelligence techniques operated.[30] The Committee satisfied itself on these and other points before taking some half dozen rollcall votes on the matter.

It is possible that never before had so much expertise and thought gone into a declassification decision. For this, the Committee was accused of being irresponsible.[31] To protect national security, the "President" invoked a cut-off, perhaps before the President ever heard of what was going on.

The Committee later learned that in a biography of Dr. Kissinger a year earlier, the subject to which the four words referred had been spelled out in great detail. So much for the validity of the classification argument. No "high State Department official" had been cut off from information or forced to turn over his files as a result of that earlier publication. So much for protecting against irresponsibility.

Police guarding Committee offices were instructed to prevent any takeover of files by the Executive, and nothing more was heard of that.

Nevertheless, the cut-off from information struck at the heart of Committee operations. One month out of our five-month investigative period was lost while the issue was negotiated. With little choice, the Committee agreed that for purposes of getting the investigation under way again, future disputes would be referred to the President.[34] This was agreed to on the assurance of the President that the Committee would have no further problem with access to information.[35]

It is perhaps significant that the day the Committee was cut off was also the day hearings were scheduled on the 1974 Cyprus coup. Hearings were to be focused on the State Department's handling of intelligence, and of Dr. Kissinger's role therein.[36] Those hearings had to be cancelled. However, the Committee located a State Department witness who was to testify about Cyprus, even in the absence of classified evidence from the Executive—his name was Thomas Boyatt.

Thomas Boyatt was the State Department officer in charge of the Cyprus desk during the period in question. The Committee was interested in what kind of intelligence had been supplied to Boyatt regarding the 1974 coup against Archbishop Makarios and the consequent Turkish invasion.

More important, the Committee wanted to examine how that intelligence, as well as Mr. Boyatt's analysis of it, was handled by the decisionmakers at State. Mr. Boyatt had, in fact, advised one of our staff members that he vigorously criticized the handling of intelligence at the time of the Cyprus crisis. This criticism was embodied in a written report which was sent through the State Department's "dissent channels."[37]

[Page 25 of the Draft Final Report not available—*editor's note.*]

Footnotes:

[21]Rex E. Loe, Assistant Attorney General, Civil Division, delivered the order:

". . . [T]he President's responsibilities for the national security and foreign relations of the United States leave him no alternative but to request the immediate return of all classified materials heretofore provided by any department or agency of the executive Branch and direct all departments to decline to provide the Select Committee with classified materials, including testimony and interviews which disclose such materials, until the Committee satisfactorily alters its position."

[22]When Mr. Rex Lee appeared before the Committee to announce the President's cut-off of information it became evident that the executive branch had not given the matter equally careful consideration.

'Chairman PIKE. Mr. Lee, you say it revealed certain foreign communications activities of the United States. Is that your language?

'Mr. Lee. That is what I am advised, Mr. Chairman.

'Chairman PIKE. Did you look at the language of what the Committee released?

"Mr. LEE. I did not.

"Chairman PIKE. You are sitting here making a statement, saying that we have released language relating to the communications activities of the U.S. Government, and you did not even look at the language we released."

[23]In his appearance before the Committee, the Assistant Attorney General asserted that the disposition of security information is solely within the prerogative of the executive branch:

"Chairman PIKE. You say the legislative branch of Government had no right whatsoever to make anything public that the executive branch of Government does not want public. Is that your position?

"Mr. LEE. That is our position as far as classified information is concerned.

. . . .

"Chairman PIKE. So what you say is that in this great democracy, one branch of Government, and one branch . . . alone may decide what is secret, and one branch of Government . . . alone may decide what is not secret."

In support of his position, Mr. Lee did not assert that the Congress or the Committee was bound, as a matter of law, by Executive Order 11652, which established the current classification system, nor did he offer any contrary interpretation of Section 6(a) of H. Res. 591, which explicitly authorized the Committee to release such information as it deemed advisable.

[24]This quotation is taken from the summary conclusion of a post-mortem prepared by the intelligence community itself. The principle conclusions of the post-mortem began as follows:

"1. There *was* an intelligence failure in the weeks preceding the outbreak of war in the Middle East on October 6. Those elements of the intelligence community responsible for the production of finished intelligence did not perceive the growing possibility of an Arab attack and thus did not warn of its imminence.

"The information provided by those parts of the community responsible for intelligence collection was sufficient to prompt such a warning." The Performance of the Intelligence Community Before the Arab-Israeli War of October 1973: A Preliminary Post-Mortem Report, Director of Central Intelligence December 1973).

[25]The two verbatim quotes which were voluntarily declassified by the CIA were:

"We continue to believe that an outbreak of major Arab-Israeli hostilities remains unlikely for the im-

40

mediate future *although the risk of localized fighting has increased slightly.* . . . 4 October 1973 (emphasis in original).

"There are reports that Syria is preparing for an attack on Israel but conclusive evidence is lacking. In our view, the political climate in the Arab states argues against a major Syrian military move against Israel at this time. *The possibility of a more limited Syrian strike—perhaps one designed to retaliate for the pounding the Syrian Air Force took from the Israelis on September 13—cannot, of course, be excluded.*" INR Memorandum to the Secretary, 30 September 1973 (emphasis in original).

[26]The first of five quotes, which was later released, is as follows:

"Syria-Egypt—The movement of Syrian troops and Egyptian military readiness are considered to be coincidental and not designed to lead to major hostilities." DIA Intelligence Summary, 3 October 1973.

The text was the subject of an extensive discussion among the Chairman and representatives of the CIA:

"Chairman PIKE. Mr. Parmenter, before we go into questioning, would you tell me why you have omitted from your sanitized statement here the actual predictions, as contained in the report from which you read, i. e., the DIA Intelligence Summary Statement of 3 October 1973? I want you to look at what the original report says and tell me why we should not, here in open session, hear what the DIA actually said on October 3, 1973.

. . . .

"Mr. PARMENTER. There are sources and methods here that we will be happy to discuss in executive session.

"Chairman PIKE. Sources and methods in that statement?

"Mr. PARMENTER. Yes, sir.

"Chairman PIKE. I find that incredible. How does

that differ from the one you read on the preceding page (INR Memorandum to the Secretary) as far as sources and methods are concerned? . . . All I am asking you is, could you tell us why the reading of this plain, blank conclusion by the DIA as to the likelihood of the outbreak of war, would reveal a source or a method?

Mr. ROGOVIN. I will assume that the reason for the deletion was the manner in which the information was secured—

"Chairman PIKE. It doesn't say how the information is secured. This is a conclusion.

"Chairman PIKE. Mr. Rogovin, I find, as I look at what has been deleted and what has been omitted and what has been retained and read, differs not as to sources and methods, not as to the necessity of protecting the sensitivity of stuff, but whether it is in fact rather self-serving. . . ." Sept. 11, 1975.

[27]All five quotes are reprinted in the Mid-East War Post-Mortem in an appendix to this report. The first two quotes are typical:

"Syria-Egypt—The movement of Syrian troops and Egyptian military readiness are considered to be coincidental and not designed to lead to major hostilities." DIA Intelligence Summary, 3 October 1973.

"Egypt—The exercise and alert activities in Egypt may be on a somewhat larger scale and more realistic than previous exercises, but they do not appear to be preparing for a military offensive against Israel. Central Intelligence Bulletin, 5 October 1973." Post-Mortem, DCI, 6 (December 1975).

[28]Of the nine words which the Committee agreed not to release, few of them would have revealed, directly, any sensitive intelligence sources or methods. Instead, in most cases, they constituted personal characterizations, the publication of which might have been embarrassing to the United States or to individual foreign officials.

[29]"Sec. 7. In the interests of the security of the foreign intelligence activities of the United States and in order further to implement the proviso of section 102(d) (3) of the National Security Act of 1947 (Public Law 253, Eightieth Congress, first session) that the Director of Central Intelligence shall be responsible for protecting intelligence sources and methods from unauthorized disclosure . . ." 50 U.S.C. § 403 (1973).

[30]In the closed session, Mr. Rogovin, Special Counsel to the CIA, stated: ". . . [T]he experts feel very confident this is the bottom line that can be made public. These are references to real time reporting. . . ." Comm. Execs. Sess., Sept. 11, 1975. . . .

[31]Mr. Lee referred to what he characterized as the traditional procedures by which the Congress has received and treated classified information, a characterization which elicited the following colloquy:

"Chairman PIKE. If it is your position that we may never disclose information, how can we carry out our responsibilities?

"Mr. LEE. The same way, Mr. Chairman, that for decades other committees in Congress. . . .

"Chairman PIKE. That is exactly what is wrong, Mr. Lee. For decades other committees of Congress have not done their job, and you have loved it in the executive branch. You tell us that Congress has been advised of this. What does that mean? It means the executive branch comes up and whispers in one friendly Congressman's ear or another friendly Congressman's ear, and that is exactly what you want to continue, and that is exactly what I think has led us into the mess we are in."

[34]Text of letter from Mr. William Colby, Director of Central Intelligence, to the Chairman, dated September 30, 1975:

"With the approval of the President, I am forwarding herewith the classified material, additional to the unclassified material forwarded with my letter of 29

43

September 1975, which is responsive to your subpoena of September 12, 1975. This is forwarded on loan with the understanding that there will be no public disclosure of this classified material (nor of testimony, depositions or interviews concerning it) without a reasonable opportunity for us to consult with respect to it. In the event of disagreement, the matter will be referred to the President. If the President then certifies in writing that the disclosure of the material would be detrimental to the national security of the United States, the matter will not be disclosed by the Committee, except that the Committe would reserve its right to submit the matter to judicial determination."

[35]On September 26, 1975, Mr. McClory described the President's position as follows:

"We have assurance, in my opinion, of getting everything we need, and I would hope we would find we were getting everything we need."

[36]Mr. William Hyland, Director of Intelligence and Research, Department of State, was scheduled to be the key witness on September 11, 1975. It was unfortunate that the cut-off and later restrictions on testimony from Foreign Service officers, prevented the Committee from a full investigation of the Cyprus crisis. There is a closely held State Department report identifying the people who killed the American Ambassador, Rodger Davies, during that crisis, and a public protest has perhaps not been raised because these same murderers are now officials in the Cyprus government. Questions related to that intelligence report should, and must, be cleared up.

[37]"The 'Dissent Channel,' through which this memorandum was submitted, provides those officers of the Department of State who disagree with established policy, or who have new policies to recommend, a means for communicating their views to the highest levels of the Department." Letter to Chairman Pike from Dr. Kissinger, Dept. of State, Oct. 14, 1975.

3. Silenced Witnesses

In response, a new tactic was fashioned—the silenced witness.

On September 22, 1975, Mr. Boyatt was ordered not to tell the Committee "information which would disclose options considered by or recommended to more senior officers in the Department."[38] The order was added on to the existing ban on classified information.

That was not the end. Anything Mr. Boyatt did say would have to be in the presence of State Department monitors, by order of the Secretary.

It is worth pointing out that this prohibition extended to more than Mr. Boyatt's options or advice. Any information that would disclose those options was also banned. An attempted interview by the staff, with monitors, demonstrated that this covered almost everything the man ever did or said.[40]

The State Department's order was issued in spite of two United States laws which protect and guarantee the right of a federal employee to provide information to Congress.

One statute says that the right of a federal employee "to furnish information to either House of Congress, or to a Committee or Member thereof, may not be interfered with or denied."[41] The second law, which directly bears on the Boyatt situation, was specifically designed to encourage candid testimony of employees from federal agencies, including the Department of State.[42]

The authority invoked by the Secretary of State was neither "classification," nor "executive privilege," but a new doctrine that can best be characterized as "secretarial privilege."[43]

The Secretary of State was demanding special treatment. If this Committee could not have received testimony from CIA officers or FBI agents about ad-

45

vice or options they presented to senior officials, it would have had no choice but to shut down.[44] Oversight would be dead.

Fortunately, the CIA, the FBI, and the other intelligence agencies had either not heard of "secretarial privilege," or did not believe it existed.

On October 2, 1975, the Committee voted to issue a subpoena for Mr. Boyatt's Cyprus critique. Dr. Kissinger responded on October 14, 1975, referring to the subpoena as a "request." It was denied, even though it was not a request, but a legal order to produce a document.[46]

Time and control are, as we noted at the outset, in the hands of those who have possession of documents. Therefore, the Committee, more than one month after issuing its subpoena, accepted from Mr. Boyatt no testimony and no document, but something less. We were given Mr. Boyatt's memo after it had been mixed into a number of other paragraphs drafted elsewhere in the State Department—ostensibly to protect Mr. Boyatt. It ended up very much like the proverbial "riddle wrapped in a mystery inside an enigma."[47]

This time the euphemism was "an amalgam."[48]

Footnotes:

[38]This order was embodied in a September 22, 1975, memorandum from Lawrence S. Eagleburger, Deputy Undersecretary of State for Management, to William G. Hyland, the Department's Director of Intelligence and Research. This directive stated that "the following conditions will pertain to sworn interviews by the Pike Committee staff:

"The Department of State insists that a State Department representative be present during the interviews. Should the interviewees wish to be represented by their own legal counsel, the State Department representative will be in addition to that private legal counsel.

"The interviewees are to decline, by order of the President, to discuss classified material.

"The interviewees are to decline, by order of the Secretary of State, to give information which would disclose options considered by or recommended to more senior officers in the Department of State."

When Mr. Eagleburger appeared before the Committee on September 25, he stated that the orders contained in his memorandum of September 22 were issued at the verbal direction of the Secretary of State.

[40]This was clearly indicated by the following exchange among Mr. Field, on behalf of the Committee, Mr. Boyatt, and Mr. Hitchcock, the Department's monitor:

"MR. FIELD. Mr. Boyatt, would you please describe for us in detail what was done in the State Department not with respect to classified intelligence reports or information, but . . . knowledge of any of these events, who was involved, and what they were doing? Would you please describe that for us in some detail?

"MR. BOYATT. I would like to ask Mr. Hitchcock's advice.

"MR. HITCHCOCK. I regret but it appears to me that this comes to the problem of the description of the decision-making process which my instructions seem to indicate is proscribed.

"MR. FIELD. In other words, it is your position that who was doing what in the State Department has something to do with decision-making?

"Mr. HITCHCOCK. Yes.
. . . .

"MR. FIELD. We can't discuss this activity? We can't discuss where he went to, what he did, who

47

he told, what that person told him in response? We can't discuss as I understand it, whether or not he is aware of any moves made by the Secretary of State towards Turkey, towards Cyprus, either preceding or during this period."

[41]"The right of employees, individually or collectively to petition Congress or a Member of Congress, or to furnish information to either House of Congress, or to a committee or Member thereof, may not be interfered with or denied." 5 U.S.C. § 7102 (1973).

[42]"Upon the request of a committee of either House of Congress, a joint committee of Congress, or a member of such committee, any officer or employee of the Department of State, the United States information Agency, the Agency for International Development, the United States Arms Control and Disarmament Agency, or any other department, agency, or independent establishment of the United States Government primarily concerned with matters relating to foreign countries or multilateral organizations, may express his views and opinions, and make recommendations he considers appropriate, if the request of the committee or member of the committee relates to a subject which is within the jurisdiction of that committee." 2 U.S.C. § 194a (1973).

[43]Chairman Pike, questioning Dr. Kissinger in an open hearing on Oct. 31, 1975, stated, "I feel that you are alleging a privilege which has heretofore been reserved only to Presidents." Dr. Kissinger responded, "I have deliberately not asked the President to exercise executive privilege, nor am I asserting a secretarial privilege."

[44]One example comes from reports on the Cyprus crisis: "On the basis of a single CIA report from Athens, the analysts, notwithstanding their earlier concern, conveyed the impression to the policymakers that the world had been granted a reprieve." CIA Post Mortem on Cyprus, p. iii (January 1975).

Not only were we told about the report, we were also told about its impact on policymakers.

[46]The Committee Counsel, on Nov. 6, 1975, noted that, "MR. DONNER . . . A subpoena is not an invitation to negotiate. A subpoena is a command by a duly authorized body of government to deliver information."

[47]Winston S. Churchill, radio broadcast.

[48]On November 4, the Committee, by a vote of 8 to 5, agreed to the following resolution:

"Resolved by the Select Committee on Intelligence of the House of Representatives that an amalgamation of Department of State documents to include in its entirety the papers described as the Dissent Memorandum prepared by Thomas Boyatt while Director of Cypriot Affairs in the Department, fulfills the requirement of the subpoena issued by the Committee on the 2nd day of October, 1975.

"Provided the amalgamation is accompanied by an affidavit signed by a person mutually acceptable to the Department of State and the Committee as represented by the Chairman and the ranking minority member, attesting that the aforementioned Boyatt memorandum is contained unabridged in the amalgamation:

"The adoption of this resolution shall in no way be considered as a precedent affecting the right of this Committee with respect to access to Executive Branch testimony or documents."

4. Flank Attack

On September 24, 1975, two days after written instructions to Mr. Boyatt were issued, the Deputy Secretary of State raised for the first time an innuendo that the Committee's action resembled McCarthyism.[49] The Committee's initial reaction was to dismiss any such inference as a temporary lapse into poor taste.

Unfortunately, it was not a temporary lapse.

The next day, on September 25, 1975, Deputy Secretary Eagleburger appeared before the Committee to explain the Boyatt order. His statement again referred to State Department employees' problems with Congress in past times—a clear reference to the McCarthy period of the 1950's, as his subsequent testimony made clear.[50] On October 14, 1957, Dr. Kissinger's written response to the subpoena of Boyatt's intelligence critique again raised a reference to McCarthyism.[51]

The implication was baseless,[52] as both Mr. Eagleburger and Dr. Kissinger admitted under questioning.[53]

Facts seemed to make no difference. Within days of the innuendo being raised by Dr. Kissinger and his reply, newspaper columns and editorials were reporting their charges of McCarthyism.[54]

To the extent that such media activity may have been inspired, directly or indirectly, by the State Department, it helped erode support within and outside the Committee for pursuing the plain truth. With that opinion, the fiction of an amalgam became feasible.

Some day the full story of Cyprus may be told, but not by this Committee.

a. An Attack Averted

If no "flank" attack was launched by the FBI to discredit the Committee, it may have been because one was averted by the Committee.

On October 9, 1975, Mr. Martin Kaiser, a manufacturer of wiretap equipment, testified before the Committee. He indicated that the FBI bought his equipment through a middleman, U.S. Recording, who added a 10 percent markup. There was no justification for the markup, and it later developed that the president of U.S. Recording and a top FBI official were close friends.

The Committee began an investigation of U.S. Recording and its FBI friends. The Justice Department and FBI later began their own probe of the same matter.

On December 23, 1975, two and one-half months after Mr. Kaiser testified, he was subjected to a six-hour interview by two FBI agents. The agents were allegedly carrying out an internal FBI investigation regarding the agency's contractual dealings with U.S. Recording Company.

Mr. Kaiser called the Committee to relay his concern, and offered to give a statement under oath as to the conduct of the FBI agents.

In a Committee deposition of December 30, 1975, Kaiser claimed that the FBI agents were more concerned with discrediting the Committee's inquiry and personnel than conducting their investigation of U.S. Recording. Ultimately, the agents had elicited from him a statement, written by an FBI agent, which in some insignificant details recanted portions of his testimony. Mr. Kaiser then repudiated that written statement, which he had signed while agents stood over him and thrust it in front of him.

Taking the initiative, the Committee, on December 31, 1975, released a copy of the written statement, a full copy of Mr. Kaiser's December 30, 1975, deposition, and the text of a letter to the Attorney General demanding a full explanation of the entire incident.[56] This was done to head off any FBI "leak" of

the statement its agents had taken while Kaiser was
under some duress.

Footnotes:

[49]Mr. Eagleburger's statement, delivered to the
Committee offices on September 24, 1975, read:
"Mr. Chairman, this is far from a hypothetical
issue. To cite but a single example, the Foreign
Service and the Department of State were torn apart
in the late 1940's and early 1950's over an issue that
raised some of the same concerns that are before us
today—the ability of Foreign Service Officers to give
to the Secretary and their other superiors their candid advice, secure in the knowledge that this advice
will remain confidential. The events of those years
not only injured individuals, but also did significant
damage to the process by which foreign policy .is
made. Who can be certain how many recommendations during the years that followed were colored by
memories of those experiences?"

[50]"I must say again, as I said in the statement
today, the issue for me right now is an issue of principle. It is the question of our duty to protect junior
and middle-grade officers of the Department in the
conduct of their duties within the Department . . ."

[51]"While I know that the Select Committee has
no intention of embarrassing or exploiting junior and
middle-grade officers of the Department, there have
been other times and other committees—and there
may be again—where positions taken by Foreign
Service Officers were exposed to *ex post facto* public
examination and recrimination." Letter to Chairman
Pike from Dr. Kissinger, Oct. 14, 1975.

[52]The plain facts are that Senator McCarthy destroyed the careers of State Department employees

52

on the basis of their beliefs and politics. This Committee never sought the political views of any federal employee. Senator McCarthy operated without evidence. This Committee sought only evidence. Senator McCarthy forced people to testify. Mr. Boyatt wanted to testify. McCarthyism grew out of a lack of character and integrity, and from a climate of hysteria. Restrictive rules are no answer to such problems.

[53]"MR. HAYES. [O]ne of the things that has deeply offended me . . . has been the implication, the very clear implication, that your position of protecting middle and lower level Foreign Service officers is a position of protecting them from McCarthyism...

"SECRETARY KISSINGER. With respect to the charge of McCarthyism, I want to make clear that I do not accuse this committee of engaging in McCarthyism and I know indeed that the Chairman has a record in this regard, and from the convictions of many of the members that I am familiar with, I know that this is not the intention of this committee."

"MR. HAYES . . . I don't think there has been one instance that you can cite or that Mr. Leigh can cite, where this Committee has ever taken it upon itself in the tradition of the McCarthys . . . to, in essence, run a purge operation.

"MR. EAGLEBURGER. Mr. Hayes, there is no implication in my statement that this Committee is performing in the way I described the Department went through in the late '40's and early '50's. That is not, sir, my point." Sept. 25, 1975.

[54]The New York Times editorial of October 19, 1975, was entitled, "Neo-McCarthyism?"

"In view of the facts, the Intelligence Committee's insistence that it has the right to reach into the interior of the State Department to subpoena the dissenting memoranda of junior and middle-rank officials—and to summon them to testify on policy issues—is clearly contrary to the national interest...."

The Washington Post editorial of October 6, 1975, entitled "Mr. Pike's Committee" had this to say:

"The analogy with McCarthyism evoked by the State Department is a relevant one, even though it appears that in this case the committee of Congress wishing to question Mr. Boyatt apparently is inclined to praise him for his views, not persecute him—and to use his testimony to fault Secretary Kissinger. Certainly Mr. Kissinger should be faulted for his Cyprus policy. . . ."

[56]One of the most disturbing aspects of the incident—quite aside from the propriety of interrogating a Committee witness about the Committee—was that the interview was replete with FBI suggestions of prejudice on the part of the Committee Counsel. Vigor was apparently seen as prejudice, and by two agents who had never met the Committee personnel they were denigrating.

5. Deletions

In early November, about the same time the Boyatt problems were being resolved, the Committee moved on from the subjects of money and what our money buys. The third topic of our hearings was risks, and how well those risks are controlled.

Seven new subpoenas were issued. Four were for materials pertaining to subjects of prior hearings. They were honored.[57] The remaining three were directed to Dr. Kissinger, for materials pertaining to upcoming hearings. Not surprisingly, those subpoenas went unanswered.[58]

Once again, some background is helpful.

Two of the three subpoenas were for covert action recommendations made by non-CIA officials, since the CIA had already opened up the covert action files to us. The third subpoena was for intelligence records on Soviet compliance with strategic arms limitation agreement (SALT).

When considering risks, covert actions rank as perhaps the highest risk operations in the government, short of war. The law allows CIA "to perform such other functions and duties related to intelligence affecting the National Security as the National Security Council may from time to time direct."[60] This is the legal authority for covert action. A subcommittee of the National Security Council, presently called the Party Committee, has been assigned the task of directing these actions.

By tracing money, the Committee came across millions of rounds of ammunition and weapons being purchased in the early 1970's. The purchases were destined for a questionable military venture in a far-off war that most Americans had probably never heard of, much less felt they had any national interest in.

The CIA's military escapade was bad enough, but, on examining documents, the Committee discovered that the Forty Committee appeared not to have met or voted on the operation. In fact, internal documents showed that CIA and the State Department had turned the project down three times in the previous two years.

It turned out that during a trip overseas, President Nixon and Dr. Kissinger had met alone with the head of a foreign government [the Shah of Iran—*editor's note*]. At that man's request, the Administration had involved CIA in an internal war in the head of state's neighboring country [the Kurdish rebellion in Iraq—*editor's note*]. John Connally, on the verge of heading Democrats for Nixon," was sent back to the foreign leader, apparently to bring him the good news of final approval.

A month later, after training for the project had already begun, Forty Committee members were sent a memo by Dr. Kissinger informing them, for the first time, of President Nixon's decision.

In a separate matter, this Committee was told by former CIA Director Richard Helms of a decision to undertake a covert action project in Chile. Mr. Helms had been called into the Oval office and told by President Nixon, with Dr. Kissinger and Mr. John Mitchell present, that he was to undertake the project in spite of CIA reservations. He was also told "not to inform the other members of the Forty Committee."[64]

A pattern was emerging.

Not all covert actions were generated by the CIA. In particular, paramilitary operations of the worst type seemed to come from outside the CIA. Some projects came from the President. Some projects came from his Assistant for National Security Affairs, and some had their beginning in the Department of State.

Forty Committee records were subpoenaed to see if the pattern was valid.[66] The subpoena was limited to the official document by which a covert action was approved. These records were often no more than one paragraph long.

What arrived in response to our subpoenas showed nothing—because it was mostly deletions.

The deletions came in all shapes and forms. Typically, there would be one line left on a page, saying, "A CIA project was telephonically approved," or, "The Committee voted to approve a CIA paper entitled [title deleted]." Ofen. if there had been numerous items considered at a meeting, the deletions themselves had been cut and pasted together. For example, item eight might follow item one, giving the impression that only two items had been considered that day.[67] Sometimes there would be only one word left on a page—"Chile"—nothing else, anywhere; but it was still classified top secret. The information, needless to say, was worthless.[68]

Wholesale deletions were encountered in the Committee's investigation of domestic covert activities as well.

COINTELPRO, the FBI'S program for disruption of the "New Left," like nearly all FBI actions, was extremely well documented. The Committee requested the appropriate documents in July.[69] What it received were summaries so heavily excised as to be unusable.

One memorandum, for example, referring only generically to the "New Left," contained the subheading. "Recommended Procedure," on one page, and "Results" on the next. The pages were otherwise blank. Another document with the same type generic reference, "Black Extremist Organization," was likewise excised in its entirety.

The Committee protested. Negotiations followed.[70]

Finally, in mid-October, an agreement was reached whereby less excised memos were made available to Committee staff, at FBI headquarters. The Committee persisted, selecting a representative number of memoranda to be delivered to its own offices. After some delay, they were delivered, still excised.

Requests for the documents pertaining to FBI national security wiretaps led to a similar experience. One set of documents was delivered, excised beyond use. Negotiations took place for almost a month. Finally a second set of documents was provided, but, again, without identifying targets of electronic surveillance.

Footnotes:

[57]The following subpoenas were honored:

1) To the Assistant to the President for National Security Affairs, for all minutes of the National Security Council Intelligence Committee, its Working Group and its Economic Intelligence Subcommittee;

2) To the Assistant to the President for National Security Affairs, for the minutes of all meetings of the Washington Special Action Group concerning the Mideast War, the Cyprus crisis, and the Portugal coup;

3) To the Assistant to the President for National Security Affairs, for all intelligence reports furnished to the National Security Council between October 5 and October 28, 1973, relating to the Mideast war;

4) To the Director of Central Intelligence, for all written requests and memoranda of requests from the CIA to the Internal Revenue Service since July 1, 1961, for tax information or official action by IRS.

[58]These subpoenas were not complied with:

1) To the Assistant to the President for National

Security Affairs for all Forty Committee records of decisions taken since January 20, 1965, reflecting approval of covert action projects;

2 To the Assistant to the President for National Security Affairs for documents relating to the Soviet Union's adherence to the provisions of the Strategic Arms Limitation Treaty of 1972 and the Vladivostok agreement of 1974; and

3) To the Secretary of State for all State Department documents recommending covert actions to the National Security Council since January 20, 1961.

[60]The National Security Act of 1947 states:

"(d) Powers and Duties.

"For the purpose of coordinating the intelligence activities of the several Government departments and agencies in the interest of national security, it shall be the duty of the Agency, under the direction of the National Security Council—

. . . .

"5) to perform such other functions and duties related to intelligence affecting the national security as the National Security Council may from time to time direct." 50 U.S.S. 403(d) (1973).

[64]"MR. FIELD. In the case of the Chile operation, could you describe very briefly how that was directed?

"MR. HELMS. Well, there was a part—

"MR. FIELD. How you came to be told—

"MR. HELMS. There was some activity undertaken at the President's direction in Chile by his saying to me that he wanted this effort made and that I was not to inform the other members of the Forty Committee.

"MR. FIELD. In other words, in the case of the Chilean operation, were you called to the Oval Office?

"Mr. HELMS. I was in the Oval Office.

"Mr. FIELD. You were called into the Oval Office and who was present?

"MR. HELMS. The Attorney General and Dr. Kissinger." Exec. Sess., Oct. 23, 1975.

[66]"CHAIRMAN PIKE. The question then becomes —and Mr. Field stated this yesterday—are those operations which are generally within the CIA, and in the normal course of business, normally more responsible? Do they normally get our nation into less difficulties than those which somebody outside of the intelligence operation department tells them to do?"

"CHAIRMAN PIKE. Well, here we are seeking to look at the genesis of all oversight and the degree of control and the degree of responsibility by which these operations get launched.

"You and I, and Mr. Dellums, and Mr. Treen, as members of the Armed Services Committee, for years heard the magic word, "The Forty Committee." It has seemed to us as we get deeper and deeper into this that the Forty Committee really has not been all that relevant in the decision-making process in the oversight process. The Forty Committee is always held forth as being that body which exercises judicial restraint, perhaps, in authorizing these various operations. It has seemed to me and I think most of the members of this committee that the activities of the Forty Committee have been relatively negligible in authorizing these operations.

"We are trying to get the information to see whether anybody ever really argues about these things, to see whether anybody votes no on these things, to see whether the Forty Committee is a reality or a rubber stamp."

[67]"MR. FIELD. I think this is the best example of the kind of deletions. The items skip from Item 1 to Item 4. Items 2 and 3 are clearly cut and pasted out of the document. It then skips from 4 to 7. In other words, here is a document that could conceivably be two or three or four pages long. It gives you the feeling that you have gotten a reasonable amount of in-

formation, but in fact all somebody has done is snip out little sections and paste them together and compact them and make it look like it is a complete document."

[68]"MR PIKE. I think that as any of us look at what they have given us, we will simply make a pretty easy judgment that what they have given us is so heavily censored and deleted as to be meaningless for our purposes."

[69]It was part of a general request on July 22, 1975, for all documents previously provided the Senate Select Committee.

[70]The Senate, which received the same excised material, also objected, with more or less the same results. All of this happened before July 22, 1975. Much time could have been saved had that information been volunteered to the House.

6. Privileges

The second Kissinger subpoena brought even less than the first one.

For the first time in the history of the Ford Administration, executive privilege was invoked. The subpoena which caused this historic assertion was directed to Dr. Kissinger as Secretary of State. It was intended for the purpose of examining the type of covert actions recommended by the State Department since 1965.

The State Department reported that it had recommended only eight projects—this was later changed to 16, and still later to 20—but that none of the documents could be provided to the Committee.

Although only a few of the recommendations were from a Secretary of State to a President, all documents were being withheld because they were deemed privileged communications with Presidents. They included recommendations from lesser State officials to the staff of the National Security Council, with no apparent intention that the document be for the eyes or the use of the President.

The communication did not take place in this President's administration. All privileges recognized by law are controlled specifically and personally by the person whose communication is being protected, and this President was not in that position as to all the documents.[74] It must be noted, again, that no other intelligence agency or department withheld recommendations for covert action—or anything else —sent to the National Security Council. If they had, the Committee's work would have come to a halt.

In any event, nothing came forth from the State Department.

At no time was there a legitimate question as to which documents the Committee was seeking, under either this subpoena or the subpoena for Forty Committee documents. At no time was the physical amount of paper a problem, since only a few hundred sheets of paper were at issue. At all times, this Committee, as well as the Congress, had a right—and, in fact, an obligation under law[75]—to review the information at issue.

With no other recourse, the Committee cited Dr. Kissinger for contempt on November 14, 1975.[76]

On November 20, 1975, the Committee approved a report to the House of Representatives, asking that the Committee's contempt citation be supported by the House itself and referred to the U.S. Attorney for prosecution. Contempt proceedings began to produce results with respect to the Forty Committee records. Revised editions, with fewer deletions, were soon provided.

Nothing came forth from the State Department.

The Committee then entered its last two weeks of hearings, having endured more than three months of uninterrupted delays, cut-offs, silenced witnesses, amalgams, attacks, deletions, and privileges.

Finally, the evening before the Committee was to take a contempt citation of Dr. Kissinger to the floor of the House for a vote, the Committee was given access to State Department recommendations for covert action.[78]

Footnotes:

[74]"MR. JOHNSON. . . . I don't think we ought to even acknowledge that this is a possibility that a President can control everything that has happened in the government files and government documents; that the President has absolute control over this since the time of the inception of the Republic."

[75]"Sec. 2. The select committee is authorized and directed to conduct an inquiry into—

. . . .

"(5) the necessity, nature, and extent of overt and covert intelligence activities by United States intelligence instrumentalities in the United States and abroad;" H. Res. 591, 94th Cong., 1st Sess. (1975).

[76]"Resolved, That the Speaker of the House of Representatives certify the report of the Select Committee on Intelligence of the House of Representatives as to the contumacious conduct of Henry A. Kissinger, as Secretary of State, in failing and refusing to produce certain pertinent materials in compliance with a subpoena duces tecum of said Select Committee served upon Henry A. Kissinger, as Secretary of State; and as ordered by the Select Committee, together with all the facts in connection therewith, under the seal of the House of Representatives to the United States Attorney for the District of Columbia, to the end that Henry A. Kissinger, as Secretary of State, may be proceeded against in the manner and form provided by law."

[78]"MR. FIELD. . . . Mr. Hyland . . . had both the State Department recommendations and the Forty Committee minutes before him. He read verbatim from the Forty Committee minutes, and he used the State Department recommendations to verify the date, the country, and the type of program that was recommended by the State Department, and in response to our questions, he was very forthcoming."

7. More Delay

The third so-called Kissinger subpoena was intended for the review of strategic arms limitation agreement (SALT) intelligence handling, but brought instead a return to the delay.

What is SALT, and why was the Committee so interested in the intelligence aspects of it? Briefly, SALT covers the strategic arms limitation agreements signed with the Russians in 1972, to limit the arms race. The agreements specifically limit such things as missile production, deployment, and testing by the United States and the Soviet Union. The ability of our intelligence services to detect whether the Russians are violating this agreement is of vital strategic interest. More important, SALT intelligence must be able to move through channels, uninfluenced by bias or ulterior motives, to appropriate decisionmakers.

The Committee had earlier received testimony that, during the Vietnam War, a desire to please highlevel officials may have caused some intelligence to reflect what the upper levels wanted to hear. Vietnam is history, but SALT is not.

To check how intelligence was being handled at the highest levels, and whether it was ever withheld from top Executive officials or Congress, the Committee subpoenaed all reports on Soviet compliance that had been sent to the National Security Council.

At first, Committee staff went to the White House and was given a few SALT monitoring reports. These, it was said, were absolutely all that the National Security Council had in its files on the subject of SALT compliance. It did not seem possible.

For one reason, the Verification Panel, which exists primarily to review SALT matters, is part of the National Security Council and has been quite active. For another, the Committee had already identified dozens of pertinent documents from the intelligence community which had been sent to the National Security Council.[82]

The skepticism proved accurate. After Committee proceedings to cite Dr. Kissinger for contempt of the SALT subpoena, on November 14. 1975, volumes of SALT intelligence materials began to come forth.

A week had passed since the return date of the subpoena before the documents we needed were even identified. making preparations for hearings most difficult.[83] This was the last of the subpoenas, however.

In reviewing the oversight experience, access to information, even when it was backed up by subpoena, was not satisfactory. As an example, at the State Department we found that lower level officials had eventually been ordered not to testify before the Committee; their documents were likewise refused to Congress. Upper level officials at State had become inaccessible because of executive privilege; and diplomatic exchanges, an important element of intelligence, were similarly off limits to the Committee.

To place the importance of this in perspective, intelligence has two primary consumers: military and diplomatic. Diplomacy is preferable to war; yet it is nearly impossible, today, to evaluate how well intelligence serves diplomatic ends. If it does not serve well, it is hard to imagine how anything could be known or done about it by Congress.

The passion for confidentiality and secrecy at State is curious, because in many cases the Russians and other adversaries were either directly informed of the name secrets the Committee sought, or the Russians know of them by other means.[84] It is hard to imagine a justification for allowing the unelected to keep elected officials in the dark, in a democracy.

Footnotes:

[82]We had not received any documents from the Verification Panel or its subcommittee, the Restricted Working Group. In addition, we had identified some 40 documents sent to the NSC from CIA that should have been included in the subpoenaed material.

[83]The lack of access to documents was the primary reason no administration witness was called to testify at the Committee's first SALT hearing. Without documents to identify issues, we called a SALT critic, Admiral Elmo Zumwalt, to testify.

Ironically, the same officials who withheld primary source materials from us criticized the Committee for not presenting administration witnesses. However, we had no evidence to question them about.

After documents were sent to the Committee, a hearing was held to receive testimony from two senior administration officials with reference to certain documents that appeared to show withholding of intelligence. The point is that until the Executive opened access to documents we could not select appropriate witnesses or be prepared with issues; nevertheless, that same Executive made it seem that responsibility for not calling their witnesses rested with the Committee.

[84]For example, SALT intelligence was put on "hold"— which means it was not only classified, but not even generally distributed in the executive branch. Mr. Hyland testified as to one of these "hold" items:

"MR FIELD. But the Russians were told it twice while it was on hold.

"MR. HYLAND. That is the purpose of the system. If you decide not to do it, that is one decision.

"MR. FIELD. Who was it kept from?

"MR. HYLAND. As far as I am concerned, officials who had an operational policy decision, were informed.

"MR. FIELD. That is not the question. Whom are we keeping it a secret from?

"MR. HYLAND. We are keeping a hold item secret from people who might read the Central Intelligence Bulletin that is disseminated in several hundred copies.

"MR. FIELD. We tell the Russians.

"MR. HYLAND. Of course."

8. Routine Problems

When legal proceedings were not in the offing, the access experience was frequently one of foot-dragging, stonewalling, and careful deception.

A few examples should suffice.

The President went on television June 10, 1975, and reassured the nation that the uncompleted work of the Rockefeller Commission would be carried forward by the two intelligence committees of the Congress. The files of the Commission, President Ford announced, would be turned over to both committees immediately.[85]

The Committee began requesting those files within the week. We requested and requested.[86] We negotiated.

Finally, by threatening to announce publicly that the President's word had not been kept, the files were turned over—in mid-October, some four months late.

In another case, likewise involving basic research information, the Committee in early August, requested a complete set of what has become known as the "Family Jewels." This 693-page document was the very foundation of the current investigations. It had come into existence as the result of an order by former CIA Director James Schlesinger, on May 9, 1973, in the wake of Watergate revelations. Dr. Schlesinger had ordered CIA employees to report any possible past wrongdoing, and those reports were compiled into the "Jewels" on May 21, 1973.[87]

By the end of August, the Committee had been provided only a sanitized version of the document. Letters were sent and negotiations proceeded throughout September. On October 7, 1975, the staff was told that they would not be allowed to see the complete record of wrongdoing as assembled in May 1973.[88]

A second sanitized version was sent in mid-October,

but it was hardly less sanitized than the first. As an interesting sidelight, the second version did have one page that was not in the first. It was a photocopy of a Jack Anderson newspaper article, nothing more. In the first version, that page had been blanked out, with the message, "This information deleted because it reveals sensitive operational techniques and methods." The second version was not deleted, but it was classified.

The Chairman demanded a complete copy of the report, and was told that one would be forthcoming. None was. As a result, he scheduled a press conference for 12:00 noon on October 11, 1975.

At 11:45 a.m. on October 11, 1975, the report was finally delivered,[89] after the life of the Committee's investigation was more than half over.

These two examples represent some of the most basic research materials available to the Committee. Their contents were crimes, abuses, and questionable conduct, not sophisticated or legitimate intelligence secrets.

Other important information was withheld, such as a Committee request for certain records of the President's Foreign Intelligence Advisory Board. On August 25, 1975, a letter was sent asking for a copy of the Board's agendas since 1961. No written response to that letter has even been received.

The Board interested the Committee from the standpoint of command and control. There have been numerous recommendations, for example, that a pending executive reorganization make this group the key command and control unit for foreign intelligence.[91]

The Committee is still waiting for the Board's documents to be delivered, despite the fact that the ranking minority member of the Committee took a personal interest in the matter. A month of his efforts produced only a limited right to see certain information, not the documents themselves.

Another important piece of information the Committee requested was the names and relationships of newsmen who worked for both the CIA and the American news media at the same time. Congressman Dellums asked for this in executive session on August 6, 1975.[92] The information was re-requested by letter on October 14, 1975, and on October 21, 1975, and on October 31, 1975, and on September 2, 1975.[93]

The Committee is still waiting for answers about the newsmen. The only information it did receive was in response to inquiries about specific newsmen, after we had determined from other sources that there was a CIA connection. In fact, in one case, the CIA denied the relationship until confronted with irrefutable proof.

As a final example, there is a category of intelligence that is sent to the Secretary of State, who then controls its further dissemination. It is called "NODIS CHEROKEE."[94]

The Committee specifically requested NODIS CHEROKEE information with reference to the Cyprus crisis in 1974. It was told none existed. Two months later other officials revealed that the materials do exist. When the Committee went back to State with this new information, it was simply told NODIS CHEROKEE was not going to be given to us.[96] By then, there was no time left to issue a subpoena.

a. The Right Question

Perhaps the most difficult problem in developing information about intelligence activities is knowing the right question to ask.[97]

As an illustration, Committee staff obtained the names of CIA proprietaries, after lengthy negotiations. Some time later, staff members noticed that certain names were not on the list. The explanation was that those were "fronts," and we had not asked for fronts.

Nor was this sort of semantic contest confined to staff inquiries. In one public hearing, Congressman Stanton and the FBI's Raymond Wannall consumed more than five minutes drawing distinctions among "surreptitious entry," "burglary," and "illegal break-in."

Another example grew out of a Committee investigation of a covert action project that had taken place some years ago. This particular project was the subject of unusual interest by the Committee, both because of the country involved and because it entailed tampering in the free election of an allied nation. The Committee's objections to the project were strong enough that it voted to recommend to the President that the project no longer be kept secret.

Astonishingly, while the Committee was in the midst of objecting to this past project, CIA was obtaining approval for re-instituting the same type of project in the same country. The CIA never told the Committee about this renewal. When newspapers revealed the new project, Committee staff asked the CIA why it had not been told. The response was, "You didn't ask the right question."

Time and again, a question had to be repeated and variously repeated. Only then would the sought-after facts emerge, even though the intent of the questions had been readily apparent. The operable ground rules were, as one official put it, "After all, we're not a Coke machine; you don't just put in a quarter and expect something to come out."

Examples of the difficulty in asking the right question are a bit like trying to prove a negative; the full impact may not be possible to illustrate. It was, however, the most nagging factor in attempting to exhaust the items that deserved Congressional insight. The significance is that it reflects an attitude which cannot be expected to change; and, as long as that is the case, ready access to documentary evidence and primary source material is all the more imperative.

Footnotes:

[85]"Because the investigation of the political assassination allegations is incomplete . . . I will make available to the Senate and House Select Committees these [Rockefeller Commission] materials together with other related materials in the executive branch. . . . I should add, that the Senate and House Committees are also in the process of making further investigations as they have been charged with the responsibility by the Congress; so there's not going to be any possibility of any cover-up because we're giving them the material that the Rockefeller Commission developed in their hearings. . . ." President's News Conference, Washington, D.C., June 10, 1975.

[86]More than two dozen phone calls were made, by three separate members of the staff, over a three-month period.

[87]"MR. JOHNSON. On May 9th of '73, Mr. Schlesinger issued a directive calling on all CIA employees to report any and all abuses by the CIA. That is a matter of public records, there isn't any question about that, is there?

"MR. COLBY. No, sir.

"MR. JOHNSON. And is it also a fact that by May 21, just 11 days later, there were several hundred separate reports of abuses which had been reported to him?

"MR. COLBY. There were a number of abuses. I couldn't give you a quantitative statement.

"MR. JOHNSON. That is the report that has been

called by a variety of names, it has been called potential flap activities, or jewels, or the family jewels; isn't that the report we are talking about?

"MR. COLBY. Yes."

[88]"On 4 September I formally requested to see the original copy of the unsanitized 'family jewels' from the Review Staff at CIA. I was put off. Then Seymour Bolten, Chief of Review Staff, countered with an offer to have someone sit with Mr. Pike and let him read a version. This was unacceptable, so they further 'compromised' and offered to let Jack Boos and A. Searle Field sit at CIA with the sanitized 'family jewels' and ask for each sanitization as it came up. This was also unacceptable and the access flap started.

"Now, I have been told by Donald Gregg and Seymour Bolten that 'no one will see the original, unsanitized family jewels.'" Memorandum to Mr. A. Searle Field, from Emily Sheketoff, Oct. 7, 1975.

[89]"Pike told reporters the documents had been turned over to him, for Committee use, 'a few minutes before noon.

"'We have been trying to get documents with hard evidence and a particular document including the report generated by Mr. Schlesinger about alleged improprieties within the CIA,' [Pike] said.

"Defense Secretary James R. Schlesinger served as CIA director for a few months in 1973 and held an in-house investigation of the agency before he left that post." "Pike Gets a New Report," The Washington Star, p. A-10, Oct. 11, 1975.

[91]From time to time, the Board has examined the scope and effectiveness of covert action and the technical means of gathering intelligence. Staff was informed of current discussions to enhance the responsibilities and resources of the Board. Another concern was the role and interrelationships of members of the Board with the business community. Many of these

members are affiliated with major intelligence community contractors.

[92]"MR. DELLUMS. Describe the existence and nature of the CIA secret propaganda operations in the U.S. I would appreciate detail. How many U.S. journalists overseas are in contact with the CIA? How many outlets for media operations does the CIA have in the U.S.?"

[93]This set of requests was for "a complete list of all people now in the news media who have ever had a relationship, contractual or otherwise, with the Agency." Letter to Donald Gregg, Assistant to the Director, CIA, from Emily Sheketoff, Oct. 21, 1975.

[94]"MR. HITCHCOCK. NODIS CHEROKEE is a particularly sensitive category of NODIS messages limited in use to relatively few embassies, covering intelligence materials of extraordinary sensitivity, handled virtually only by the Secretary, the President, if he is involved, and the Chief of Mission. And virtually one-man dissemination in Washington and the field."

[96]"All of them (NODIS CHEROKEE) . . . contain diplomatic correspondence between the capitals and Washington. . . . Thus, these messages do not deal with the intelligence matters of concern to the committee and do not relate to your request of 16 October." Letter to Gregory Rushford from J. J. Hitchcock, Department of State, Jan. 5, 1976.

[97]"MR. PIKE. It has been my experience and judgment that if you [Mr. Colby] are asked precisely the right question, you will give an honest answer. You do not lead us into those areas which would help us know what the right question was to ask. You do not make it easy for us to ask the right question. Anyone who thinks you have been running back and forth to Capitol Hill with briefcases bulging with secrets which you are eager to bestow upon us hasn't sat on my side of the desk."

Congress and the Secrecy Dilemma

Classified information presents a classic paradox: without it, government sometimes cannot function; with it, government sometimes cannot function.

Spy agencies cannot publish details about their operations. At the same time, Congress cannot fail to report to its constituents about abuses of their government. What it all means is that there must be a responsible system of classification, accompanied by an equally responsible and effective system of declassification.

We have neither.

It has been easy to create secrets, but this government has yet to construct an adequate way to handle the problems too many secrets create. We have no Official Secrets Act—which would make it a crime to publish secrets—because such a law would be unconstitutional.[100] Therefore, the only real enforcement of classification is sanctioning those who depend on access to secrets,[101] such as Congress. Congress can be, and has been, either cut off from classified information or convinced to receive secrets selectively.

That is only the beginning of classification problems.

The law says that there are to be only three categories of classifications: top secret, secret, and confidential.[102] In spite of this, intelligence agencies spawn all sorts of "higher" classification, such as "code word" or compartment" categories. Just as often, information is simply withheld from Congress under ad hoc arrangements. This Committee was frequently told that, whereas its mandate was legal authority to receive classified information, that was not enough.

Footnotes:

[100]Mr. Colby stated: "I do believe that the question of an Official Secrets Act has to be looked at in the context of our Constitution . . . I would not apply it to the press, for example, because I think that would run into real conflict with our Constitution."

Chairman Pike summarized the witnesses' testimony as follows: "I gather that you are all agreed there should be no Official Secrets Act or the equivalent thereof, and that our Constitution simply doesn't allow it, for openers."

[101]In the course of the investigation, one official reminded Committee staff of an anecdote involving President Kennedy and Chairman Khrushchev. During one of their visits, President Kennedy apparently asked the Russian leader about a Soviet citizen who had been sentenced to 23 years for running naked through Red Square shouting, "The Party Leader is a moron." Chairman Khrushchev allegedly replied, "He got one year for indecent exposure, two years for insulting the Chairman, and twenty years for revealing a state secret."

[102]The classification categories and criteria used by the executive branch are defined in Section 1 of Executive Order 11652, as follows:

"SECTION 1. Security Classification Categories. Official information or material which requires protection against unauthorized disclosure in the interest of the national defense of foreign relations of the United States (hereinafter collectively termed "national security") shall be classified in one of three categories, namely "Top Secret," "Secret," or "Confidential," depending upon the degree of its significance to national security. No other categories shall be used to identify official information or material as requiring protection in the interest of national security, except as otherwise expressly provided by statute."

1. Oaths and Agreements

The first matter of business between the CIA and the Committee was a request by the Agency that all of the staff be required to sign six pages of CIA oaths.

These elaborate oaths stipulated, in effect, acceptable conduct for Congressional employees with respect to things CIA had determined were secret. Without oaths, secrets would not be forthcoming. The staff represents, of course, Committee members, but the members were not asked to sign oaths. Perhaps this was because members would not do anything untoward with secrets. More likely, it was because they would protest loudly.

The Committee reminded CIA that subjecting our employees to Executive oaths would violate the concept that Congress is an independent and co-equal branch of government.

It is the Constitutional responsibility of Congress to control its own staff, and this is the course the Committee followed. It required every employee to sign a statement, drafted by the Committee, reflecting the needs and considerations of Congress, and enforced by Congress.[107]

This may seem like so much posturing; but it is important not to underestimate the significance of firmly establishing the premise that a target of an investigation does not lay down ground rules. As the Agency noted, this has not been the case in the past; and it may be one of the reasons this investigation had become necessary.[108]

The next move was to require the Committee to enter into agreements.

The proposed agreements outlined certain categories of information so sensitive that the Committee was to agree in advance not to see them. When this was rejected, a modified version of those agreements set forth proposed rules and regulations the Committee would abide by if certain classified information were to be made available.[109] These agreements also included a proposal to "compartment" our staff.[110] Compartmenting would mean dividing them up and restricting their access to each other's work.

The Committee refused to sign. It refused even to agree, as a matter of "understanding," that Executive rules would be binding. Such proposed understandings included allowing intelligence officials to review the notes of investigators before notes could be brought back to Committee offices. Other committees have consistently been subjected to that arrangement.[111]

The FBI then came forward with a six-page agreement that they requested be signed before classified information could be handled by the Committee.

The FBI proposal was even more restrictive than CIA's. Secret documents would be made available in special rooms at the FBI, with FBI monitors present. Notes would be reviewed by FBI agents. After notes had been appropriately sanitized, they would be sent to our offices.[112]

Once again, the Committee refused to sign. It did agree orally to put all future requests for documents in writing. The repercussions of this oral agreement illustrate quite nicely the problem with agreements. A few days later the Committee received a letter from the Justice Department stating that requests for materials that had been made a month earlier by Committee members in public hearings had not been fulfilled. Even though FBI officials had publicly agreed to furnish the documents promptly, the requests had not been "in writing."[113]

While the Committee was negotiating an end to the cut-off from classified information, another agreement for handling secrets was proposed by the Executive. The Committee was asked to agree that certain categories of information be inaccessible.[114] Other categories would be available only to senior members, by means of selective briefings. Again, it was not agreed to.

Footnotes:

[107]The following excerpts are from the agreement signed and honored by the members of the Committee's staff:

"EMPLOYEE AGREEMENT

"1. I have read House resolution 591, 94th Congress, establishing the House Select Committee on Intelligence, and the Committee's Rules and Security Regulations.

"2. I understand that as a condition of employment with the Committee I am required to, and hereby agree to, abide by House Resolution 591 94th Congress, and by the Committee's Rules and Security Regulations.

. . . .

"4. I further agree that I will not divulge to any unauthorized person in any way, form, shape or manner the contents of classified information received or obtained pursuant to House Resolution 591, 94th Congress. I understand that it is my responsibility to ascertain whether information so received or obtained is classified. I further understand and agree that the obligations hereby placed on me by this paragraph continue after my employment with the Committee has terminated."

[108]As the Chairman expressed it to Mr. Rex Lee of the Justice Department: "It means the Executive Branch comes up and whispers in one friendly Con-

gressman's ear or another friendly Congressman's ear, and that is exactly what you want to continue, and that is exactly what I think has led us into the mess we are in."

[109]"c. The compartmentation procedures of the Intelligence Community have been established pursuant to statute and National Security Council Intelligence Directives. The simplest way for the staff to obtain access to this compartmented material would be to accept the normal secrecy arrangements as modified in the enclosed. This would ensure against difficulties in access to such compartmented material throughout the Intelligence Community." Letter to Chairman Pike, from Mr. Colby, CIA, July 28, 1975.

[110]The specific suggestion came in a letter to the Chairman: "The security principle of 'compartmentation' involving special access and information dissemination controls is designed to ensure that only those individuals whose 'need to know' have been specifically approved by some higher authority, who have been specially indoctrinated, and who undertake special commitments to protect it are provided access to a particularly sensitive category of foreign intelligence sources and methods. Compartmentation assists in the application of the 'need-to-know' principle by ensuring that individuals are provided access to only that information clearly essential to the performance of their duties. . . .

"For your information, in addition to the Senate Select Committee's use of the modified secrecy oath dealing with compartmented access, the following House and Senate committees have obtained compartmented access for their staffs, which was granted after the normal briefings and signing of the secrecy oath:

"Armed Services Committee
"Appropriations Committee
"Aeronautical and Space Sciences Committee"

Letter to Chairman Pike, from Mr. Colby, CIA, July 28, 1975.

[111]The CIA has also informed this Committee that all other Congressional committees leave their personal notes at Agency headquarters.

[112]"(3) The Department will furnish access at the Hoover Building in Room 4171 to those materials requested:

"(a) only to the members of the Committee, where it is determined by the Attorney General that the materials involve peculiarly sensitive foreign intelligence sources of peculiarly sensitive ongoing foreign intelligence operations.

. . . .

"(c) An exception to (a) and (b) above is made for the identities of so-called "live" informants or potential informants as defined in the FBI Manual of Instructions as to which no access will be furnished unless the identity of the individual as an informant or potential informant has already been made known to the Committee. . . .

. . . .

"(a) Before the copies of . . . materials are taken to the Committee's offices, the Bureau shall, within 24 hours of the selection, make appropriate excisions and paraphrases of information which might, if inadvertently disclosed, endanger sensitive FBI sources or sensitive ongoing operations.

. . . .

"The Committee staff may remove notes on unscreened materials only if such notes are reviewed and cleared by the Bureau under the provisions of (6) (a) thru (c) above." Procedures, submitted by the Department of Justice, to the House Select Committee on Intelligence, Aug. 19, 1975.

[113]"You will recall that the Committee agreed to put all requests for materials, documents, information, and briefings in writing. . . .

"To date the Department has not received written requests which encompass all of the oral requests which were made by the different Committee members during the testimony of Messrs. Pommerening and Walsh before the Committee on August 7, 1975. Letter to Mr. Field, from Mr. Steven Blackhurst, Department of Justice, Aug. 21, 1975.

[114]"1. Identities of secret agents, sources and persons and organizations involved in operations which, if disclosed, would be subject to personal physical danger, or to extreme harassment, or to economic or other reprisals, as well as material provided confidentially by cooperating foreign intelligence services; diplomatic exchanges or other material the disclosure of which would be embarrassing to foreign governments and damaging to the foreign relations of the United States; and

"2. Specific details of sensitive intelligence methods and techniques of collection. . . .

"Verification procedures will continue to be available in case of Committee questions concerning matters deleted by the Executive agency.

"Other matters, the complete confidentiality of which the President personally certifies is essential to the effective discharge of Presidential powers, may be withheld." Draft Agreement, submitted to the Committee, Sept. 28, 1975.

2. Selective Briefings

Soon after the opening hearings, staff began investigating a high-risk, secret program. A request was made to interview the official in charge of the program. The interview was granted, but the official refused to talk about the program. He sat with a thick book of documents, but he refused to let any documents be reviewed. They were too secret.

Intelligence officials made a proposal the Committee would hear again and again. The Chairman and perhaps the ranking minority Member could be briefed on the program.[117] In light of the fact that the Committee had been told that clearances would not be used to block the staff's work, it protested. When the Chairman refused to be briefed alone, intelligence officials relented and allowed staff to have access to the information, so long as the Chairman was briefed first.

A second example illustrates the problem with selective briefings. The Committee inquired into a project that included foreign military assistance via the CIA. It was "too sensitive" to discuss with staff. Once again, intelligence officials asked to brief the Chairman and senior Members.

The full Committee and staff were briefed, and the consensus was that the project had turned out to be one of the more outrageous ventures by CIA. Some months later, this same project was the subject of a Committee action to ask the President that the full story be made public.

A recent CIA operation in Africa followed the same awkward course of senior Member and senior staff briefings first, then full and prompt disclosure to the Committee. This Committee consistently maintained this policy that everything told to senior members was promptly told to the full Committee.[119] If Congress wanted a one- or two-man Committee, it had every opportunity to set one up. It has not done so to date. Preventing this from happening de facto was, and is, a serious challenge.[119a]

Footnotes:

[117]This request was a constant problem, as illustrated by the Chairman's remarks with reference to subpoenaed Forty Committee materials:

"Chairman PIKE. It has been indicated to me that I would be permitted to go down and look at these documents. That is not satisfactory to me. We subpoenaed these documents for the Committee. One of the difficulties which my predecessor had was that he was in possession of information which the rest of the Committee did not have. This Chairman has made it clear from the outset that when we subpoena documents for the Committee and when there is information which the Committee feels it is essential that the Committee have, I am not going to look at the information and deprive the rest of the Committee of it."

[119]"Chairman PIKE. I have two problems with that verification situation.

"We have had this situation time and time again in the House of Representatives where the members of a committee, and the members of the House are asked to trust the discretion of the Chairman, or of the Chairman and the ranking Member.

"I have a great deal of problem with the concept that I should be privy to information which is withheld from the rest of the Committee. That is No. 1."

[119a]Intelligence agencies are constantly maneuvering to keep information from Congress:

"MEMORANDUM FOR
THE RECORD   23 February 1973
FROM: [deleted], CHIEF, WESTERN HEMIS-
      PHERE DIVISION
RE: MEETING WITH SENATOR JACKSON
      TO DISCUSS HOW CIA SHOULD
      HANDLE INQUIRIES FROM SENATOR
      CHURCH'S SUBCOMMITTEE ON MUL-
      TINATIONAL CORPORATIONS, IN RE-
      GARD TO CIA INVOLVEMENT WITH
      ITT IN CHILE IN 1970.

"*TOPICS DISCUSSED*. Senator Jackson's advice to us was as follows:

"1. Senator Jackson felt strongly that the first order of business for CIA in terms of handling the basic issues that were involved in the Senate Foreign Relations Subcommittee on Multinational Corporations asking the Agency about its activities in Chile in 1970, was to discuss the problem with the White House. (Jackson) was quite explicit that this conversation should be carried out by Schlesinger and that he should talk with no one other than President Nixon and Mr. Halderman (sic). The Senator stressed repeatedly that the Church Subcommittee on Multinational Corporations had focused on ITT only in the sense that this was the top of the iceberg. . . .

"2. Senator Jackson felt that the ultimate solution to the problem facing the Agency . . . could be found in getting Senator McClellan, acting on behalf of Senator Stennis, to call a session of the CIA Oversight Committee. This Committee would then look into the nature and scope of CIA's activities in Chile in 1970. Once that was accomplished, the Oversight Committee would handle the Foreign Relations Committee. Senator Jackson repeatedly made the comment that in his view the CIA Oversight Committee had the responsibility of protecting the Agency in the type of situation that was inherent in the Church

Subcommittee. As a result of this conviction, Senator Jackson would work with the Agency to see that we got this protection . . .

"4. Once the Oversight Committee had heard the details provided on the CIA's involvement, 'the Agency could send a brief statement to the Church Subcommittee staff members in response to the questions which they had previously posed to CIA. Senator Jackson agreed that the following statement would be perfectly adequate for this purpose:

" 'The testimony of Mr. Helms on 5 and 7 February before the Senate Foreign Relations Committee clearly established that CIA neither gave to nor received from ITT funds for use in Chile in 1970 for support of political parties. In addition, Mr. Helms' testimony brought out the fact that there were no joint action programs established in the context of the 1970 political developments in Chile. CIA regards Mr. Helms' testimony on this topic to be accurate thus, no further elaboration is planned.'. . .

"9. *Comment.* Senator Jackson was extremely helpful throughout 23 February on the issue of the Agency's problems with the Church Subcommittee. Senator Jackson is convinced that it is essential that the procedure not be established whereby CIA can be called upon to testify before a wide range of Congressional committees."

3. Special Restrictions

Committee Members are not the only object of secrecy arrangements proposed by intelligence officials. Other Members of Congress apparently cannot be trusted with secret information about the government they govern.

Time and again, staff was told that it would be difficult to turn over documents because of Rule 11. Rule 11 is a House rule that allows members of the House of Representatives to have access to all "committee hearings, records, data, charts, and files . . ."[120]

The Committee was asked to sign letters affirming that it would not turn over any documents to another Member of the House. The Committee was eventually asked to pass a Resolution to that effect. Sometimes this acted to delay the forwarding of documents. The primary result was that most materials the Committee received in the closing months of its investigations were "on loan."[121]

The concept of loaning materials to the Committee had other advantages for the intelligence community.

The first advantage is the right to possession and control of final disposition of our files. Without a loan arrangement, staff was told that certain papers could not be provided.

The other advantage in loaning documents pertained to a possible court contest over release of classified information. If release of a document were going to be legally disputed, the Executive clearly wanted to be in the position of having legal possession of that document. Unfortunately, release or publication of Committee information raised far more immediate, and practical, problems.

Footnotes:

[120]Specifically, House Rule XI (2) (e) (2) provides that:

"All committee hearings, records, data, charts, and files shall be kept separate and distinct from the congressional office records of the Member serving as chairman of the committee; and such records shall be the property of the House and all Members of the House shall have access thereto."

[121]The standard caveat, which accompanied all materials turned over to the Committee, was adopted from a letter of Sept. 30, 1975:

"This is forwarded on loan with the understanding that there will be no public disclosure of this classified material (nor of testimony, depositions or interviews concerning it) without a reasonable opportunity for us to consult with respect to it." Letter to Chairman Pike, from Mr. Colby, CIA.

4. The Release of Information

One of the most troubling problems the Committee faced was what information to release and what process to follow in making its decision. A corollary problem was what to do about unauthorized release of information.

Existing standards for classifications are vague, arbitrary, and overused. Almost anything can be a "source" or "method" of intelligence—which are the primary criteria for foreign intelligence classifications. As a result, the sources or methods by-line is used to classify items that have practically no bearing at all on intelligence, but was extremely embarrassing.[123]

Overuse of classifications is inevitable when, by the Executive's most recent estimate, some 15,466 persons can classify information.[124]

The difficulty is that no one in Congress can declassify. The Executive Branch claims exclusive and sole jurisdiction. This gives an administration the power to use the classification system in a manner that can result in manipulation of news by declassifying information that can be used to justify policy, while maintaining classification of information that may lead to contrary conclusions. Another aspect to be recognized is that classification can hide conduct from the American people that is well-known to the foreign country involved. Castro knew of the assassination attempts, the Cambodians knew they were being bombed, but the American people, whose government was engaging in these practices, were not aware of the activities because of the classification system.

The dilemma arises when a Congressman or Committee receives information which one or the other decides should be brought before the people they represent. This Committee faced that problem and did not reach a satisfactory solution.

The procedure followed by the Committee was that when it decided to consider making public certain information taken directly from classified documents or testimony, it would give appropriate executive branch officials 48 hours' notice. It would then allow those officials to appear before the Committee, in closed session, and present arguments against release of all or part of the information. If no agreement could be reached, the materials at issue would be forwarded to the President. They would be released unless the President asserted, personally and in writing, that release would be "detrimental to the national security."[126]

The Committee used this process with three separate pieces of information. All three were covert CIA projects. Their release was proposed in separate motions placed before the Committee by Congressman Johnson.

The initial Johnson motions were introduced in November 1975, and voted down by the Committee, with five Members not present. Some weeks later, the motions were made again, with all but one Member present, and approved by the majority. [128] This began the release of information process.

The next step was to draft a short statement outlining the significant aspects of each covert operation.[129] The statements were forwarded to the Special Counsel to the Director of Central Intelligence, with an accompanying letter notifying him of an opportunity to present the Intelligence Community's views in a hearing three days later.

The Director of Central Intelligence, Mr. Colby, appeared, accompanied by appropriate officials, to present any specific objections he might have. His response was specific, but sweeping. He objected to everything, no matter how it was worded, and no matter how impossible it would be to identify a country, a source, or an operational method.[131]

Mr. Colby's response seemed to end any good faith effort to work out mutually acceptable release of information, but the Committee made one more effort. The three statements were rewritten, making them even more general than before. Names of countries were taken out; only gross dollar totals were used; and innumerable generic descriptions were inserted. In one case, far less remained than had appeared in newspaper articles attributed to high executive branch officials.

In a hearing the next day, Mr. Colby still objected to the release of anything.[132]

This meant that all the materials had to be forwarded to the President for a decision on whether release would be detrimental to the national security. The President, of course, turned to CIA for guidance.

More than three weeks later, the Chairman was informed in writing by the President that the Committee could not implement its decision to release the two statements.

Incredibly, the President's letter was classified "secret." The secret stamp was unnecessary, because there were no facts at all about the covert projects in his letter. The types of projects at issue were not even mentioned. The letter was simply a rhetorical pronouncement of how important confidentiality is, and how telling the American people what their government is doing in these matters would harm our best interests.

It should be noted that one of the items that allegedly would harm this nation's security if made public had already been made public—by Dr. Kissinger.[134]

Footnotes:

[123] A typical example was the CIA refusal, at first, to declassify part of the 1973 Mid-East War Post-Mortem. That position produced the following exchange with the CIA Special Counsel:

"Chairman PIKE. Mr. Rogovin, I find, as I look at what has been deleted and what has been omitted and what has been retained and read, differs not as to sources or methods, not as to the necessity of protecting the sensitivity of stuff, but whether it is in fact rather self-serving, or whether it is in fact rather damaging."

[124] This estimate was provided to the Committee by the Interagency Classification Review Committee, which was established by President Nixon in Executive Order 11652, which also established the security classification system now in force. . . .

[126] In the event of disagreement, the matter will be referred to the President. If the President then certifies in writing that the disclosure of the material would be detrimental to the national security of the United States, the matter will not be disclosed by the Committee, except that the Committee would reserve its right to submit the matter to judicial determination." Letter to Chairman Pike, from Mr. Colby, CIA, Sept. 30, 1975.

[128] The votes were 10-2, 10-2, and 10-2.

[129] The shortest statement was two pages; the longest was 14 pages.

[131] Mr. COLBY. Mr. Chairman, we have several difficulties with this report. We looked through it. We tried to identify what things might be released and what things might not. There are a few odd sentences that might be released."

[132] "Mr. NELSON. . . I consulted with the Director. It is his position that he would object to the declassification of either of these papers as I described them to him over the phone."

[134]"Tokyo-U.S. assistance prevented a takeover by Soviet-backed elements in Angola in July, a senior official aboard U.S. Secretary of State Henry A. Kissinger's plane said en route to Tokyo yesterday." Washington Post. A-17, Dec. 8, 1975.

This was the first administration acknowledgement of U.S. involvement in Angola.

"Secretary of State Henry A. Kissinger's admission that the United States is trying to be helpful to some neighbors of strife-torn Angola is a surprise only because Kissinger has openly acknowledged it." Jeremiah O'Leary, "U.S. Admits Indirect Aid to Angola," Washington Star, A-4, Dec. 10, 1975. ☐

Section Two:

The Select Committee's Investigative Record

Costs

No money shall be drawn from the Treasury, but in Consequence of Appropriations made by law; and a regular Statement and Account of the Receipts and Expenditures of all public Money shall be published from time to time. Art. 1, Sec. 9, cl. vii, U.S. Const.

Money and spending were the first topics of Committee hearings. This choice of a beginning was founded on Constitutional responsibilities, and it implemented a straightforward investigative technique—by following the dollars, the Committee would locate activities and priorities of our intelligence services.

The inquiry was fruitful and interesting. By the time it was over, GAO accountants on loan to the Committee had concluded that the foreign intelligence budget is three to four times more costly than Congress has been told. [135] An OMB review of the domestic intelligence budget, conducted at the Committee's request, concluded that it may be five times the estimate given to Congress by federal officials.

Totals do not tell the whole story. Congressional and Executive scrutiny of these budgets was found to range somewhere between cursory and nonexistent. Spending controls by the agencies themselves were, likewise, often inadequate, as a few preliminary examples indicate.

• A CIA Station in a small country spent $41,000 on liquor, in one year.

• Taxpayer monies were spent to provide heads of state with female companions, and to pay people with questionable reputations to make pornographic movies[137] for blackmail.

• The "accommodation procurement" mechanism was used to buy limousines for foreign dignitaries, with cash payments that were difficult to verify.

• A huge arsenal of weapons and access to ammunition have been developed by CIA, giving it a capability that exceeds most armies of the world.

• A middleman who is a close friend of top FBI officials tacked thousands, if not millions, of dollars of unwarranted markups on to covert purchases.

These examples reflect the wide range of problems with secret financing of secret activities. A more detailed review of these and other examples, along with the basic processes or mechanisms that accompany them, is a good base for suggested reforms.

1. Deceptive Budgets

Much attention is paid to numbers when the foreign and domestic intelligence budgets are prepared. Not much attention is paid to substance.

The Office of Management and Budget (OMB), the Director of Central Intelligence (DCI), and other officials go through an elaborate process in arriving at budget numbers. As described to Congress, it is an impressive procedure.

What is not described is the close, almost inbred relationship between OMB officials and intelligence budgetmakers. OMB also does not point out that it completely lacks the expertise to evaluate huge technological expenditures by the National Security Agency.

Executive officials do not stress the lack of a centralized budget authority in the intelligence services, which causes enormous waste, duplication and hidden costs in military intelligence. There is little consideration given to the extraordinary spending latitude granted to CIA, or to the CIA's heavy use of "unvouchered" funds. There is no explanation from FBI of the reasons for millions of dollars of "confidential" purchases.

When appearing before Congress, executive officials do not review the inadequacies of internal Agency auditors. No mention is made of items transferred elsewhere in the federal budget to keep the intelligence budget small.

These officials do not remind Congress that our government's auditors, the General Accounting Office, have been denied access to secret intelligence budgets for more than a decade. They do not explain abuses of covert purchasing mechanisms, domestic as well as foreign.

These same officials do, however, stress that anything they can or will say must be kept a secret

All this adds up to more than $10 billion being spent by a handful of people, with little independent supervision, with inadequate controls, even less auditing, and an overabundance of secrecy.

It begins with OMB officials and their counterparts in the various agencies. Testimony before this Committee revealed that only six OMB employees work full-time on the foreign intelligence budget. Of those six, three are former CIA employees. In turn, the CIA official in charge of the Agency's budget has recently arrived from OMB, where he had primary responsibility for CIA's budget.

This, in itself, does not bode well for a vigorous review of the merits of intelligence programs. It is set back further by the fact that OMB is not told of sensitive projects as they are being planned. Even after it is told, OMB's officials are not free to evaluate all details of sensitive projects.

The absence of real involvement by outsiders in intelligence spending continues.

For example, CIA's budget appears as only a single line item in the published Federal budget. This is done in the name of secrecy, but it gives CIA an unusual advantage. Congress requires any agency wishing to transfer funds from one line item to another to come back to Congress for approval.

This is called reprogramming. Most agencies have many line items, giving Congress some check on their spending. CIA has had no reprogramming problems in the past. It could tell Congress it was spending a certain amount on covert action, then proceed to transfer large amounts to covert programs without Congress' approval.[148]

This is not however, the most significant lack of knowledge about intelligence spending. Billions of dollars spent every year for intelligence are not included in the "official" intelligence budgets.

One way this has been accomplished has been by

shifting items that have traditionally appeared in the intelligence budget into other budget categories. For example, the Department of Defense has switched the following items, by reclassifying them as "communications": Counterintelligence and Investigative Activities; Mapping, Charting, and Geodesy; and the Advance Location Strike Program. A sizeable secret reconnaissance activity at Defense was switched to "research and development." All of these activities and many more were, until recently, in Defense's intelligence budget.[149] Defense is not alone in using this tactic.

The costs given Congress for military intelligence do not include expenditures for tactical military intelligence, which would approximately double intelligence budgets for the three armed services.[150] Roughly 20 percent of the National Security Agency's budget is not added into the intelligence budget. It should be noted that NSA does nothing else except gather and analyze technical intelligence, and it has one of the largest budgets in the intelligence community.

Sometimes entire agencies, such as the Defense Advanced Research Projects Agency, are completely omitted from estimates of intelligence-related costs as well as the intelligence budget.

The budget for the National Security Council is omitted completely, although a sizeable portion of their staff and subcommittees work exclusively on intelligence matters.[153]

Still another technique is undervaluation of the real cost of certain operations. The Committee analyzed one covert operation and found that the dollar amounts given by CIA for weapons supplied were about half of the Defense Department's contract prices.

At the Committee's request, OMB did add up the total cost for all federal domestic intelligence, for the

100

first time ever. The total they came up with was more than five times the amount that had been given to the Committee in testimony by domestic intelligence officials.[155] The FBI, for example, had neglected to include such clear intelligence functions as the National Bomb Data Center, or Counterintelligence. More significantly, there had never been an attempt to add up all the divergent intelligence operations in the federal government.[156]

By using the new OMB figures for domestic intelligence, and by adding such items as transferred expenditures, the full NSA budget, and revalued cost figures, the Committee estimated that the cost of intelligence today is at least three to four times the amount reported to Congress.

An obvious question is how can there be such a difference in total cost estimates? One answer is the lack of coordination in approaching the budget. Another is that there are no adequate standards for what is, and is not, intelligence spending. A final answer may be that there is a conscious desire to keep the totals small, by dividing and confusing the estimates.

It should be obvious that if nobody has ever added up the costs of the many domestic intelligence units, then certainly nobody is coordinating their budgets, as intelligence per se. In foreign intelligence, the problem is, to a large degree, a lack of centralized authority. For example, the DCI presents the entire foreign intelligence budget to Congress and the President, but he only has authority for CIA's budget. Defense officials testified that a substantial part of their intelligence budget is considered the responsibility of the Secretary of Defense. The DCI, they say, merely reviews their work.

Fragmented authority leads to overall coordination problems. A good illustration is the existence of separate counterintelligence budgets in FBI, CIA, NSA, DIA, Army, Navy, and Air Force.[159] Some are included in the intelligence budget; some are not. Some coordinate with other counterintelligence programs; some do not. The FBI testified, for example, that it does not know if CIA has a counterintelligence group, that it does not know how much CIA's operations cost, and that it does not know if CIA duplicates FBI's work.[160]

Fragmented authority and coordination leave the budget wide open to distortions. Each agency applies its own budget standards. . . .

There is, for example, no standard for allocating the cost of a military base whose primary purpose is to support intelligence operations. The repair of a submarine damaged on intelligence duty may or may not be included in spy costs. The Committee asked OMB, GAO, and all the intelligence agencies for their standards for allocating support costs. No agency had any to offer. No agency had even a basic definition of intelligence.

In a statement prepared for the Committee, the DCI made it clear that there are no good definitions in use today. As he said, ". . . [I]n essence, it boils down to a judgment call."

The Committee has compiled it own set of suggested guidelines.[164] In addition, a good first step would be to include the same items in the intelligence budget from one year to the next. This alone would have prevented the official intelligence budgets from remaining at constant levels over the past few years, which is fundamentally deceptive.

Footnotes:

[135]A special study done in 1971 by Dr. Schlesinger, as head of OMB, concluded that the foreign intelli-

gence budget was nearly double the amount being told to Congress at that time. *See, A Review of the Intelligence Community*, OMB (March 10, 1971).

[137]One of these was titled "Happy Days," with Mr. Robert Maheu as casting director, make-up man, cameraman and director.

[148]"MR. ASPIN. For the record again, tell us who has to approve reprogramming, who is informed, and who approves reprogramming?

"MR. COLBY. I do.

"MR. ASPIN. And that is all?

"MR. COLBY. Yes. . . ."

. . . Comm. Hearings . . . Aug. 4, 1975.

[149]In total, the transfer of these programs from the "intelligence" portion of DoD's budget to "Communications" and "Research & Development" by themselves involved hundreds of millions of dollars and thousands of personnel.

[150]Some costs for military/tactical activities are disclosed to Congressional Committees in chart form, entitled "Intelligence Related". However, after examination, the staff believes that the charts vastly understate the costs of military/tactical intelligence activities.

[153]Examples of this would be the Forty Committee whose sole task is to approve covert action projects, or the Verification Panel and its Restricted Working Group who verify intelligence indicating alleged Soviet violations of SALT.

[155]Letter to Staff Director, from Mr. Ogilvie, OMB, **Nov. 12, 1975:**

"**Department of Justice**

| | FY76 except as noted | |
	$ in K	Personnel
Deputy Attorney General's Office	125	5
Federal Bureau of Investigation	87,119	3385

Drug Enforcement Administration	11,913	463
Immigration & Naturalization Service	814	38
Criminal Division	1,262	51
	101,233	3942

Civil Service Commission

National Agency Check & Inquiry	3,366	265
Full Field Investigations	15,386	722
Other Investigations	3,082	95
	21,834	1082

Department of Treasury

Bureau of Alcohol, Tobacco & Firearms	62,929	2269 .
Customs Service	183,441	7748
Internal Revenue Service Intelligence Division	101,942	3813
Internal Security (Inspection)	12,141	553
Secret Service	94,466	2934
INTERPOL dues	140*	—
INTERPOL other	388*	—
	455,447	17,317

Energy Research & Development

Administration	295	15
TOTALS	578,809	22,356"

*1975 costs

[156]Testimony on Aug. 7, 1975 by Eugene W. Walsh, Assistant Director, Administrative Division, Federal Bureau of Investigation:

"MR. FIELD. It sounds like that is all they are over there for and that it is a way of shifting the real cost of intelligence out of that budget. How about the National Bomb Data Center?

"MR. WALSH. Yes, sir.

"MR. FIELD. That is intelligence?

"MR. WALSH. It may be in the dictionary's definition, sir, but it is not in ours." Comm. Hearings . . . Aug 7, 1975.

[159]When Mr. Walsh appeared before the Committee on Aug. 7, 1975, he was asked if FBI was aware of the multitude of counterintelligence programs:

"Are you aware that the CIA, the DIA, the Army, the Navy, the Air Force and NSA, all have their counterintelligence programs?

"MR. WALSH. I haven't acquainted myself with their programs, sir." Comm. Hearings . . . Aug. 7, 1975.

[160]Mr. Walsh was also asked: "Do you know if the CIA spends more than you do?

"MR. WALSH. I would certainly think so.

"MR. FIELD. Has anybody in the administration ever told all of these people, who spend multi-multi millions of dollars, over and over again—really on the same program—has anybody in the vernacular of my generation, told them to 'get their act together'?

"MR. WALSH. I have no knowledge on that, no sir." Comm. Hearings . . . Aug. 7, 1975.

[164]The Committee used three major classifications:

1. Foreign/National—This intelligence relates to "national" programs (i.e., overhead reconnaissance with various detection and sensing devices) targeted against foreign countries. Intelligence of this nature is "national" in the sense that it is a concerted effort of the CIA, DoD components and State Department.

a. National intelligence is intelligence bearing on the broad aspects of U.S. national policy and national security transcending the competence of a single agency to produce.

2. Domestic Intelligence—This intelligence includes activities of civil departments and agencies such as DEA, IRS, FBI. It is conducted within the United States and directed at U.S. citizenry.

3. Military/Tactical—Intelligence of this nature includes a variety of DoD activities to support military commanders ranging from detailed weapons performance assessments of our adversaries, to R & D projects for upgrading present radar early warning and ocean surveillance and patrol systems.

   a. Tactical intelligence is intelligence in support of military plans and operations at the military unit level.

   b. Strategic intelligence is intelligence in support of military plans and operations at national and international levels.

2. An Absence of Accountability

The General Accounting Office (GAO) is the auditing arm of Congress. When it comes to intelligence agencies, that arm is no arm at all.

In the early years, GAO was generally limited to an auditing function. With the passage of time, Congress has turned to GAO for more than balancing books. Today, under authority of law, GAO is empowered to analyze the economy and efficiency with which government funds are spent.

The Comptroller General, who heads GAO, testified that he cannot even balance CIA's books, let alone analyze its efficiency. Specifically, he said that from 1962, GAO has made no attempt to audit the CIA, because it was allowed scant access to classified spending.

Last year GAO was directed to compile basic budgetary information on federal investigative and intelligence functions. It was refused information by CIA, NSA, and intelligence agencies of the Defense Department. In another recent instance, the FBI refused to permit GAO to examine case files. The Bureau offered special summaries, but refused to allow any verification of those summaries.

The Executive agencies' treatment of GAO is curious. In January 1966, the CIA enter into a sole-source contract with the management consulting firm of Peat, Marwick, Livingston & Co., for a total contract price of $55,725.00. CIA could have saved taxpayers some money, if it had given GAO access.

CIA officials conceded that these independent consultants were given complete and free access to all classified procurement documents, as well as all personnel concerned with Agency procurement activities. In June 1966, the firm completed its work and issued a full report of findings and recommendations. A cover memorandum addressed to the Inspector General expressed appreciation for the Agency's full cooperation.

By contrast, this Committee's staff encountered lengthy delays in gaining limited access to similar documents and personnel, including the report of Peat, Marwick, Livingston & Co.

The issue is not really whether Congress—with Constitutional responsibility for federal spending—should have equal access with a private company. The issue is whether an objective look at secret expenditures ever takes place.

It does not take place at OMB. GAO cannot look. Even this Congressional investigating committee has now tested access and come up wanting.

Do intelligence agencies themselves adequately audit their own operations? No.

The CIA is a good example. Their audit staff is undermanned for a comprehensive review of complex and extensive agency spending that takes place worldwide. They are allowed to balance books, but they are not always allowed to know the exact purpose of expenditures. Only five percent of all vouchered transactions are checked, even though these add up to 20 percent of CIA's entire burget. Substantive corroborating records are not kept. Their audits deviate from the standards of professional Certified Public Accountants, and CIA has not compiled a list of these exceptions to control the deviances.

These and other shortcomings in audit and control, for both foreign and domestic intelligence agencies, lead to an inevitable result—spending abuses.

3. Spending Abuses

The easiest way to illustrate problems encountered in secret spending is to examine a number of mechanisms currently in use, and a number of situations that have grown out of those mechanisms.

a. Covert Procurement

Many CIA covert actions and clandestine operations must be supported in a "non-attributable" manner, which led CIA to establish a covert procurement branch. Unfortunately, covert procurement has become an overused, expensive, and often uncontrollable technique for questionable purchasing.

The branch's activities include support of overseas stations and the procurement of weapons and paramilitary materials. To facilitate these requirements, covert procurement has under its control a number of operational proprietaries and "notional" companies. Notional companies are merely paper firms, with appropriate stationery and checking accounts. These companies make requests to the proprietaries so the proprietary can bill an apparently legitimate company for covert requirements. Needless to say, it is an expensive way to buy a refrigerator, and should not be used unnecessarily.

When an overseas station requires an item that cannot be traced to the United States government, it sends a requisition with a special code. One code is for items that should not be traceable to CIA. Another code means it should not be traceable to the U.S. government.

Theoretically, once these codes, called "sterility codes,"[180] are attached, there is no more traceable involvement with the government. However, the Committee reviewed documents which showed that items purchased in a non-traceable manner are sometimes transported by U.S. military air-pouch, rather than sent by private carrier as a truly non-government purchase would be.

Another procedure which the Committee staff questioned was the routing of requests for small quantity, low-cost, and even non-traceable items through the expensive covert process. The logical alternative would be to have the item purchased either overseas or here with petty cash, avoiding the expense of covert procurement. These included such items as quantities of ball point pens, ping-pong paddles, or hams.

The staff was also unable to determine the reason for certain high-cost items being purchased through this mechanism. Hundreds of refrigerators, televisions, cameras, and watches are purchased each year, along with a variety of home furnishings.

The question is why an American television would be purchased here and sent to Europe if someone was trying to conceal his involvement with the United States. This is especially true because the power requirements abroad are different, and a transformer has to be installed on an appliance bought in the U.S. before it will work. In fact, a large percentage of electrical appliances did not have transformers added, which raises the possibility that these items are being covertly purchased for use in the United States.

The same question arises with the purchases of home furnishings. A review of overseas station purchases showed, for example, that one station bought more than one hundred thousand dollars of furnishings in the past few years. In that context, additional covert purchases here at home seem excessive. Finally, why not buy a Smithfield ham through normal purchasing channels? There is no way that ham could be traced to the CIA or the U.S. government, no matter how it was bought.

As in every other component of the Agency, the effort to maintain secrecy, even within the branch itself, is highly emphasized.

The Committee was told that because proprietary employees do not have a "need to know," they are not put in a position to question any request the Agency might make. Three high procurement officials have conceded that the sterility code is not questioned by the covert procurement staff. The 1966 study by Peat, Marwick, Livingston & Co., stated that there was excessive use of these codes, without justification. [188] The Committee's investigation indicates that this situation has not been remedied.

b. Local Procurement

The Committee's investigation of the covert procurement mechanism led to a review of records from local, or in-field, procurement. The staff reviewed records for the past five fiscal years from three typical overseas stations varying in size and number of employees. Over-spending and under-auditing seemed to be prevalent.

An example is a medium-sized station that purchased over $86,000 in liquor and cigarettes during the past five years. [189] The majority of these purchases were designated "operational gifts"—gifts to friendly agents or officials in return for information or assistance.

It would appear that spending practices have an uncanny way of changing with new station chiefs. A station that purchased $41,000 in liquor in 1971, had a new chief in 1972. Liquor purchases dropped to $25,000, which is still a lot of liquor. [190]

One station had purchased over $175,00 in furnishings for leased quarters and safehouses. [191]

In an effort to determine whether this kind of spending is questioned by CIA auditors, the staff interviewed the CIA audit official who audited these stations. He recalled the liquor, and that when he inquired as to the quantity, he was told by the Station Chief that they would "try to hold it down in the future."[192] The same auditor had audited the station that purchased over $175,000 in furnishings. When questioned, he was not even aware of the total figure.

This experience led the Committee staff to interview several members of the Internal Audit Division, as well as eight overseas case officers and chiefs of station. From these interviews, several things became apparent.

Auditors do not perform thorough reviews of case officers' "advance accounts." At all overseas stations, each case officer is allotted an advance, which is nothing more than a petty cash fund. From this fund, the officer pays operating expenses and the salaries of his agents. He is required by Agency regulations to obtain a receipt for every expenditure, but, due to manpower considerations, these are only spot-checked when audited—which is not often. [195] Such funds run into millions of dollars each year.

Every case officer and Internal Audit officer conceded that the Agency must "rely solely on the integrity of its case officer." When a case officer's agents refuse to sign receipts, the case officer "certifies" that he expended the funds. A case officer might have as many as ten agents working for him, each of whom may receive between $50 and $3,000 per month, all in cash.

Finally, audits of all overseas stations are not performed on a regular basis. It may be two or three years, or more, before a station is audited. Even then, the Committee discovered that recommendations made by auditors are usually not disclosed in the auditor's report to headquarters.

c. Accommodation Procurements

In addition to procuring goods and services for its own use, CIA makes "accommodation procurements" for foreign governments, officials, agents, and others.

The Agency serves more or less as a purchasing agent for an undisclosed principal. Although the individual for whom the accommodation procurement was made advances the necessary funds or repays the Agency after delivery, the indirect administrative costs are borne by American taxpayers. These costs include the salary of the agency purchaser, certain transportation charges, accounting costs, and in some cases the salaries of training and technical personnel.

In investigating one series of accommodation procurements, the Committee learned that a foreign government received a 20 percent discount by having CIA buy equipment in the name of the U.S. government.

If the foreign government had contracted for the same items in its own name, this discount would not have been available. In just two of these actions CIA saved the foreign government over $200,000, at the expense of American suppliers.

The Agency will usually refuse to make such procurements only if the requested item might appear to be beyond the requester's financial means, and might therefore give rise to questions about the requester's sources of income. Agency security officers feel that such questions might lead to disclosure of the requester's relationship with the agency.

Accommodation procurements involving less than $3,000 require only the approval of a CIA chief of station. When larger sums are involved, approval must be obtained from the Deputy Director for Operations. When the amount is more than $500,000, it must also be approved by the Director of Central Intelligence.

The Committee examined a number of accommodation procurement records. The following two examples illustrate that the facilities and resources of the United States government are sometimes used to satisfy little more than the whims of foreign officials.

In one instance, a foreign official described his son's enthusiasm for model airplanes to the chief of station. The foreign official wanted three model airplane kits, and even advised the CIA officer precisely where the kits could be purchased in the United States. A cable was sent to Agency headquarters asking for the purchase of three kits from the store in Baltimore suggested by the foreign official. Further, the cable instructed that the items were to be designated by a "sterility code," to indicate that the purchase of the kits could not be attributable to the United States government. Documents provided to the Committee in this case by the Agency were sanitized.[206]

In another instance, the President of an allied nation was preparing to play golf on a hot afternoon. Anticipating his thirst after several hours in the sun, he made a "priority" request to the local chief of station for six bottles of Gatorade. An Agency employee was immediately relieved of his ordinary duties and assigned to make the accommodation procurement.[207]

Nor was this the chief of state's only experience with the Agency's merchandising talents. In the past, the Agency has purchased for him several automobiles, including at least two custom-built armored limousines,[208] and, among other things, an entire electronic security system for his official residence. It is worth noting that these security devices are being supplied to a man who runs a police-state.

Accommodation procurements have also involved more expensive and politically sensitive items. For example, another head of a one-party state had long been fascinated by certain highly sophisticated electronic intelligence gathering equipment. He wished to develop his own independent collection capability. As an accommodation, and to "share the take," the Agency procured an entire electronic intelligence network for him in two phases. Phase I involved contract costs in excess of $85,000, and Phase II cost more than $500,000.

In investigating one series of accommodation procurements for an oil exporting country, the Committee asked CIA officials about the coordination and effect of the Agency's purchasing favors on the foreign country's oil pricing policy. The country's oil policy, incidentally, has not been among the most favorable to the United States. Agency officials were uncertain as to the effect, but they indicated that the two policies are largely considered separate issues.

In return for making accommodation procurements, the Agency is usually reimbursed by the requesting party. Although reimbursement may be in U.S. dollars, it is usually made in local foreign currency.[210] The Committee was unable to learn whether the Agency has any firm policy on what rate of currency exchange is to be used in making reimbursement. In many countries, U.S. dollars exchanged for local currency at the official rate bring fewer units of local currency than if exchanged at an unofficial, but more commonly used, rate.

d. Research and Development

CIA has long prided itself on technological capability, and many of its projects operate at far reaches of the "state of the art." Such accomplishments are made by the Agency with assistance and advice from the private sector.

Each year, CIA's Deputy Director for Science and Technology enters into hundreds of contracts with industry, usually in the name of other government agencies.[211] These contracts total millions of dollars for Agency contracts alone. Not only does the Agency contract for its own research and development programs, but also for national intelligence programs. Total contracts for both programs amount to hundreds of millions of dollars, annually.

Committee Staff interviewed numerous members of the Science and Technology Staff. A major target of this investigation was "contractor selection" practices. Although Mr. Colby testified before the Committee that CIA has established management controls to insure that contracting is carried out according to the intent of Congress, the investigation revealed that 84 percent of these contracts are "sole source contracts."

Staff also examined "cost overrun" aspects of research and development contracting. CIA claimed two and one-half percent of all research and development contracts involved cost overruns of 15 percent or more. There is no reason to doubt the figures; however, certain caveats must be considered. Contractors' cost estimates in sole-source contracts can easily be inflated to cover anticipated cost increases. Overruns can also be labeled "changes in scope."

In several interviews with contracting officers, "by the book" answers were given to questions regarding which officer is authorized, and does, accept contract changes. However, one former Agency contracting officer indicated that, to a considerable degree, the technical representative actually makes the contractual decisions, and the contracting officer then has to "catch up" by preparing contract amendments to legitimize changes already made.

Another target of the investigation was the disposal of Government Furnished Equipment (GFE). Regulations regarding GFE appear to be precise in determining when to "abandon" this equipment. However, the Office of Communications, for example, contracted in 1965 with an electronics company to do research work. The contract required the purchase of a large piece of industrial equipment, as well as related testing equipment. CIA provided funds for the equipment as well as the research.[221] The testing equipment cost $74,000 and the industrial equipment over $243,000. At the termination of the contract in 1975, the testing equipment was sold to the contractor for $18,500, the large piece of industrial [equipment] was abandoned, in place.

Calls to the manufacturer of this piece of machinery, as well as two "experts" in the field of this particular type of testing, revealed that the machinery which was abandoned, while perhaps "useless" to the Agency, was not a "worthless" piece of equipment which should have been "abandoned." According to documents provided to the Committee, CIA made no attempt to contact other government agencies, to see if the chamber could have been used by another agency.

c. Colleges and Universities

In 1967 *Ramparts Magazine* disclosed CIA support to the National Students Association. As a result, President Johnson issued a flat prohibition against covert assistance to educational institutions; but the Agency unilaterally reserved the right to, and does, depart from the Presidential order when it has the need to do so.[224]

There is no evidence that a President authorized this departure from the Johnson directive.

As background, President Johnson had appointed a committee to investigate the matter and make policy recommendations.

Under Secretary of State, Nicholas deB. Katzenbach, and CIA Director, Richard H. Helms, served on the Committee. It recommended that "no federal agency shall provide any covert financial assistance or support, direct or indirect, to any of the nation's educational or private voluntary organizations."

On March 29, 1967, President Johnson issued a statement accepting the recommendation and directing "all agencies of the government to implement it fully."

The Agency then issued internal policy statements to implement the President's orders, stating that, whenever possible, the Agency's identity and sponsorship are to be made known. But the Agency was to clearly retain the option of entering into a covert contract with colleges and universities, after obtaining approval from the Deputy Director for Administration.

Mr. Carl Duckett, Deputy Director for Science and Technology, testified before the Committee on November 4, 1975, that the Agency still has on-going contracts with "a small number of universities." Mr. Duckett also revealed that some of the contracts involved "classified work," and some are covert.

f. U.S. Recording

On October 9, 1975, the Committee held hearings on electronic surveillance in the United States. One of the witnesses, Mr. Martin Kaiser, was a manufacturer of electronic surveillance and counter-measure equipment. In the course of his testimony, he revealed that all sales of his equipment were routed—pursuant to FBI instructions—through a cut-out or middle-man, U.S. Recording Company, of Washington, D.C.[232]

The equipment was neither modified nor serviced by U.S. Recording. Kaiser testified that he delivered 80 percent of his equipment directly to the FBI. On one such occasion Kaiser noticed an invoice from U.S. Recording for equipment he had supplied, and it showed that U.S. Recording had tacked on 30 percent more than it had paid for the devices.[235]

The mark-up interested Committee investigators because, according to Kaiser, the middle-man had handled only paperwork and deliveries. The staff therefore acquired records of all sales between U.S. Recording and the FBI involving Kaiser's equipment. A Committee staff accountant did a detailed study and

118

determined that the 30 percent mark-up on the invoice seen by Mr. Kaiser was representative of all such sales.

As a result of numerous interviews, it became apparent that Mr. Joseph Tait—the President of U.S. Recording—was a long time friend and poker-playing companion of Mr. John P. Mohr, the Associate Director of the FBI in charge of Administration until 1972.[236]

During the course of investigation, the staff learned the poker games had been held at the Blue Ridge Club near Harpers Ferry, West Virginia, on several weekends each year for the past decade.[237] Guest lists included FBI officials connected with the Administrative Division, OMB officials, and a procurement officer from CIA. The only non-governmental officials at the poker games were Tait, and Mr. Gus Oberdick—the President of Fargo International—a supplier of police equipment to the FBI and CIA.[238] Mr. Mohr had invited all the guests, although Mr. Tait was the only person in the poker games 'who possessed membership in the Blue Ridge Club.

Interestingly, the Blue Ridge Club burned to the ground the evening before two staff attorneys traveled to Harpers Ferry to examine its records.

Most purchasing procedures of the FBI are governed by General Services Administration (GSO) regulations. However, confidential contracts are not subject to GSA regulations or supervision. The U.S. Recording Company was the sole company serving as an FBI cutout.[239] Interviews revealed that there was virtually no control exercised over the confidential contracts between U.S. Recording Company [and] the FBI.

Neither the Laboratory Division, which initiated the equipment requisitions, nor the Administrative Division, which authorized the requisitions, had any knowledge of the percentage markup being charged. The General Services Administration was consulted and gave an opinion that an appropriate mark-up for similar services would have been in the 5 percent range.

FBI's use of U.S. Recording was apparently motivated by the need for secrecy in purchases of sensitive electronic equipment. That justification appears questionable. In most instances, FBI Laboratory Division personnel negotiated for equipment directly with the manufacturers. When manufacturers later received purchase orders from U.S. Recording, for equipment with corresponding model number, quantities, and prices, it was apparent that the equipment was indeed going to FBI. In fact, the FBI told Kaiser that they were using U.S. Recording Company and not to worry about it.

FBI's use of U.S. Recording represents a grossly inefficient expenditure for intelligence equipment. Similarly, the fact that the persons within the FBI responsible for requisitioning and purchasing the equipment had no clear knowledge of the chain of authority regarding the arrangement, is at best, nonfeasance. Further ramifications are presently being investigated by the Criminal Division of the Justice Department, and by the IRS. The Committee has made its information on this matter available to both authorities.

Footnotes:

180"Sterility Codes," as they are termed within the Agency, designate the "degree of traceability" which can accompany an item procured or shipped. These codes range from "unclassified," which may be attributed to CIA, to a code which designates that a purchase is so sensitive that it is an "off-shore purchase of a foreign item."

188. . . This was one of many deficiencies and recommendations highlighted by the study. Some of the rec-

ommendations were adopted; most were not, according to the Committee's investigation.

[189]This figure was computed by Committee staff during several reviews of Local Procurement expenditures for one of the three typical overseas situations.

[190]Those two figures were likewise computed by Committee staff during reviews of Local Procurement records. The same Agency employee who was chief of the station in 1971, is now responsible for CIA operations in Angola.

[191]Figures computed by staff during review of local procurement expenditures. "Leased Quarters" are housing units supplied by CIA for staff or contract employees at field stations. "Safehouses" are housing units where the Agency's primary interest is that of a secure location to conduct clandestine meetings; its housing function, per se, is only incidental. The Agency also provides furnishings for these quarters, such as refrigerators, ranges, and living room furniture, and at times provides luxury items, such as china or crystal ware.

[192]Interview with Agency auditor, by S. A. Zeune, Oct. 29, 1975. The auditor concurred, with another high level Agency official, that in the country in question, it was "traditional" to give liquor and cigarettes as gifts. He also stated, "the controls on the issuances [of liquor] are not so stiff."

[195]Ibid. Agency regulations permit expenditures of less than $15.00 without receipts.

[197]Staff interviews with case officers and a former Chief of Station revealed this fact. Interviews, by S. A. Zeune, Oct. 17 & 24, 1975, copies on file with Sel. Comm. on Intell. Further, it was revealed during these interviews that polygraph examinations of staff employees, at one time carried out on a regular basis, are no longer performed except during pre-employment investigations. The agency continues, however, to polygraph indigenous agents on a regular basis.

121

206This information first came to the attention of the Committee from staff review of requisition documents in Sept., 1975. Further inquiry about the model plane purchases led CIA to give staff access to the cables.

207This was related to Staff, in response to questions concerning "accommodation procurements" made for the President of the allied country. The response was supplied by the former Chief of Station in the country. Interview with Chief of Station, by S.A. Zeune, Oct. 31, 1975, copy on file with Sel. Comm. on Intell.

208CIA documents made available to the Committee revealed that the Agency made three such accommodation procurements for the Chief of State. In all three instances—three times in the last ten years— the Chief of State requested that CIA procure the limousines. A Staff interview with the former Chief of Station disclosed that in the instances concerning the limousines, the Agency was reimbursed by way of American currency, hand delivered in bags or briefcases to the Station. In one instance, the transaction involved the equivalent of (U.S.) $50,000. Further, the documents appeared to reveal that the Agency was not disturbed by the fact that the President, in two instances, did not reimburse the full balance to the Agency until some months after the transaction had taken place. Interview with Chief of Station, by S.A. Zeune, Oct. 31, 1975, copy on file with Sel. Comm. on Intell.

210A Staff interview with the member of CIA Review Staff (and former Chief of Station) revealed that this is considered a further accommodation to the requesting party, inasmuch as the local currency is certain to be more readily available than U.S. dollars.

211For security reasons, CIA usually contracts in the name of other government agencies, such as Department of Defense, Air Force, or Army. Contractor employees are usually unwitting of CIA's association, although in most cases a high company officer will be briefed by the Agency on a "need to know" basis.

[221] In this instance, CIA did not advance the funds to the contractor for the purchase of the test equipment or the industrial equipment. The cost of both was added to the contractor's fee to the Agency. Interview with Office of Communications staff members, by S.A. Zeune and J.C. Mingee, Oct. 28, 1975, copy on file with Sel. Com. on Intell.

[224] "3. It is proposed that upon your approval:

"a. The attached guidelines be applied immediately to all future contractual arrangements with U.S. educational institutions.

"b. Contracts and grants now in existence be conformed to these guidelines as rapidly as feasible and wherever possible, no later than 30 December 67 for relationships that will extend beyond that date . . . The thrust of the review of existing contracts and the placement of future contracts will be that our contractor relationships with academic institutions will be strongly on the premise that CIA will be identified as the contractor . . . Any special contract arrangement will be considered only when there is extremely strong justification warranting a variance from the principles of CIA identification as the contractor. It is felt that the Agency must retain some flexibility for contracting arrangements with academic institutions and this can be carefully monitored and accomplished within the policies and principles expressed in the Katzenbach report . . ." Memorandum for Director of Central Intelligence, June 21, 1967.

[232] "I began my relationship with the FBI around 1967 or 1968. All my correspondence was sent directly to the FBI. However, I think it was on only one occasion that the Bureau ever contacted me personally. All other addresses were made personally or verbally. Once they began purchasing equipment I was directed not to send this equipment to the FBI, but

rather sell it to a company known as United States Recording, a private company operating on South Capitol Street in Washington, D.C. I informed the Bureau, as if they needed that piece of information, that Federal law would not allow me to sell equipment to anyone except bona fide governmental agencies. The FBI agents assured me my actions were proper and subsequently supplied a stamp to United States Recording which purported to certify on the purchase order that the transaction was in accordance with Federal law." Comm. Hearings . . . Oct. 9, 1975.

235"I might point out at this time, by the way, that nearly all the equipment deliveries I made to the Equipment Bureau involving orders to United States Recording were handled by me and billed to United States Recording. So the paperwork went through that route. I discovered at one time that United States Recording was adding a 30 percent markup on the bills for the equipment. During my dealings with the Federal Bureau of Investigation I sold them approximately $100,000 worth of electronic equipment." Comm. Hearings, . . . Oct 9, 1975.

236"MR. VERMEIRE. Mr. Tait, I believe at the last deposition, November 21, you mentioned that you had played poker on a number of occasions with Mr. John Mohr, former Assistant Director of the FBI.

"MR. TAIT. Yes." Interview with Mr. Tait, by J. B. F. Oliphant and R. Vermeire, Dec. 1, 1975, copy on file with Sel. Comm. on Intell.

237"MR. VERMEIRE. And I think you testified that you had played poker with him not only privately at each other's homes or homes in the area but also at a club up in Harpers Ferry. I think at the time that is all that was said; it was up in Harpers Ferry.

"MR. TAIT. That's right.

"MR. VERMEIRE. What was the name of that club?

"MR. TAIT. Blue Ridge.

"MR. VERMEIRE. How did you become a member of the club?

"MR TAIT. I used to play cards up there . . . with another man by the name of Parsons, Donald Parsons, (former Chief of the FBI Laboratory Division).

"MR. VERMEIRE. And was Mr. Parsons alive when you became a member?

"MR. TAIT. No.

"MR. VERMEIRE. How long had you been playing at the club prior to becoming a member?

"MR. TAIT. I don't know. I'd say probably four or five years.

"MR. VERMEIRE. Who is the one business person who was connected with private enterprise that was there?

"MR. TAIT. A man by the name of Oberdick.

"MR. VERMEIRE. Mr. Oberdick?

"MR. TAIT. Yes.

"MR. VERMEIRE. May I have his first name?

"MR. TAIT. Godfrey.

"MR. VERMEIRE. What business was he in?

"MR. TAIT. He is—I don't know exactly what you would say. He is a representative to various companies that supply equipment. What companies, I'm not sure.

"MR. VERMEIRE. What kind of equipment?

"MR. TAIT. Firearms, tear gas." *Ibid.*

[239]This fact was established through numerous staff interviews with knowledgeable FBI personnel in the Laboratory and Administrative Divisions.

"MR. VERMIERE. Were there other companies that you dealt with in that way?

"MR. HARWARD. I don't know of any company.

"MR. VERMEIRE. U.S. Recording is the only company that you know of that you had this confidential relationship with?

"MR. HARWARD. Yes." Interview with Mr. Harward.

4. Budget Secrecy

During Senate hearings in 1973, to confirm James Schlesinger as Secretary of Defense, Mr. Schlesinger indicated it might be possible to make public the total budget cost of foreign intelligence. When William Colby was confirmed as head of CIA in 1973, he, likewise, testified that publication of budget totals might not be harmful.[244]

In a television interview some years later, Dr. Schlesinger inadvertently revealed the size of the foreign intelligence budget. No great harm apparently came from that disclosure.

In 1973, a recommendation to publish the annual costs of intelligence was made by a Senate Special Committee to Study Questions Related to Secret and Confidential Documents.

On June 4, 1974, Senator J. William Proxmire of Wisconsin offered a floor amendment to a defense procurement authorization bill. His amendment would have required the Director of Central Intelligence to provide Congress with an annual, unclassified report describing the total amount requested for the "national intelligence program" in the budget submitted by the President.

In June 1975, the report of the Rockefeller Commission recommended that Congress carefully consider whether all or part of the CIA budget should be made public.

On October 1, 1975, Representative Robert N. Giaimo of Connecticut offered a floor amendment to a defense appropriations bill, prohibiting any of the funds provided for "Other Procurement, Air Force" from being expended by the CIA. Had the amendment been adopted, a subsequent amendment would have been offered to restore funds for the CIA, and a specific total for the agency would have been disclosed. .

Today, however, taxpayers and most Congressmen

do not know, and cannot find out, how much they spend on spy activities.

This is in direct conflict with the Constitution, which requires a regular and public accounting for all funds spent by the federal government.

Those who argue for secrecy do not mention the Constitution. They do not mention taxpayers. Instead, they talk of rather obscure understandings the Russians might derive about some specific operation,[251] even if all the Russians knew was a single total which would be in the billions of dollars and would cover dozens of diverse agencies.

How the Russians would do this is not clear. The Committee asked, but there was no real answer. What is clear is that the Russians probably already have a detailed account of our intelligence spending, far more than just the budget total.[252] In all likelihood, the only people who care to know and do not know these costs today are American taxpayers.

Footnotes:

[244]"When the same question was put to William E. Colby during his confirmation hearings to be Director of Central Intelligence, he replied: I would propose to leave that question, Mr. Chairman, in the hands of the Congress to decide . . . We are not going to run the kind of intelligence service that other countries run. We are going to run one in the American society and the American constitutional structure, and I can see there may be a requirement to expose to the American people a great deal more than might be convenient from the narrow intelligence point of view." Cong. Rec. S. 9603, June 4, 1974.

[251]"CHAIRMAN PIKE. . . . Do you think the Soviets know what our intelligence effort is?

"MR. COLBY. They know a good deal about it,

from the various books that have been published by 'X' members of the intelligence community." Comm. Hearings . . . Aug. 6, 1975.

252"CHAIRMAN PIKE. . . . Don't you think really that the Soviets have a far better estimate of what we are spending for intelligence than the average taxpayer in America has?

"MR. COLBY. I think they have put a great deal of time and attention trying to identify that, and they undoubtedly have a better perception of it than the average taxpayer who just takes the general statements he gets in the press. But—and that comes from the careful analysis of the material that is released. This does help you get a more accurate estimate of what it is." *Ibid.*

Performance

It is one thing to conclude that tens of billions of intelligence dollars have been rather independently spent, and sometimes misspent, over the past few years.

The important issues are whether this spending sufficiently meets our needs, whether Americans have received their money's worth, and whether non-monetary costs sometimes outweigh the benefits.

The latter question is a matter of risks. . . . To test the first two questions, the Committee investigated a representative spectrum of recent events. Some involved war; some involved law enforcement. Some involved American lives overseas; some involved personal freedoms at home. All involved important interests.

How did intelligence perform? Let the events speak for themselves.

1. Tet: Failure to Adapt to a New Kind of War

War in Vietnam meant that intelligence had to adapt to an unconventional war, and true perceptions could spell life or death for Americans. In Tet, perceptions were shattered.

Taking advantage of the Vietnamese lunar holiday, the North Vietnamese and Viet Cong forces launched an all-out offensive on January 30, 1968, against virtually every urban center and base in South Vietnam. The scale of attacks was unprecedented in the history of American involvement in the Vietnam War and flatly challenged the reassuring picture intelligence officials in Saigon and Washington had helped present to the American people.

With nearly all provincial capitals under siege, the American embassy compound was penetrated by the Viet Cong, and the pacification program set back in all areas; predictions of successes, announced scant months before, had turned into one of the greatest misjudgments of the war.

The Committee's investigation of Tet focused on the questions of warning in a combat situation and communicating the realities of a guerrilla war to executive branch policy-makers. Both are interrelated. Mr. William Colby and the post-mortems certify, "warning of the Tet offensive had not fully anticipated the intensity, coordination and timing of the enemy attack." A chief cause was our degraded image of the enemy.

There were at least two primary causes for such degradation. First, the dispute between CIA and MACV (Military Assistance Command, Vietnam) over enemy strength—called Order of Battle figures—created false perceptions of the enemy U.S. forces faced, and prevented measurement of changes in enemy strength over time. Second, pressure from policy-making officials to produce positive intelligence indicators reinforced erroneous assessments of allied progress and enemy capabilities.

a. The Order of Battle Controversy

According to Mr. Colby, the CIA had been suspicious of MACV's numerical estimate of the Vietnamese enemy since at least mid-1966. At an order of Battle conference held in Saigon in September, 1967, the differences between Washington and the field, and between CIA and MACV, were thrashed out; but according to Mr. Colby, to neither's satisfaction.

A resulting compromise represented the best resolution of MACV's preoccupation with viewing the order of battle in the classic military sense and CIA's assessment of enemy capabilities as a much broader people's war. The Special National Intelligence estimate that emerged from this conference quantified the order of battle in MACV terms, and merely described other potential enemy forces. Categories now proposed from previous estimates of order of battle detailed as much as 200,000 irregular personnel, self-[one word illegible] and secret self-defense forces, and assault [one word illegible] and political cadre.

As foot soldiers realized at the time, and as different studies by the Army Surgeon General confirm, the destructiveness of mines and booby traps, which irregular forces set out, was increasingly responsible for American losses. This was primarily because American forces were engaging the enemy with increased frequency in his defensive positions. Documents indicate that, even during the Order of Battle Conference, there was a large increase in sabotage for which irregulars and civilians were responsible. It appears clear in retrospect that, given the nature of protracted guerrilla war, irregular forces were basic determinants of the nature and scope of combat.

The numbers game not only diverted a direct confrontation with the realities of war in Vietnam, but also prevented the intelligence community, perhaps the President, and certainly Members of Congress, from judging the real changes in Vietnam over time.

The Saigon Order of Battle Conference dropped numbers that had been used since 1962, and used those that were left in what appears to have been an arbitrary attempt to maintain some ceiling. It prompted Secretary of State Dean Rusk to cable the American Embassy in Saigon, on October 21, 1967: "Need your recommendation how to resolve problem of unknown percentage of enemy KIA (Killed in Action) and WIA (Wounded in Action) which comes from ranks of self-defense, assault youth and VC civilian supporters. Since these others not carried as part of VC strength, indicators of attrition could be misleading."

When the Systems Analysis office in the Department of Defense examined the results of the conference and reinterpreted them in terms consistent with prior quantification, it remarked that the new estimate should have been 395,000–480,000 if computed on the same basis as before. "The computations do not show that enemy strength has increased, but that previous estimates of enemy strength were too low."

In the context of the late 1960's, numbers were not at all an academic exercise. Mr. Colby has testified that "(T)he effort to develop a number with respect to the enemy strength was a part of the advising of our government as to the amount of effort we would have to spend to counter that kind of (guerrilla) effort by the Viet Cong. They were also used to inform Members of Congress and the American public on the progress in Vietnam.

The validity of most of the numbers was significantly dubious. Unfortunately, they were relied on for optimistic presentations. For example, while mentioning in parenthetical and classified comments that the numbers supporting its indicators of progress in Vietnam were suspect, the Bureau of Intelligence and Research provided Assistant Secretary of State William Bundy with quantified measures of success.[263] General Westmoreland used such figures to support his contentions in the fall of 1967, that the enemy's "guerrilla force is declining at a steady rate."

In testimony before this Committee, Mr. Colby has stated that the "infatuation with numbers" was "one of the more trying experiences the Intelligence Community has had to endure." In the context of the period it appears that considerable pressure was placed on the Intelligence Community to generate numbers, less out of tactical necessity than for political purposes.

The Administration's need was for confirmation of the contention that there was light at the end of the tunnel, that the pacification program was working and generally that American involvement in Vietnam was not only correct, but effective.[266] In this sense, the Intelligence Community could not help but find its powers to effect objective analysis substantially undermined. Whether this was by conspiracy or not is somewhat irrelevant.

b. The Consequences

Four months after the Saigon Order of Battle Conference, the Tet offensive began. On February 1, hours after the initial mass assaults, General Westmoreland explained to a press conference, "I'm frank to admit I didn't know he (the enemy) would do it on the occasion of Tet itself. I thought he would do it before or after." The U.S. naval officer in command of the river forces in the Mekong Delta and his army counterpart were similarly caught off guard. Appalled at how poorly positioned they were to provide quick and efficient response, the naval officer, now a retired Vice Admiral, has told the Committee that he "well remember(s) the words of the Army General who brought us the orders to extricate ourselves from the mudflats as fast as possible. They were, 'It's Pearl Harbor all over again.'"

The April, 1968, post-mortem done by a collection of intelligence officers discussed the general question of warning. It concluded that while units in one corps area were on alert, allied forces throughout the country generally were caught unprepared for what was unfolding. Certain forces even while "on a higher than normal state of alert" were postured to meet "inevitable cease-fire violations rather than attacks on the cities." In other areas "the nature and extent of the enemy's attacks were almost totally unexpected." One-half of the South Vietnamese army was on leave at the time of the attacks, observing a 36-hour standdown.

In testimony before this Committee, both General Graham and William Colby confirmed the fact of some amount of surprise. General Graham preferred to label it surprise at the enemy's "rashness." Mr. Colby spoke of a misjudgment of their potential "intensity, coordination and timing."

Even though quick corrective action was taken to salvage American equipment and protect U.S. personnel, the ultimate ramifications on political and military fronts were considerable. General Westmoreland requested a dramatic increase of 206,000 in U.S. troop strength, and additional equipment supplies. Secretary of Defense Clark Clifford began rethinking the substance of intelligence. A collection of intelligence officers finally briefed the President of the United States on the realities of the Vietnam War in mid-March, and a few days later he announced he would not seek re-election.[271]

c. The Aftermath

The Committee received testimony that problems with intelligence in Vietnam were not confined to Tet. Up to the last days of South Vietnam's existence, certain blinders prevented objective reporting from the field and an accurate assessment of the field situation by Washington. Tet raised the issue of whether American intelligence could effectively account for enemy strength. Later events, among them the collapse of the Saigon government, pointed to a failure to properly acknowledge weaknesses of allies.

A real attempt to address the shortcomings of friendly forces in Vietnam was hampered by many factors. During the time of massive American presence, there was a failure to attribute at least partial South Vietnamese "success" to American air power and logistics support. Consequently, projected ARVN performance in 1975, after the U.S. pullout, was measured against the yardstick of the Easter Offensive of 1972, when American support was crucial.

Mission restrictions curtailed necessary collection activity by professional intelligence officers, and forced reliance on officials charged with military aid responsibilities. This promoted biased interpretations.[274]

The sum total of restrictions, manipulations, and censorship no doubt led to the conclusion Secretary of Defense, James R. Schlesinger reached at an April, 1975, news conference. He pointed out that "the strength, resiliency and steadfastness of those forces (South Vietnamese) were more highly valued than they should have been, so that the misestimate, I think, applied largely to Saigon's capabilities rather than Hanoi's intentions."

Ultimately, the Vietnam intelligence experience is a sobering reminder of the limitations and pitfalls the United States can expect to encounter if it chooses to align itself in unconventional battle with unconventional allies. It illustrates how very different guerrilla war is from World War II, and how much more problematic an alliance with emerging and unstable Third World governments will be.

Reviewing the American experience in Indochina, an Assistant Secretary of Defense for Intelligence wrote a note of caution to the Secretary of Defense emphasizing the following view:

"The problems that occurred in Vietnam or Cambodia can now be occurring in our efforts to assess [an allied and an adversary Third World country's] forces, forces in the Persian Gulf or forces in the Middle East. These problems must be addressed before the U.S. becomes involved in any future crisis in the Third World that requires objective and timely intelligence analysis."

Given the substantial American involvement in these areas, strong remedies and honest restrospect appear necessary, to overcome and prevent intelligence output that fails, for whatever reason, to present comprehensive and undisguised perceptions of war.

Footnotes:

263The memorandum to William Bundy is from Fred Greene of the State Department's Bureau of Intelligence and Research and is dated Sept. 22, 1967. It notes that claims of enemy captured, enemy recruited, weapons lost, desertions, incidents of battalion size attacks, killed in action, vital roads opened, and the percentage of population under South Vietnamese control are not supported by the statistics. The memorandum also advises that Mr. Bundy not bring to light other figures that present a negative picture.

After alleging that the VC was having difficulties in its recruitment, Mr. Greene goes on to point out, in a confidential comment, that "Recruitment statistics should be avoided since they are based on a relatively small number of reports of dubious reliability. Moreover, any use of recruitment figures might well be used by our critics to question the reliability of our estimates on Communist order of battle, a subject which almost certainly will soon cause us considerable public relations problems."

[264]"It is significant that the enemy has not won a major battle in more than a year. In general, he can fight his large forces only at the edges of his sanctuaries . . . His Viet Cong military units can no longer fill their ranks from the South but must depend increasingly on replacements from North Viet Nam. His guerrilla force is declining at a steady rate. Morale problems are developing within his ranks." He concluded by saying, "The enemy has many problems: He is losing control of the scattered population under his influence. He is losing credibility with the population he still controls. He is alienating the people by his increased demands and taxes, where he can impose them. He sees the strength of his forces steadily declining. He can no longer recruit in the South to any meaningful extent; he must plug the gap with North Vietnamese. His monsoon offensives have been failures. He was dealt a mortal blow by the installation of a freely elected representative government. And he failed in his desperate effort to take the world's headlines from the inauguration by a military victory." General Westmoreland, "Progress Report on the War in Viet Nam," before the National Press Club, Washington, D. C., Nov. 21, 1967.

[266]According to George Allen, pressure was put on CIA by Walt Rostow, Assistant to the President for National Security Affairs, to prepare positive indicators of progress in the pacification program. When

Mr. Allen suggested that there were few, he received the reply, "I am amazed at your unwillingness to support your President in his time of need." Rostow then requested that the Office of Current Intelligence produce a compilation of extracts showing progress, which OCI did, while attaching a cover letter caveat. Rostow removed the cover letter and reported to the President "at last an objective appraisal from CIA." Staff interview with George Allen, Dec. 1, 1975.

[271]Immediately after the Tet offensive, President Johnson began to seek independent assessments of the US role in Vietnam. Turning first to Dean Acheson, the former Secretary of State, he solicited opinions from an informal study group, known as the "Wise Men." Startled by the pessimism of these advisors from outside of the government, the President demanded an individual presentation of three briefings provided to the group, in order to discover "who poisoned the well." George Carver from CIA opined that the President had a two-audience problem and could not very well continue to tell the Americans one thing and the Vietnamese another.

Staff interview with George Carver, Jan. 9, 1975.

[274]Defense attaches in Vietnam held the dual responsibilities of monitoring military aid and coordinating intelligence reporting on friendly forces. The former tended to affect the latter, and attaches would use supply figures to interpret South Vietnamese capabilities toward the end of the war.

The Ambassador in Vietnam in 1975 "personally and through his Political Section monitored very closely the intelligence reporting from Vietnam." Reports on the political and economic conditions (including reports on corruption) were either censored or retained within the Embassy. (See Henry A. Shockley, "Intelligence Collection in Vietnam, March 1974-March 1975" in Appendix.)

2. Czechoslovakia: Failure Of Tactical Warning

The Czechoslovakia crisis challenged our ability to monitor an attack by the Soviet Union—our prime military adversary. We "lost" the Russian army, for two weeks.

Forces of the Warsaw Pact invaded Czechoslovakia on August 20, 1968, to overthrow the Dubcek regime which, since spring, had been moving toward liberal, independent policies the Soviets could not tolerate. U.S. intelligence had understood and reported the basic issues in the developing Soviet-Czech confrontation, and concluded that the Soviets were capable of launching an invasion at any time.

Intelligence failed, however, to provide a warning that the Soviets had "decided to intervene with force." Consequently, President Johnson first learned of the invasion when Soviet Ambassador Dobrynin visited the White House and told him.

A review of U.S. intelligence performance during the Czech crisis indicates the agencies were not up to the difficult task of divining Soviet intentions. We knew Soviet capabilities, and that the tactical decision to invade might leave only hours of advance warning. The CIA, DIA, and NSA should have been prepared for lightning-quick reaction to Soviet military moves.

Czech radio broadcasted news of the invasion at 8:50 p.m., Washington time. CIA translated and transmitted its reports of invasion to Washington at 9:15 p.m. By that time, President Johnson had already met his appointment with the Soviet Ambassador.

U.S. technical intelligence learned of the Soviet invasion several hours before—but the information did not reach Washington until after the Czech radio message. The CIA later concluded that the information "might have made a difference" in our ability to provide the tactical warning.

One alarming failure of intelligence prior to the invasion occurred during the first two weeks in August, when U.S. intelligence could not locate a Soviet combat formation, which had moved into northern Poland. Director Helms later admitted he was not "happy about those two weeks" when he could not locate the Soviet troops.

Information from technical intelligence, which would have been helpful, was not available until days later. Clandestine reporting in the previous weeks had been so slow to arrive it proved of little value to current intelligence publications.

Director of Central Intelligence Richard Helms reported to the President's Foreign Intelligence Advisory Board in October, 1968, that the intelligence record of failing to detect the actual attack "distresses me." The Director provided reassurances that the record would have been better "if West Germany had been the target rather than Czechoslovakia."

In 1971, a Presidential Commission reported to President Nixon that its review of U.S. ability to respond to sudden attack had found serious weaknesses. The Pentagon was directed to improve its warning system. Improvement to the very best possible degree is, of course, the minimum acceptable standard. There will be no more important area for Congressional oversight committees to explore thoroughly.

3. The Mid-East War: The System Breaks Down

The Mid-East war gave the intelligence community a real test of how it can perform when all its best technology and human skills are focused on a known world "hot spot." It failed.

On October 6, 1973, Egypt and Syria launched a major assault across the Suez Canal and Golan Heights against a stunned Israel. Although Israel eventually repelled the attack, at a cost of thousands of lives, the war's consequences cannot be measured in purely military terms.

For Americans, the subsequent U.S.-Soviet confrontation of October 24–25, 1973, when the Soviets threatened to unilaterally intervene in the conflict, and the Arab oil embargo are reminders that war in the Middle East has a direct impact on our own national interests.

The Committee's analysis of the U.S. intelligence performance in this crisis confirms the judgment of an intelligence community post-mortem that "the principal conclusions concerning the imminence of hostilities . . . were—quite simply, obviously, and starkly— wrong." Even after the conflict had begun, we did not accurately monitor the course of events.

The important question is what went wrong?

The last relevant National Intelligence Estimate before the October War was published five months earlier, in May, 1973, during a particularly bad period in Arab-Israeli relations. That estimate addressed the likelihood of war "in the next few weeks." No long-range view was presented, and the crisis soon passed.

The only intelligence report concerned with future political-military issues was a May 31, 1973, Bureau of Intelligence and Research (INR) memorandum to

Secretary of State Rogers. The authors reasoned correctly that Egypt's President Sadat, for political reasons, would be strongly tempted to resort to arms if diplomacy proved fruitless. Accordingly, the report concluded, the "resumption of hostilities by autumn will become a better than even bet" should the diplomatic impasse continue.

By September 30, 1975—less than a week before the attack—INR had lost "the wisdom of the Spring." By then, all U.S. intelligence agencies argued that the political climate in the Arab nations was not conducive to a major war. Intelligence consumers were reassured that hostilities were not likely.[292]

The next question is why this happened.

Analytical bias was part of the problem.[293] In the summer of 1973, the Defense Intelligence Agency (DIA), CIA, and INR all flatly asserted that Egypt was not capable of a major assault across the Suez Canal. Syria, they said, was not much of a threat either, despite recent acquisitions of sophisticated Soviet . . . missile systems and other material.

One reason for the analysts' optimism can be found in a 1971 CIA handbook, in a passage reiterated and reinforced in discussions in early October, 1973. The Arab fighting man, it reported, "lacks the necessary physical and cultural qualities for performing effective military services." The Arabs were thought to be so clearly inferior that another attack would be irrational and, thus, out of the question.

No doubt this attitude was not far in the background when CIA advised Dr. Kissinger on September 30, 1975, that "the whole thrust of President Sadat's activities since last spring has been in the direction of bringing moral, political, and economic force to bear on Israel in tacit acknowledgment of Arab unreadiness to make war."

That analysis is quite surprising, in light of information acquired during that period, which indicated that imminent war was a distinct possibility. By late September, for example, CIA had acquired vital evidence of the timing and warlike intentions of the Arabs. The source was disbelieved, for reasons still unclear.

There were other positive indications. In late September, the National Security Agency began picking up clear signs that Egypt and Syria were preparing for a major offensive. NSA information indicated that [a major foreign nation] had become extremely sensitive to the prospect of war and concerned about their citizens and dependents in Egypt. NSA's warning escaped the serious attention of most intelligence analysts responsible for the Middle East.[299]

The fault may well lie in the system itself. NSA intercepts of Egyptian-Syrian war preparations in this period were so voluminous—an average of hundreds of reports each week—that few analysts had time to digest more than a small portion of them. Even fewer analysts were qualified by technical training to read raw NSA traffic. Costly intercepts had scant impact on estimates.

These reports lacked visibility and prestige to such a degree that when, two days before the war, an NSA briefer insisted to General Daniel Graham of CIA that unusual Arab movements suggested imminent hostilities, Graham retorted that his staff had reported a "ho-hum" day in the Middle East. Later, a key military analyst claimed that if he had only seen certain NSA reports, which were so "sensitive" they had not been disseminated until after the war began, he would have forecast hostilities.[302]

There was testimony that Dr. Kissinger's secrecy may also have thwarted effective intelligence analysis. Kissinger had been in close contact with both the Soviets and the Arabs throughout the pre-war period. He, presumably, was in a unique position to pick up indications of Arab dissatisfaction with diplomatic

143

talks, and signs of an ever-increasing Soviet belief that war would soon break out. When the Committee was denied its request for high-level reports, it was unable to learn whether Kissinger elicited this information in any usable form. It is clear, however, that the Secretary passed no such warning to the intelligence community.[303]

The Committee was told by high U.S. intelligence officials and policy-makers that information from high-level diplomatic contacts is of great intelligence value as an often-reliable indicator of both capabilities and intentions. Despite the obvious usefulness of this information, Dr. Kissinger has continued to deny intelligence officials access to notes of his talks with foreign leaders.

The morning of the Arab attack, the Watch Committee—which is responsible for crisis alerts—met to assess the likehood of major hostilities. It concluded that no major, coordinated offensive was in the offing.[305] Perhaps one of the reasons for this was that some participants were not "cleared" for all intelligence data, so the subject and its implications could not be fully discussed.

The entire system had malfunctioned. Massive amounts of data had proven indigestible by analysts. Analysts, reluctant to raise false alarms and lulled by anti-Arab biases, ignored clear warnings. Top-level policy-makers declined to share perceptions gained from talks with key Arab and Soviet diplomats during the critical period. The fact that Israeli intelligence, to which the U.S. often deferred in this period, had been wrong was small consolation.

Performance did not measurably improve after the war's outbreak, when the full resources of the U.S. intelligence community were focused [there].

The Defense Intelligence Agency, having no military contingency plan for the area, proved unable to deal with a deluge of reports from the war zone, and quickly found itself in chaos. CIA and INR also engulfed Washington and each other with situation reports, notable for their redundancy.

Technical intelligence-gathering was untimely, as well as indiscriminate. U.S. national technical means of overhead coverage of the Middle East, according to the post-mortem, was "of no practical value" because of time problems. Two overflight reconnaissance missions, on October 13 and 25, "straddled the most critical phase of the war and were, therefore, of little use."[310]

The U.S. failure to accurately track war developments may have contributed to a U.S.-Soviet confrontation and troop alert called by President Nixon on October 24, 1973.[311]

A second intelligence community post-mortem, the existence of which was not disclosed to the Committee until after its hearing,[312] reported that CIA and DIA almost unquestionably relied on overly-optimistic Israeli battle reports. Thus misled, the U.S. clashed with the better-informed Soviets on the latter's strong reaction to Israeli cease-fire violations. Soviet threats to intervene militarily were met with a worldwide U.S. troop alert. Poor intelligence had brought America to the brink of war.

Administration witnesses assured the Committee that analysts who had performed poorly during the crisis had been replaced.[313] The broader record suggests, however, that the intelligence system faults have survived largely intact. New analysts will continue to find themselves harassed and deluged with largely equivocal, unreadable, or unusable data from CIA, DIA, INR, and the collection-conscious NSA. At the same time, they can expect to be cut off, by top-level policy-makers, from some of the best indicators of hostile intentions.

Footnotes:

[292]"If analysts did not provide forewarning, what did they offer in its stead? *Instead of warnings, the Community's analytical effort in effect produced reassurances.* That is to say, the analysts, in reacting to indicators which could be interpreted in themselves as portents of hostile Arab actions against Israel, sought in effect to reassure their audience that the Arabs would *not* resort to war, at least not deliberately." (Emphasis in original.) CIA's Post-Mortem, page 3.

[293]CIA-DIA-INR Arab-Israeli Handbook, July 1973. The CIA's Post-Mortem at 13 characterizes this Handbook and analytic preconceptions: "No preconceptions seem to have had a greater impact on analytical attitudes than those concerning relative Arab and Israeli military prowess. The June War was frequently invoked by analysts as proof of fundamental and perhaps permanent weaknesses in the Arab forces and, inferentially, of Israeli invincibility. The Arabs, despite the continuing acquisition of modern weapons from the Russians, remained about as far behind the Israelis as ever." At page 14 the Post-Mortem concludes: "There was, in addition, a fairly widespread notion based largely (though perhaps not entirely) on past performances that many Arabs, as Arabs, simply weren't up to the demands of modern warfare and that they lacked understanding, motivation, and probably in some cases courage as well. These judgments were often alluded to in conversations between analysts. . . ."

[299]The draft CIA Post-Mortem states that NSA SIGINT Summaries probably did not convey the full significance of these technical indicators to the reader. The conclusion of all intelligence officials interviewed by the Committee staff was unanimous: the National Security Agency products—particularly raw products—are difficult to understand. The CIA's Post-Mortem,

page 9, states the problem with NSA products as seen by Middle East intelligence analysts: "Two particular problems associated with SIGINT should be mentioned here: (1) Certain highly classified and specially handled categories of COMINT reached their consumers only several days after intercept, a circumstance which perhaps had unfortunate effects; (2) SIGINT reporting is very voluminous; in a typical non-crisis week, hundreds of SIGINT reports on the Middle East cross the desk of the area specialist in a production office. Moreover, partly because of the requirements levied on it by a wide variety of consumers, NSA issues most SIGINT reports (not merely ELINT) in very technical language. SIGINT can thus challenge the ingenuity of even the most experienced, all-source analyst searching for meaning and patterns in a mountain of material.". . . .

[302]From the Draft CIA Post-Mortem: "If the information contained in the NSA messages had been available prior to the time of the outbreak of hostilities, we could have clearly predicted that [a foreign nation] knew in advance that renewed hostilities were imminent in the Middle East." This particular type of NSA-acquired intelligence was delayed "a minimum of ten days."

[303]Among such reports on Soviet and Arab attitudes were "The Secretary Afternoon Summary," 27 Sept., 1973 which reported an intelligence finding that a high Arab official "has said that Kissinger's statement before the Senate Foreign Relations Committee, that U.S. policy in the Middle East remains the same, destroyed the recent Egyptian hope aroused by President Nixon's comment that the U.S. is partial neither to the Arabs or to Israel." . . .

[305]"The Watch Committee met in special session at 0900 on 6 October 1973 to consider the outbreak of Israeli-Arab hostilities and Soviet actions with respect to the situation.

"We can find no hard evidence of a major, coordinated Egyptian/Syrian offensive across the Canal and in the Golan Heights area. Rather, the weight of evidence indicates an action-reaction situation where a series of responses by each side to preconceived threats created an increasingly dangerous potential for confrontation. The current hostilities are apparently a result of that situation, although we are in a position to clarify the sequence of events. It is possible that the Egyptians or Syrians, particularly the latter, may have been preparing a raid or other small-scale action." Special Meeting of the Watch Committee, Oct. 7, 1973.

[311]"We do not know whether, in fact, these differing appreciations contributed to the development of a confrontation between the U.S. and U.S.S.R. during the final three days of the crisis (24-26 October). But this seems to be a real possibility. And it is clear in any event that in certain crises and under certain circumstances an accurate view of the *tactical military situation* can be of critical importance to decision-makers." Also: "If U.S. decision-makers had had a more accurate view of the tactical situation around Suez between 21 and 25 October, they might have had better insight into why the Soviets reacted as they did to the Israeli violations." *Ibid*. . . .

[312]The second post-mortem . . . was not given to any Congressional Committee, even those who were told of the first post-mortem.

[313]Three DIA officials were removed from their positions; there were no changes at the CIA, INR, or NSA. Community analysts interviewed by Committee staff all agreed the reassignments involved internal DIA controversies more than any effort to revamp the agency after the Middle East War.

4. Portugal: The U.S. Caught Napping

Do our intelligence services know what is going on beneath the surface in allied nations that are not making headlines? Quiet Portugal exploded in 1974, leaving serious questions in its aftermath.

When a group of left-leaning Portuguese junior military officers ousted the Caetano regime on April 25, 1974, State Department officials represented to the New York· Times that Washington knew those who were behind the coup well. State indicated that we were not surprised by the coup, and that no significant changes in Portugal's NATO membership were expected. Nothing could have been further from the truth.

The Committee has reviewed documents which show that the U.S. intelligence community had not even been asked to probe deeply into Portugal in the waning months of the Caetano dictatorship.[315] As a result, policy makers were given no real warning of the timing and probable ideological consequences of the coup, despite clear and public indications that a political upheaval was at hand.[316]

The State Department's Bureau of Intelligence and Research had not analyzed events in Portugal in the month before the April coup. In retrospect, four warning signals, beginning in late February and continuing through mid-March, 1974, should have sparked "speculation at that time that a crisis of major proportions was brewing," according to the Director of Intelligence and Research, William Hyland. All four events were reported in the American press:

1. The publication in February 1974, of General Antonio de Spinola's controversial book criticizing Portugal's African colonial wars, which unleashed an unprecedented public storm.

2. The refusal of General Spinola and the Armed Forces Chief of Staff, Francisco Costa Gomes, to participate in a demonstration of military unity and support for the Caetano dictatorship.

3. An abortive coup, in mid-March, when an infantry regiment attempted to march upon Lisbon. This was followed by the subsequent dismissal of Spinola and Costa Gomes from their commands.

4. A period of rising tensions, the arrests of leftists, and a purge of military officers following the first three developments.

The intelligence community, however, was too preoccupied to closely examine the Portuguese situation. Those responsible for writing current intelligence publications had deadlines to meet, meetings to attend, and relatively little time to speculate on developments in the previously sleepy Caetano dictatorship.[318]

The Committee's investigation indicates there were other, earlier warning signs which might have sparked some intelligence interest. Again, these indications of deeper unrest were not subjected to close analysis.

On October 26, 1973, the Defense Attache in Lisbon reported to DIA headquarters in the Pentagon rumors of a "coup plot," and serious discontent among Portuguese-military officers.

On November 8, 1973, the attache reported that 860 Portuguese Army Captains had signed a petition protesting conditions.[320] The attache quickly concluded these dissidents had no intentions of revolution. Nevertheless, the fact that over 800 military officers felt deeply enough to risk retribution was a good indication of the profound social revolution which Portugal faced.

The record does not suggest that the attache attempted to get to know these junior officers, understand their views, or even record their names. Nor had anyone in Washington assigned him the task of searching for signs of social and political unrest in the Portuguese military. One reason for this was that the Director of Attache Affairs was not allowed to assign duties to attaches. Assignments were done elsewhere, in an unbelievable demonstration of confusing and inefficient administration.[321]

Also in November 1973, the attache attended a social gathering at the home of a retired American officer where he heard discussion of right-wing Spanish and Portuguese countercoup plans, should "extremists" overthrow the Caetano government. Neither the identities of the counter-plotters nor of the "extremists" were reported by the attache. No further reference to this report was found in a review of subsequent attache activities prior to the April coup.

In February 1974, the attache forwarded information from December 1973, on the Portuguese government response to a petition of complaints signed by over 1,500 junior military officers.[323] There was no effort to identify the leaders of the petition campaign or to contact any of the signers. After the coup, high CIA officials would complain of the lack of in-depth biographic reporting from the attache office.

A review of all Defense Attache reports in the months prior to the coup indicated substantial delays in forwarding reports to Washington. It even took a month for the attache to send Washington the Spinola book which unleashed the public storm when it was published in February.

Twice, Defense Intelligence Agency headquarters in Washington wrote the attache office in Lisbon urging the six officers there to be more aggressive, to travel more, and frequent the diplomatic party circuit less. Only the most junior attache, a Navy lieutenant, made an attempt to probe beyond the obvious.

The Committee was also told that a serious problem in DIA is a tendency to reward senior officers, nearing the ends of their careers, by assigning them to attache posts. Not only were these officers often untrained and unmotivated for intelligence duties, but the Director of Attache Affairs testified that he was powerless to assign substantive duties to the attaches in any case.

The Committee did not have the opportunity to review raw CIA reports during the six months prior to the coup. CIA officials who relied on these reports told this Committee that the CIA Station in Lisbon was so small, and so dependent upon the official Portuguese security service for information, that very little was picked up. In fact, attaches were in a better position than CIA to get to know the Portuguese military. There is no indication that attaches and the Chief of Station attempted to pool their resources and combine CIA's knowledge of the Portuguese Community movement with attaches' supposed military contacts.

The National Intelligence Officer (NIO) for Western Europe did attempt an analysis. A draft memorandum on trends in Portugal, titled, "Cracks in the Facade," had been in preparation for nearly a month, and was almost complete when the April coup erupted. It had to be re-titled. The document itself, despite its titles, was not attuned to the real causes of intense discontent which produced a leftist-military revolt.

That same National Intelligence Officer testified that he had some twenty-five European countries to monitor, with the help of only one staff assistant. NIO's do not have command authority over CIA's intelligence or operations directorates. They cannot order that papers be written, that staffers be detached from the current intelligence office to work on an in-depth estimate. They cannot instruct clandestine operations to collect certain types of information. Nor will the NIO always be informed of covert actions that may be underway in one of his countries.

The most disturbing testimony before this Committee was official satisfaction with intelligence prior to the Portuguese coup. The Director of Attache Affairs told the Committee that intelligence performance had been "generally satisfactory and responsive to requirements." The National Intelligence Officer for Western Europe said intelligence reports had described "a situation clearly in process of change, an old order coming apart at the seams."[331]

However, both officials quickly admitted under questioning that the attaches had not, in fact, been very aggressive. Nor had any intelligence document warned when and how the old order was "coming apart at the seams." Without access to intelligence reports, this Committee might have believed official claims that the system was functioning well.

Footnotes:

[315]Interview with Dennis Clift, Senior Staff Member, National Security Council, by G. Rushfort, Oct. 3, 1975, copy on file with Sel. Comm. on Intell. Mr. Clift stated there was no National Security Council effort to levy requirements on the intelligence community, nor was there any National Security Council study memorandum addressed to Portugal.

[316]Testimony of William Hyland before the Committee: "Even a cursory review of the intelligence record indicates there was no specific warning of the coup of April 25, 1974 in Portugal. As far as the Bureau of Intelligence and Research was concerned, our last analytical reporting was in late March and we drew no conclusions that pointed to more than a continuing struggle for power but short of a military revolt." Comm. Hearings . . . October 7, 1975.

[320]Defense Attache report from Lisbon to the De-

fense Intelligence Agency: "These younger officers are not disloyal and desire to serve Portugal as military officers and have no intention of revolution. They are patriots who want to make changes for the improvement of the P.A. [Portuguese Army—*editor's note*] and Portugal."

[323]Defense Attache report also commented on the Spinola appointment as Deputy Chief of Staff, Armed Forces: "Although there are some political reasons in back of this appointment, it is reported that he will concern himself mainly with personnel and logistics in the Metropole." Defense Attache report, Feb. 6, 1974

[331]Testimony of Keith Clark and Samuel V. Wilson. Only William Hyland, Director of INR, testified without prodding that the system had not functioned well in the Portugal crisis.

5. India: Priorities Lost

How well does U.S. intelligence keep track of non-military events that affect our foreign policy interests? Not very well, if the first nuclear test in the Third World is any indication.

The intelligence community estimated, in 1965, that India was capable of conducting a nuclear test, and probably would produce a nuclear device within the next few years. In 1972, a special estimate said the "chances are roughly even that India will conduct a [nuclear] test at some time in the next several years and label it a peaceful explosion."

DIA, in reports distributed only within the Joint Chiefs of Staff, had stated since 1971 that India might already have a nuclear device. However, when India did explode a nuclear device on May 18, 1974, U.S. intelligence was caught off-guard. As the CIA's post-mortem says of the community's surprise: "This failure denied the U.S. Government the option of considering diplomatic or other initiatives to try to prevent this significant step in nuclear proliferation."

Only one current intelligence article was published in the six months before the May explosion. That article, by DIA, stated for the first time that India might already possess such a device. Perhaps one reason the article did not provoke more debate and initiative was the title: "India: A nuclear weapons program will not likely be pursued in the near term."

In 1972, U.S. intelligence had picked up 26 reports that India would soon test a device, or that she was capable of doing so if the government made the decision to proceed. There were only two reports on the subject from August 1972, to May 1974, when the device was exploded. Neither was pursued with what the CIA can claim was a "real follow-up."

An April 17, 1974 report indicated that India might have already conducted an unsuccessful nuclear test in the Rajasthan Desert. The CIA did not disseminate this report to other agencies, nor did CIA officials pursue the subject.

The Director of Central Intelligence had established the bureacratic device of "Key Intelligence Questions" in 1974. Although nuclear proliferation was on the list, few officials outside the upper reaches of the bureaucracy expressed much interest. The CIA's general nuclear developments priority list did not address India, and the military attaches received no clear instructions on nuclear matters. Nevertheless, previous estimates on India had identified "gaps" in our information.

After India exploded the nuclear device in May 1974, Director Colby wrote Dr. Kissinger to say he intended to mount a more aggressive effort on the nuclear proliferation problem.

One of several justifications for national technical means of overhead coverage over India in the two years prior to May 1974, was the nuclear test issue. However, the Intelligence Community technical analysts were never asked to interpret the data. The CIA's post-mortem stated, in effect, the system had been tasked to obtain data, but the analysts had not been asked to examine such data. After the explosion, the analysts were able to identify the test location, from pre-test data.

Following the failure to anticipate India's test, the United States Intelligence Board agreed to hold one committee meeting a year on nuclear proliferation. Interagency "coordinating" mechanisms were established. Teams of experts traveled to various countries to impress on American embassy personnel the importance of the proliferation threat. Analysts once again were encouraged to talk to each other more.

The missing element, as the bureaucracy reshuffled its priorities after the Indian failure, is quite simple: the system itself must be reformed to promote antici-

pation of, rather than reaction to, important world events.

6. Cyprus: Failure of Intelligence Policy

Cyprus presented a complex mix of politics, personalities, and NATO allies. Unfortunately, a crisis turned to war, while intelligence tried to unravel events—and America offended all participants.

On the morning of July 15, 1974, Greek strongman General Dimitrios Ioannides and his military forces on Cyprus overthrew the elected government of Archbishop Makarios. Five days later, Turkey invaded the island, ostensibly to protect the Turkish minority there and to prevent the Greek annexation long promoted by the new Cyprus leadership. Unsatisfied with its initial military success, Turkey renewed its offensive on August 14, 1974.

The failure of U.S. intelligence to forcast the coup, despite strong strategic and tactical signs, may be attributed to several factors: poor reporting from the U.S. Embassy in Athens, in part due to CIA's exclusive access to Ioannides; the general analytical assumption of rational behavior; and analysts' reluctance to raise false claims of an impending crisis.[346]

The failure to predict the coup is puzzling in view of the abundance of strategic warnings. When Ioannides wrested power from George Papadopoulos in November, 1974, analysts concluded that relations between Greece and Makarios were destined to worsen. Ioannides' hatred of Makarios, whom he considered pro-Communist or worse, has been described as having "bordered on the pathological." Moreover, Makarios was seen as a stumbling block to Ioannides' hopes for *onosis*. Observers agreed that a serious confrontation was only a matter of time.

By spring of 1974, that confrontation would at times appear imminent, with intervening lulls. Each trip to the brink elicited dire warnings to policy officials from Near East desks in the State Department. However, the nuances of these events, indicating a gathering of storm clouds, were largely lost on analysts as their attention remained focused on the Greek-Turkish clash over mineral rights in the Aegean. Cyprus remained a side issue despite growing evidence that the Ioannides-Makarios relationship was reaching a critical stage.

There would soon be several tactical indications that a coup was in the works. On June 7, 1974, the National Intelligence Daily warned that Ioannides was actively considering the ouster of Makarios if the Archbishop made an "extremely provocative move."[350] On June 29, intelligence officials reported that Ioannides had again told his CIA contact nine days before, that if Makarios continued his provocation, the Greek would have only two options: to write-off Cyprus, with its sizeable Greek majority, or eliminate the Archbishop as a factor.

On July 3, 1974, Makarios made that "extremely provocative move," by demanding the immediate withdrawal of a Greek National Guard contingent on Cyprus. The ultimatum was delivered in an extraordinary open-letter to the Greek government, accusing Ioannides' associates of attempting his physical as well as political liquidation.[352]

On June 29, 1974, Secretary Kisinger, responding to alarms sounded by State Department desk officers, approved a cable to U.S. Ambassador Henry J. Tasca in Athens, instructing that he personally tell Ioannides of U.S. opposition to any adventure on Cyprus.[353] The instruction was only partially heeded.

Tasca, assured by the CIA station chief that Ioannides would continue to deal only with CIA, and not sharing the State Department desk officer's alarm, was content to pass a message to the Greek leader indirectly.

Tasca's colleagues subsequently persuaded secretary Kissinger's top aide, Joseph Sisco, that a general message passed through regular government channels would have sufficient impact. The Ambassador told Committee staff that Sisco agreed it was unnecessary for Tasco himself to approach Ioannides, who had no official government position. That interpretation has been vigorously disputed. It is clear, however, that the Embassy took no steps to underscore for Ioannides the depth of U.S. concern over a possible Cyprus coup attempt.

This episode, the exclusive CIA access to Ioannides, Tasca's indications that he may not have seen all important messages to and from the CIA Station, Ioannides' suggestions of U.S. acquiescence, and Washington's well-known coolness to Makarios, have led to public speculation that either U.S. officials were inattentive to the reports of the developing crisis or simply allowed it to happen, by not strongly, directly, and unequivocally warning Ioannides against it.[358]

Due to State Department access policies. the Committee was unsuccessful in obtaining closely-held cables to and from the Secretary of State during this period including a message the Secretary sent to Ioannides through the CIA the day after the coup. Accordingly, it is impossible to reach a definitive conclusion.

On July 3, 1974, a CIA report stated that an individual, later described as "an untested source," had passed the word that despite new aggressiveness on Makarios' part, Ioannides had changed his mind: there would be no coup after all. For reasons still unclear, this CIA report was embraced and heeded until July 15, the day of the coup. The Intelligence Community post-mortem, appears to have concluded that the "tip" was probably a ruse.

Ioannides' dubious change of heart went virtually unquestioned despite Makarios' open-letter, despite

160

further ultimatums from the Archbishop to remove the Greek officers, and despite the en masse resignations of three high-level Greek Foreign Ministry officials known to be soft-liners on Cyprus. In this setting, the grotesquely erroneous National Intelligence Bulletin of July 15, 1974, is not surprising, nor are Ambassador Tasca's protestations that he saw no coup on the horizon.

Almost at the moment Ioannides unleashed his forces, a National Intelligence Bulletin was reassuring intelligence consumers with the headline: "Ioannides is taking a moderate line while he plays for time in his dispute with Archbishop Makarios."

Results of the events triggered by the coup included: thousands of Cypriot casualties and refugees, a narrowly-averted war between NATO allies Greece and Turkey, a tragic worsening of U.S. relations with all three nations, and the death of an American Ambassador. U.S. intelligence must be accorded a share of the responsibility.

The intelligence community somewhat generously termed its performance during the Cyprus crisis as "a mixture of strengths and weaknesses." The Committee's conclusion, after an analysis of the record, is less sanguine. Intelligence clearly failed to provide adequate warning of the coup, and it performed indifferently once the crisis had begun.

The analytical failure in the Cyprus crisis brings to mind several parallels with the 1973 Middle East debacle. In both cases, analysts and policymakers were afflicted both with a past history of false alarms, and with the rigid notion, unsupported in fact, that foreign leaders invariably act "rationally." In the Cyprus crisis, as in the Mid-East, analysts were deluged with unreadable and redundant data subsequent to the initial intelligence failure.[363] Still, given the ample indications that Makarios had sufficiently aroused Ioannides' ire, these analytical quirks should

161

not have prevented a correct interpretation of events.

There appear to have been collection failures in this period, although additional evidence could probably not have overcome the analytical deficiencies that caused erroneous conclusions. For example, CIA personnel had been instructed by the U.S. Ambassador not to establish contacts within the Turkish minority, and to obviate any allegations of collusion with the anti-Makarios EOKA-B movement. They were told to seek intelligence on EOKA-B by indirect means, rather than through direct contact with members of that organization. Finally, signals intelligence in the area was focused elsewhere and even after the coup was not a significant factor.[366]

Since the coup inevitably led to the two Turkish invasions and the Greek-Turkish confrontation, the performance of intelligence in predicting military hostilities after the coup is both less important and unremarkable in its successes.

Along with most newspaper articles of the time, U.S. intelligence concluded that Ioannides' installation of Nicos Sampson, notoriously anti-Turk, as Cypriot President insured a Turkish invasion of the island. Despite prominent stories in Turkish newspapers and undisguised troop movements at the coast, DIA did not predict the invasion until literally hours before Turkish forces hit the beaches on July 20, 1974. A National Intelligence Officer's report had picked July 20 as a likely invasion date, but was never disseminated to the intelligence community.[368]

Perhaps flushed by its "success" in calling the first Turkish invasion just after the Turkish press did, U.S. intelligence appeared to lose interest, in the belief that the crisis was over. Thus, there was no real forewarning that the Turkish forces would launch an even more ambitious invasion on August 14, resulting in the capture of fully one-third of the island.

In terms of both its immediate [370] and long-range

consequences, the sum total of U.S. intelligence failure during the Cyprus crisis may have been the most damaging intelligence performance in recent years.

Footnotes:

346Former intelligence officials have described to this Committee the difficulties encountered by those who must report from an area which has frequent and intense crises. "After a while, Washington officials get tired of hearing about impending crises from your area and it actually gets embarrassing to report them." That observation gained credence when witnesses from the Department of State jokingly referred to the number of times Cypriot Desk officers had predicted coups. Interview with intelligence official, by F. Kirschstein, Sept. 29, 1975, copy on file with Sel. Comm. on Intell.

350The June 7 National Intelligence Daily was based on a June 3 Field Intelligence Report which stated that "Ioannides claimed that Greece is capable of removing Makarios and his key supporters from power in twenty-four hours with little if any blood being shed and without EOKA assistance. The Turks would quietly acquiesce to the removal of Makarios, a key enemy . . . Ioannides prayed for some unexpected favorable gift from heaven. Ioannides stated that if Makarios decides on some type of extreme provocation against Greece to obtain a tactical advantage, he (Ioannides) is not sure whether he should merely pull the Greek troops out of Cyprus and let Makarios fend for himself, or remove Makarios once and for all and have Greece deal directly with Turkey over Cyprus' future." That report has been confirmed by former CIA Athens officials interviewed by staff. Interview with CIA operations officials, by J. Boos and G. Rushford . . . copy on file with Sel. Comm. on Intell.

[352]The letter reads in part; "I have many times asked myself why an unlawful and nationally harmful organization . . . is supported by Greek officers . . . The Greek officers' support for EOKA-B constitutes an undeniable reality . . . I am sorry to say, Mr. President, that the root of evil is very deep, reaching as far as Athens. It is from there that the tree of evil, the bitter fruits of which the Greek Cypriot people are tasting today, is being fed and maintained and helped to grow and spread. In order to be absolutely clear, I say that cadres of the military regime of Greece support and direct the activity of the EOKA-B terrorist organization. This also explains the involvement of Greek officers of the National Guard in illegal activities. conspiracy and other inadmissable situations . . . You realize, Mr. President, the sad thoughts which have been preoccupying and tormenting me following the ascertainment that men of the Government of Greece are incessantly preparing conspiracies against me and, what is worse, are dividing the Greek Cypriot people and pushing them to catastrophe through civil strife. I have more than once so far felt, and some cases I have almost touched, a hand invisibly extending from Athens and seeking to liquidate my human existence . . ." Makarios went on to ask for the immediate withdrawal of all Greek officers in the Cypriot National Guard.

[353]The State cable, drafted by John Day, of the Greek desk, was dispatched to the Embassy in Athens under Undersecretary Joseph Sisco's signature. It stated in part: "We share concerns of Athens and Nicosia regarding gravity of relationship between Government of Greece and Government of Cyprus. From various reports, it is evident that Ioannides is seriously considering way to topple Makarios from

power. . . . In our view effort to remove Makarios by force contains unacceptable risks of generating chaos eventually causing Greco-Turk confrontation; involving Soviets in Cyprus situation; and complicating developing U.S.-Soviet detente.

"We know that Ioannides has long been obsessed with issue of communism both in Greece and in Cyprus and that his dislike for Makarios has bordered on the pathological. Until recently, our impression has been that he preferred to play for time on Cyprus problem until he had consolidated his position in the internal Greek context. Now, however, he apparently feels that Makarios is seeking to take advantage of Greek-Turkish tensions and the Greek regime's domestic difficulties to reduce Greek influence on the island and that this effort is a personal challenge which he cannot ignore." The cable went on to instruct Ambassador Tasca to personally tell Ioannides that the U.S. opposed any adventure on Cyprus. Department of State cable to Athens Embassy, June 29, 1974.

[358] "It is reasonable to ask whether this U.S. action was perceived in Athens as a reflection of the depth of Washington's concern about Ioannides' scheme to oust Makarios. Clearly General Ioannides had much ground to believe that in light of the direct contact he enjoyed with the CIA station, he would have prevented the crisis. This judgment is shared by the rest of the Greek language/area specialists in SE." "Criticisms of United States Policy in the Cyprus Crisis." Internal Department of State memorandum.

[363] As in the previous Mid-East crisis, many NSA SIGINT reports were too technical to be understood by lay analysts. The Post-Mortem added: "As in past crises, most of the Customers interviewed complained of the volume of . . . reporting, as well as its frequent redundancy. Many also complained of too little analysis of the facts, too few assessments of the significance of reported developments."

[366]Intelligence officials have told our staff that U.S. SIGINT resources were not focused on targets which would have the most relevance to an Athens-Nicosia crisis, i.e., Greek National Guard communications. Emergency reaction SIGINT teams were rushed into the area after the coup and later contributed to some successful intelligence. Interview with Intelligence officials, by F. Kirschstein, Dec. 2, 1975, copy on file with Sel. Comm. on Intell.

[368]The NIO responsible for the report which predicted July 20 as the invasion date was preoccupied with the production of a National Intelligence Estimate on Italy which was to be presented at a USIB meeting on the 18th of July. It should also be noted that Cypriot experts within State and CIA were in the process of being shuffled around in a bureaucratic reorganization of area responsibilities. In addition, State Department Washington experts on all three countries concerned, as well as the U.S. Ambassador to Greece, were removed from their posts at one time or another during the crisis.

[370]Some days later, Roger Davies, the U.S. Ambassador to Cyprus, was fatally wounded during an anti-American demonstration at the Embassy in Nicosia. Contemporary accounts concluded that Davies was simply struck by a stray bullet. Information made available to the Committee suggests that Davies may have been the victim of an assassin.

Ambassador Tasca disclosed to staff a report that EOKA-B had decided to kill either Davies or himself. U.S. intelligence officers have asserted not only that Davies may have been intentionally shot, but also that the identities of individuals firing at the Embassy are also known. The intelligence sources have alleged that the individuals may be officials of the Nicosia police. Despite repeated private U.S. protests, the Cypriot government is said to have declined to remove these individuals from their jobs.

Interview with Henry J. Tasca, by J. Boos, Sept. 26-27, 1975, copy on file with Sel. Comm. on Intell. Interview with CIA officials by G. Rushford and F. Kirschstein, Oct. 22, 1975, copy on file with Sel. Comm. on Intell.

7. Domestic Internal Security and Counterintelligence

The Intelligence Division of the FBI is divided into two sections: Internal Security and Counterintelligence. The Internal Security Division investigates domestic subversive or extremist groups with the goal of ascertaining whether individuals are violating federal laws.

These investigations are costly, in monetary terms and in terms of personal privacy. Are they effectively and dispassionately controlled, in keeping with criminal priorities? Are they efficiently terminated when clearly unproductive? Thirty-four years of investigating the Socialist Workers Party and over five years spying on the Institute for Policy Studies provide some examples of disturbing answers.

a. Institute for Policy Studies

The FBI Manual of Instructions allows preliminary investigations to be opened on groups espousing extremist philosophies. If these investigations do not demonstrate reasonable likelihood of uncovering criminal violations, the Manual states that they should be terminated within 90 days.

In 1968, the FBI saw sufficient connection between the Institute for Policy Studies (IPS) and the Students for a Democratic Society (SDS) to open a preliminary investigation of IPS.

The investigation was not terminated after an initial 90-day period, even though it had turned up no evidence that IPS members or their associates were violating federal laws. Six months later, at the end of a vigorous nine-month investigation of IPS, the Washington field office reported the results as "negative."

The IPS investigation was destined to continue for five more years.

The investigation had been based on an SDS connection. During the investigation, however, FBI had received information from a source, advising "that, in general, the IPS is not well thought of by the hardcore SDS leaders because members of the IPS are not activists," except for one IPS leader considered sympathetic with SDS objectives. The FBI was not discouraged by the loss of its investigative base, and went ahead reporting unrelated matters. One report, for example, described IPS as "a non-profit, non-taxable institute which studies programs to present policies." The same report noted the fact that "IPS educational curriculum centers on topics which are critical of the present U.S. system . . ."

In January, 1971, the Bureau continued reporting non-criminal matters, such as the fact that the Institute "though small . . . exerts considerable influence through contacts with educators, Congress and labor." It is important to remember that the whole probe began with an investigation of alleged contacts between one IPS staffer and an SDS leader. The FBI had effectively reversed the traditional concept of "guilt by association." Instead of a suspect group tainting an individual, the individual had tainted the group.[377]

An October 1971 Bureau report said of the Institute:

The popular impression of IPS as the "think tank" of radical United States politics is justified. It has taken and continues to take a major role in the antiwar movement and calls for disarmament. While IPS people see themselves as leaders of radical thought, they would appear to be leaders without a popular constituency.

The same report concentrated on IPS suspicions of FBI surveillance. It stated that "they suspect that they are being watched from the building across the street and from adjacent buildings." The same report went on to say that two members of the Institute had been "observed by a representative of the FBI . . . walking slowly around the block of IPS, sometimes several times, conversing with each other . . . they appear to be conversing in low tones and in a guarded manner."

In August 1972, an alert Bureau agent collected some IPS garbage.[380]

The trash revealed no evidence of criminal conduct. However, eight used typewriter ribbons were found. Even though there were no signs of crimes, and despite the fact that IPS itself was not suspected of crimes, FBI devoted time and money to the expensive process of reconstructing the documents that had been typed by the ribbon.

Part of the yield was intimate sexual gossip.

FBI officials told Committee staff, under oath, that personal information, such as sexual activities, is discarded if it does not bear on a crime. That was not true. Information from the trash retrieval, including the sexual gossip, was incorporated into a number of reports. In each report, the information was attributed to "a source who has supplied reliable information in the past."

In 1973, the Washington Field Office reported that "the organization [IPS] is fragmented into a wide variety of studies and interests, the vast majority of which appear to be within legal limits." In May 1974, the Washington Field Office concluded that a "paucity of information exists that would support the likelihood of IPS or its leaders to be functioning in violation of federal law." Only then, after five years and no evidence of law-breaking, did the investigation become inactive.

b. Socialist Workers Party

The second example involved the Socialist Workers Party (SWP). The SWP adopted a Declaration of Principles and a Constitution at their founding convention in January 1938. The Declaration of Principles was replete with revolutionary rhetoric of the Marxist Left. The fledgling Socialist Workers Party also swore allegiance to the world-wide organization of Trotsky —the Fourth International.

Nevertheless, the SWP dissolved their allegiance with the Fourth International and retracted this Declaration of Principles on December 21, 1940, in order to comply with the Voorhis Act. The FBI maintained that this disassociation with the Fourth International was merely cosmetic. However, the FBI has been unable to prove any illegal relationship between the SWP and the Fourth International.

FBI's failure to uncover illegal activity by this political party is not from lack of effort. SWP has been subjected to 34 years of intensive investigation.

On November 5, 1975, FBI officials testified that the Fourth International itself was a body made up of Marxist elements around the world and enjoyed no structural power base in the Soviet Union. Significantly, these officials demonstrated no detailed knowledge about the Fourth International. FBI officials did not mention the fact that the Socialist Workers are a legitimate American political party, that even runs a candidate for President. Equally as important, the FBI has found no evidence to support a federal prosecution of an SWP member, with the exception of several Smith Act violations in 1941. Since that time, not only have there been no further prosecutions against the SWP for any Federal offense, but the portions of the Smith Act under which these earlier convictions had been obtained have been declared unconstitutional.

The investigation, which FBI officials tacitly admit has been conducted partially under the aegis of an unprosecutable statue, has revealed that the SWP is a highly law-abiding group. The SWP has even avoided illegal and potentially violent confrontations with the authorities during any sort of civil protest. Nevertheless, this had no apparent impact on 34 years of unproductive spying.

According to the Presidential candidate of the SWP, Peter Camejo, party members are even forbidden by the SWP to smoke marijuana. The Bureau apparently formulated a philosophy, in this case, to justify their investigation.

Considerable resources have been allocated to compound the error of a continuing unproductive investigation and to back-stop the preconceptions of FBI personnel.

For example, FBI Internal Security investigators committed a massive manpower allocation to interviewing landlords, employers, fellow employees, and family relations of SWP members. The FBI also maintained intensive surveillance of most, if not all, of the SWP's 2500 members.

Americans are often concerned about privacy invasions of domestic security investigations. One-fifth of all investigations initiated by the FBI during the last decade dealt with security matters. The important issue is whether citizens receive a valuable product in the form of anticipatory intelligence which would serve as a deterrent to, and a prevention of, crime. While it is impossible to accurately gauge the deterrent effect of FBI efforts, it is obvious that the FBI failed to anticipate groups dedicated to the overthrow of the existing government and fully committed to violence.[400]

The FBI has likewise had a dismal record in the prompt apprehension of fugitives from the New Left underground.[401] Domestic intelligence appears to be suffering from a misallocation of resources and effort.

Footnotes:

[377]One group may taint another group. The FBI initiated investigation of the Vietnam Veterans Against the War because the VVAW had the misfortune of being mentioned favorably by the Communist Party. . . .

[380]"Institute for Policy Studies (IPS) is DASH, RA. On August two three last, [a Special Agent] observed a private trash truck picking up trash from IPS. The truck proceeded to a burning dump, where the trash was abandoned. [The Special Agent] obtained the IPS trash, and information obtained from this source is being assigned symbol number, [deleted]." NITEL Cable to Acting Director, FBI from SAC, WFO, Aug. 8, 1972.

[400]The S.L.A. is an example. The FBI provided staff attorneys with a detailed after-the-fact history of the S.L.A. However, the FBI was apparently unable to anticipate the formation of the group or thwart its initial criminal activities. FBI briefing on Intelligence by [W. Raymond] Wannall, et al., attended by J. B. F. Oliphant and R. Vermeire.

[401]Mark Rudd, Abbie Hoffman, et al.

8. President's Foreign Intelligence Advisory Board

In addition to day-to-day bureaucratic efforts to monitor and to improve intelligence, the executive branch oversees performance through mechanisms like the quasi-public President's Foreign Intelligence Advisory Board (PFIAB). The issue is whether such a mechanism is viable and effective.

Staff investigation suggests that reliance on PFIAB for oversight responsibility is totally without merit. The Board, admittedly part-time, meets for one- or two-day sessions about six times a year. The Chairman spends about half his time on PFIAB affairs. Only two professional staff members support the Board, and both are detailees from the very intelligence agencies they are supposed to oversee.

The meeting and staffing arrangements do not lend themselves to a responsible analysis and review of massive and complex intelligence programs. It is said that, from time to time, PFIAB submits to the President useful documents on covert action and technical collection programs. However, the Committee, denied access to these and other periodic PFIAB reports, is unable to determine whether the Board has been functioning meaningfully.[405]

Two important and limiting factors shed light on the role and performance of the Board. The Board cannot establish or even oversee policy, but is limited to advising the President with respect to objectives and conduct of the foreign intelligence and related activities. The Board's effectiveness also is limited by the interest and confidence of the President, and this has varied considerably throughout the five Administrations of the Board's existence.

The problems do not end there. Board members are chosen for distinguished careers in government, aca-

174

demia, and the business world. Not surprisingly, members of PFIAB, whose principal functions include advice on research and development goals, are typically affiliated with firms holding lucrative intelligence and defense contracts.[408]

There are no indications that a PFIAB member has ever improperly profited from his Board service. However, after searching Board records at the request of Committee staff, a PFIAB spokesman stipulated that there are no conflict-of-interest regulations applicable to its members. Likewise, there were no regulations covering the expense and confidential contracts they assess and review. Instead, members are provided, on their appointment, with the "Standards of Conduct for the White House Staff."

There are obviously difficult policy problems in gathering a group of distinguished and knowledgeable citizens and, at the same time, insuring that the Board's activities and judgments are entirely beyond reproach.

The part-time nature of PFIAB, if its work is recognized as being cursory, is not necessarily undesirable. Members can bring a fresh perspective from their other pursuits, and they are less compromised by the secrecy and insular views of intelligence agencies. On the other hand, heavy reliance on this Board for oversight, without more outside professional staff and greater Presidential commitment, is an illusion.

Footnotes:

[405]The Committee felt that access to materials relied on and prepared by the Board was the only equitable method of assessing the Board's past performance and role within the structure of the intelligence community. The Committee, without reliance on sub-

poena, attempted in vain to gain access to materials used by and prepared by the Board. After several months of negotiation, the Committee was granted access to a classified Board history, which outlined, but did not specifically enunciate, the kinds of recommendations the Board has made since its inception, and the agendas of the Board's meetings from January 1961 to the present.

[408]For example, present members of the Board whose corporations hold such contracts include William O. Baker, President, Bell Telephone Laboratories; John S. Foster, Jr., Vice-President for Energy Research and Development, TRW; Robert W. Galvin, Chairman and Chief Executive Officer of Motorola, Inc.; Edwin H. Land, Board Chairman, Polaroid Corporation; and Edward Teller, Associate Director of Lawrence Livermore Laboratory. In addition, three of the remaining four members have formidable military credentials and affiliations: George W. Anderson, Jr., former Chief of Naval Operations; Leo Cherne, member of the Board of Advisors of the Industrial College of the Armed Forces; and Gordon Gray, former Secretary of the Army and Director of the Office of Defense Mobilization.

9. National Security Council Intelligence Committee

. . . The National Security Intelligence Committee has met only twice in four years. [Membership consists of the Assistant to the President for National Security Affairs as Chairman, DCI, Deputy Secretary of State, Deputy Secretary of Defense, Chairman of the Joint Chiefs of Staff and Under Secretary of the Treasury for Monetary Affairs—*editor's note*.] It met once in December 1971, to organize, and once in August, 1974, to re-organize. It has no permanent staff, other than the NSC Director for Intelligence Coordination, Richard Ober, a CIA detailee and architect of the controversial CHAOS program. There is no indication that the Committee has been effective.

A Working Group is composed of the next lower-level of consumers. Although in existence from 1971 to 1974, it apparently did not perform any useful function. This group was revived following the 1974 Intelligence Committee meeting and met seven times thereafter. While Working Group principals assert a need for intelligence consumers to somehow institutionally convey their problems to collectors, there appears to be a general low level of interest on the part of several members and misgivings as to the effectiveness of the panel as presently constituted.

The Economic Intelligence Subcommittee's performance to date can be easily evaluated. While its purpose—to provide consumers of economic intelligence a forum to convey their needs—appears worthwhile on paper, it has produced no results. One meeting was held in May 1975, at the behest of the DCI.

The Chairman, Assistant Secretary of the Treasury for International Affairs, told Committee staff that as a consumer he was generally satisfied with intelligence input, that the group was a waste of time, and that he intended to hold as few meetings as possible. Displaying an attitude rare among government officials, the Chairman disdained formal high-level committees and called for informal communication at the working level. He has since left his post and may well be replaced by a proponent of bureaucratic committees. Nonetheless, the record strongly calls for an abolition of the Subcommittee, as presently operated and tasked.

10. The Management and Production of Defense Intelligence

The Deputy Secretary of Defense recently expressed frustration at the apparent inability of a multi-billion dollar U.S. intelligence establishment to produce timely and useful information. He reportedly complained that "In a mechanical sense the system produces the information, but it's so damn big and cumbersome and uncoordinated, that you can't get the information properly assessed and to the right people."[417]

Mismanaged and uncoordinated intelligence operations result in more than resource wastage.

During the Mideast war and Cyprus crisis, for example, uncoordinated and duplicative reports compounded the problem of interpreting events.[418]

There is a clear need to challenge organizational proliferation, duplication of activity and product, and overlapping of management layers that have plagued defense intelligence for years. The significance of these problems is contained in the fact that the Department of Defense controls nearly 80 percent of the intelligence community's resources and employs nearly 90 percent of its personnel.

Particular attention must be directed toward the Defense Intelligence Agency (DIA), an organization established in the early 1960's to integrate and align defense intelligence activities, and a major production unit in its own right.

As chartered, DIA was to function as both a supervisor and coordinator, and as centralized producer of intelligence.

Over the years, however, it became increasingly

apparent that DIA could not accomplish the ambitious management and production goals envisioned at the time of its formation. A string of overviews, including the 1969 Froehlke report, the 1970 Blue Ribbon Defense Panel, the 1971 Schlesinger study for the Office of Management and Budget, the 1974 Management Review, and the 1975 Defense Panel on Intelligence all found that organizational impediments and product imperfection have continued to persist after years of DIA operation. Each in turn recommended reorganization and substantive improvements. None solved the problems.

DIA lacks comprehensive authority to direct and control resources throughout the Defense Department, as initially envisioned. For example, the vast cryptologic resources in the armed services and the National Security Agency are not responsible to DIA. DIA's resources management functions were taken over in 1972 by an Assistant Secretary of Defense for Intelligence with a broader mandate to coordinate budgeting.

The central problem is bureaucratic politics. The three individual branches of the military resist any organization which might curb their authority to direct programs and allocate resources. They undermine the concept on which DIA was founded, by avoiding its authority and preventing it from obtaining qualified manpower.

President Nixon recognized that DIA had not achieved its purpose and issued a directive on Nov. 5, 1971, charging the DCI with responsibility for intelligence budget preparation, including the budget for tactical military intelligence. This too failed, since the DCI lacked authority for over 80 percent of the community's budget, which remained in the Department of Defense.[421]

The only noticeable effect of these reforms has been

an added layer of bureaucracy and a confused sharing of responsibilities.

The output side of DIA's operation has been criticized from a number of directions. Over the years, neither the Secretary of Defense nor the armed services have been completely satisfied with DIA product. Secretary of Defense McNamara reportedly preferred CIA's product; the services prefer their own analysis.[423] Their criticisms focus on DIA's current intelligence and its estimates. They raise questions as to DIA's capability to produce unique and quality intelligence to meet tactical and national demands.

An internal Defense Department memorandum to the Deputy Secretary of Defense in January 1974, indicated the scope of DIA inadequacy in light of the Mid-East war failures. The memorandum concluded: "What has been stated briefly are only the symptoms of the disease. The causes lie deeper . . ."

While noting the failure of DIA analysts to predict the war, the memo stated, "the blame is not theirs alone. It is a corporate failure, a chronic unsoundness of the entire DIA mechanism. Unless we make the required changes in organization, procedures, and personnel, we are going to reap another intelligence failure—and the next one could be a disaster involving U.S. Forces."

While several of the root causes of poor performance provide an argument for piecemeal reform, in general the problems are too permanent to allow for anything less than across-the-board changes.

A major obstacle to strong analytic capability within DIA results from the civilian-military nature of DIA, in a setting of independent military establishments. As long as the service branches retain viable intelligence units, DIA remains an unattractive assignment and will not attract qualified officers. In addition, manpower reductions have spread available personnel too thin for effective reporting.

Civilians in DIA are confronted with two disincentives. DIA cannot compete with CIA and NSA in appointments and promotions, and persistent military control of higher grade management positions limits mobility.[428]

Officials within DIA are ready to admit they cannot match CIA. They justify their contribution as that of "devil's advocates," or "honest brokers." Even in military intelligence, the Committee was told, "they (CIA) are at least our equals, meaning that DIA was no real improvement over CIA intelligence.

In summary, finished intelligence generated by DIA has repeatedly failed to meet consumer needs. The evidence suggests that DIA does not fulfill the ambitious expectations of the early 1960's. It is duplicative, expensive, unattractive, and its production capabilities are handicapped by the consistent weaknesses of its own organization.

Footnotes:

[417]Quoted by William Beecher, Acting Assistant Secretary of Defense for Public Affairs, in Report of the Defense Panel on Intelligence, January, 1975, p. 7 of his statement.

[418]*See*, for example, the IC Staff Preliminary Post-Mortem report on the October War which concludes, "The coordination procedures which are followed by the Community during normal times are frequently abandoned during times of crisis—because the press of time may simply not allow regular processes to continue. It thus has been said *that the Community is pretty good about coordinating, except when the intelligence becomes important.* And, in a way, this did indeed happen immediately before and during the October War in the Middle East. Coordi-

nation of the *Central Intelligence Bulletin*, for example, was suspended for a time, and the wartime Situation Reports and Spot Reports prepared by CIA, DIA and INR were unilateral and often duplicative issuances. This, if not a major problem for the analysts themselves, was certainly one for the consumers. . . ." (IC Stall., The Performance of the Intelligence Community Before the Arab-Israeli War of October 1973: A preliminary Post-Mortem Report, December, 1973, p. 19, emphasis added.) . . . .

[421]The President on November 5, 1971, citing the "need for improved intelligence product and for greater efficiency in the use of resources allocated to intelligence" charged the DCI with greater responsibility for coordinating the community intelligence effort. His Memorandum stated that the President would "look to him (DCI) to improve the performance of the community, to provide his judgments on the efficiency and effectiveness of all intelligence programs and activities (*including tactical intelligence*), and to recommend the appropriate allocation of resources to be devoted to intelligence," (emphasis added). More specifically, he directed "the Director of Central Intelligence to prepare and submit each year, through OMB, a consolidated intelligence program budget, *including tactical intelligence*," (emphasis added). These sentiments are reiterated in an October 9, 1974, Presidential Memorandum. . . .

[423]General Graham has written the committee: "I believe that much of this criticism stems from the early growing pains of the DIA, when its consumers, particularly those on Mr. McNamara's staff, turned elsewhere for intelligence analysis when the DIA product did not satisfy them." The 1975 Defense Panel on intelligence indicated dissatisfaction with DIA by Secretary of Defense Schlesinger and the Assistant Secretary of Defense for International Security Affairs, both important consumers. Vice Ad-

miral David Richardson, in the same report, offered his experience as a commander of deployed forces to point out "the institutional inability of the Agency to provide other than intelligence for background and data base purposes."

[428]The most recent density ratios (supergrades compared to total force) show that possibility of advancement for civilians is vastly better in CIA than in DIA. The Civil Service Commission has refused DIA exemption from the General Schedule that CIA maintains. A deputy director of DIA informed Committee staff that civilians are still "second class citizens" there. Staff interview with James Agersborg, DDI/DIA, Nov. 10, 1975. Statistics provided by ASDI.

Risks

The American taxpayer clearly does not receive full value for his intelligence dollar. The costs of intelligence should not, however, be measured in dollars alone. Many day-to-day activities inevitably pose real risks.

The Committe has found that when results are measured against hazards alone, certain intelligence programs may be wholly unacceptable; other projects may too easily stray from wise and worthwhile courses, without detection.

It is disturbing that the consequences of intelligence activities are sometimes apparently given scant consideration by policy makers. Even more troubling are indications that this insensitivity continues when dangers reveal themselves.

1. Covert Action

The Committee has examined CIA covert action operations and has considerable evidence that they are irregularly approved, sloppily implemented, and at times have been forced on a reluctant CIA by the President and his National Security Advisor.

"Covert action" may be defined as clandestine activity other than purely information-gathering, which is directed at producing a particular political, economic, or military result.

Successive administrations have cited Section 102 of the National Security Act of 1947 as the legal justification for covert action.[431] During the course of this investigation, the Special Counsel to the Director of Central Intelligence has argued that the President, in his conduct of foreign relations, has an inherent Constitutional mandate to authorize these activities.[432]

On the other hand, in recent years, commentators have maintained that in establishing the CIA, Congress had no specific intention that covert operations apart from intelligence-gathering missions be conducted. Witnesses before the Committee likewise disputed any inherent Constitutional power to conduct covert actions. In any event, Congress has implicitly acquiesced in covert action through the oversight process.

It may be argued that there has been explicit approval as well. Just as the War Powers Act acknowledges the authority of the President to conduct overt military hostilities, albeit for a limited period, without a Congressional declaration of war, the Ryan-Hughes Amendment to the Foreign Assistance Act of 1974[434] formally acknowledges the existence and legality of covert action.

The Committee has surveyed all Forty Committee approvals since 1965, and has delved deeply into three recent covert action projects. It is believed that the Committee's review of ten years of covert action is without precedent in the Congress or the executive branch.

a. Ten Year Survey

Our primary purpose was to determine whether the Forty Committee and its predecessors had been exercising their oversight and control responsibilities from 1965 to date.[435] To do this, it was necessary to trace the process from proposal to final approval.

Like other aspects of covert action, fixing responsibility for the initiation of various covert action projects was a difficult task. As recorded in Forty Committee records, the vast majority of projects was submitted by the CIA, 88 percent of the total projects since 1965. The high number of covert action proposals represents a general activism within the foreign affairs bureaucracy, especially within CIA.

The overall picture, however, does not support the contention that covert action has been used in furtherance of any particular principle, form of government, or identifiable national interest. Instead, the record indicates a general lack of a long-term direction in U.S. foreign policy. Covert actions, as the means for implementing a policy, reflected this band-aid approach, substituting short-term remedies for problems which required long-term cures.

Covert action proposals came from a variety of interest areas: a foreign head of state, the Department of Defense, the Department of State, an Ambassador, CIA, the Assistant to the President for National Security Affairs, a cabinet member or the President himself.

Proposals involving a large expenditure of funds or classified as "politically sensitive," required review and approval of the Forty Committee. Unfortunately, the executive branch does not have a clear definition of what constitutes a large or politically sensitive operation. Projects of less sensitivity are approved within the CIA, usually at the level of the Deputy Director for Operations, with the determination of "political sensitivity" being left to the Director of Central Intelligence.

The Forty Committee is chaired by the Assistant to the President for National Security Affairs and includes the Deputy Secretary of Defense, the Undersecretary of State for Political Affairs, the Chairman of the Joint Chiefs of Staff, and the Director of Central Intelligence. Theoretically, a detailed proposal is presented to this group. The members are then afforded an opportunity for a full discussion of the merits and a reporting of their views to the President. In practice, the Forty Committee has often been little more than a rubber stamp.

The procedures for approval of covert action have changed with administrations, political conditions and personalities. At various times, the approval process has been relatively informal, extraordinarily secretive, and pro-forma.

While on occasion some projects have been considered in depth, at Committee meetings which included the approval or disapproval by formal votes, several informal procedures have frequently been used. These informal procedures, such as telephonic votes, do not allow each member to benefit from the views of his colleagues. At times, members have been given only the barest of details, and instead of formal votes have simply been allowed the opportunity to acknowledge the project's existence.

The Forty Committee has only one full-time professional staff member. Because of the high degree of compartmentation attending these projects, committee members—who are among the busiest officials in government—are frequently in the position of evaluating a complex proposal without adequate staff support. The Assistant to the President for National Security Affairs and the Director of Central Intelligence, having the incentive and the resources to cope with Forty Committee business, clearly dominate the process.

The origin of many covert action projects is murky at best.

The CIA, as the prospective implementation arm, is often directed to produce proposals for covert action and is, therefore, incorrectly seen as a plan's original proponent. It is clear that on several occasions involving highly sensitive projects, CIA was summarily ordered by the President or his National Security advisor to carry out a covert action program. It is further clear that CIA has been ordered to engage in covert action over the Agency's strong prior objections.

All evidence in hand suggests that the CIA, far from being out of control, has been utterly responsive to the instructions of the President and the Assistant to the President for National Security Affairs. It must be remembered, however, that the CIA Director determines which CIA-initiated covert action projects are sufficiently "politically sensitive" to require Presidential attention.

From 1965 to 1972, a majority of approvals occurred subsequent to a formal committee meeting; although many telephonic approvals also took place during this period. In 1972, the process became quite informal, often involving mere notification to members that an operation had already been set in motion by the President. The Forty Committee, as the review and approval mechanism for covert action, fell into virtual disuse, with telephonic approvals being the rule and formal meetings the exception. One formal meeting was held in 1972, none in 1973 and 1974. This process did not begin to reverse itself until 1975.

b. Election Support

From 1965 to date, 32 percent of Forty Committee approved covert action projects were for providing some form of financial election support to foreign parties and individuals. Such support could be negative as well as positive. This is the largest covert action category, and its funding has occurred in large part in the developing countries. With few exceptions, financial support has been given to incumbent moderate party leaders and heads of State.

Certain projects have had a long life. One Third World leader received some $960,000 over a 14-year period. Others were financially supported for over a decade.

c. Media and Propaganda

Some 29 percent of Forty Committee-approved covert actions were for media and propaganda projects. This number is probably not representative. Staff has determined the existence of a large number of CIA internally-approved operations of this type, apparently deemed not politically sensitive. It is believed that if the correct number of all media and propaganda projects could be determined, it would exceed Election Support as the largest single category of covert action projects undertaken by the CIA.

Activities have included support of friendly media, major propaganda efforts, insertion of articles into the local press, and distribution of books and leaflets. By far the largest single recipient has been a European publishing house funded since 1951. There are a number of similar operations in the region. About 25 percent of the program has been directed at the Soviet Bloc, in the publication and clandestine import and export of Western and Soviet dissident literature.

d. Paramilitary/Arms Transfers

The 23 percent approvals in this category from 1965 to 1975 have taken one of esentially four forms: secret armies, financial support to groups engaged in hostilities; paramilitary training and advisers; and shipment of arms, ammunition and other military equipment. Military ordnance is typically supplied by CIA out of its large inventory of U.S. weaponry and captured foreign weapons.

The Committee scrutinized these projects carefully, since this category is the most expensive and represents the greatest potential for escalating hostilities and deepening American involvement. By far the most interesting, and important, fact to emerge was the recognition that the great majority of these covert action projects were proposed by parties outside CIA. Many of these programs were summarily ordered, over CIA objections. CIA misgivings, however, were at times weakly expressed, as CIA is afflicted with a "can do" attitude.

At times, CIA has been used as a conduit for arms transfers in order to bypass Congressional scrutiny. A State Department-proposed project which could have been accomplished under the Military Assistance Program was tasked on CIA because the Department of Defense did not desire to return to Congress for additional funds and approval.

e. Organizational Support

A plethora of foreign, civic, religious, professional, and labor organizations have received CIA funding. There has been no real geographical concentration, although the Third World was again well represented. For example, one labor confederation in a developing country received an annual subsidy of $30,000 in three successive years.

f. Trends

Since 1965, there has been a general decline in the number of covert action projects approved by the Forty Committee. There are indications that the low figure represents the Director of Central Intelligence's determination that not as many projects should be considered "politically sensitive" and taken to the Forty Committee for approval. This, in turn, may reflect his recognition that the Forty Committee had fallen into disuse and their approvals pro-forma.

There is no indication that the passage of the Ryan-Hughes Amendment to the Foreign Assistance Act of 1974, requiring Presidential certification and briefings of Congressional oversight committees, has had a significant impact on the national covert action program. As the events of 1975 have shown, those who had warned that the Amendment and the Congressional probes into the U.S. intelligence community would make covert action impossible, have not seen their fears realized.

g. Three Projects

The three projects examined in depth were selected from major recent operations, apart from the American experience in Indochina, and involved different types of covert activity. One was election funding of pro-U.S. elements in an allied country. The second was Presidentially-directed arms support of an insurgency movement at the behest of the foreign head of a third country. The last involved a mix of political action, military training, and assistance to pro-Western forces in Angola. The last project was also initiated in part at the request of a third party.

The Committee became aware of each of these operations through other parts of its investigation and through information provided to staff by sources outside the intelligence community. For example, a study of CIA arms inventories and shipments led to the major Agency para-military support ʼoperations.

The case studies are not representative of all covert action since 1965. The Committee does believe that they are not atypical of most major programs of this type. CIA has indicated its agreement with the completeness and factual accuracy of the staff's analysis. though not necessarily with the conclusions.

Case 1: Election Support

The U.S., perhaps needlessly, expended some $10-million in contributions to political parties, affiliated organizations, and 21 individual candidates in a recent parlimentary election [1972—editor's note] held in an allied country[447] [Italy—editor's note].

The program was initiated by our Ambassador [Graham Martin—editor's note], who later persuaded the Assistant to the President for National Security Affairs [Henry Kissinger—editor's note] to authorize him, rather than CIA, to select funding recipients and otherwise control the program's implementation. The results of the aid were mixed, and short-lived.

With national assembly elections less than two years away, the U. S. country team concluded from a CIA-contracted survey that the pro-U.S. elements, which had governed the country since the post-war period, were being seriously challenged by the Communists. The opposition, apparently heavily financed by Moscow, had scored gains in regional elections and trailed the incumbents by only a few points in the opinion polls.

Pro-West parties and affiliates had received substantial funding in the past. CIA reports total U.S. election financing over a previous 20-year period at some $65 million.[448] Despite this massive aid, the beneficiaries had suffered repeated electoral setbacks. American observers apparently concluded that another "quick fix" was necessary to see our clients through the next vote.

Anxious to gain control of the covert program, and fearing that inter-agency consideration would be inhibiting, the Ambassador has originally sought the President's personal approval of this proposed political action.[449]

This course would avoid the Forty Committee and, with it, the inevitable role of CIA in implementing the program. The Ambassador was rebuffed. Ironically, the Assistant to the President then requested that CIA draft a proposal without the knowledge of the Ambassador or the Department of State.[450]

It is known that during this period the President was indirectly approached by prominent international businessmen, who were former nationals of the allied country. Their communications to the President were not available to the Committee.[451]

The Forty Committee subsequently approved the CIA proposal, but with unusual implementation. Despite the usual near-automatic control of covert action by CIA, the Ambassador, by all accounts a man of unusual force, successfully extracted from the Assistant to the President the commitment that he would have total control of the "mix. and implementation" of the project.[452] Thus, the Ambassador, who had been in the country less than two years and did not speak the language, would determine which individuals and organizations would receive U.S. funds. The CIA station would be reduced to couriers. The Agency expressed concern that a high profile by the Ambassador would needlessly compromise the program; their complaints fell on deaf ears, despite the agreement of all that exposure would bring down the pro-West government.

A major political party received $3.4 million; a political organization created and supported by CIA,

$3.4 million; other organizations and parties, a total of $1.3 million. Substantial funds were provided to several incumbents whose seats did not appear in jeopardy. Of a total of $11.8 million approved by the Forty Committee, only $9.9 million was actually spent. The reserve was held to be spent in the following year.

CIA concurred in most of the recipients chosen by the Ambassador, although differences were expressed on precise amounts. There were serious disagreements over some recipients. One of these was a high local intelligence official to whom the Ambassador wanted to give over $800,000, to conduct a propaganda effort. The Ambassador was unmoved by CIA warnings that the man was clearly linked to anti-democratic elements of the right, and went ahead with the funding.[456]

Embassy control of the funds was poor. Participants in the program testified before the Committee that little effort was made to earmark grants or, failing that, at least seek assurances that the money was spent as intended by the Forty Committee. The Ambassador resisted most CIA control suggestions, insisting that such monitoring would insult the recipients. Thus, there was almost no accounting or control of the expenditures.[457] There is no indication that the Ambassador began to encounter interference from Washington at this point.

The fruits of this U.S. investment are difficult to assess. The pro-U.S. elements retained control of the government by a small plurality, and most of the incumbents supported were returned to office. On the other hand, the ruling coalition quickly lost public support and suffered severe reverses in subsequent local elections.

Case 2: Arms Support

[At this point in the committee report one manuscript

195

page was missing. It is clear from the context that the missing material opened a discussion of a U.S. scheme, involving the Shah of Iran, to channel secret aid to the Kurds in their rebellion against the government of Iraq.][459]

The program, ultimately to involve some $16-million, was apparently endorsed by the President after a private meeting with the foreign head of state and Dr. Kissinger.

There was no Forty Committee meeting at which a formal proposal paper containing both pros and cons could be discussed and voted on. Instead, members were simply directed to acknowledge receipt of a sparse, one-paragraph description of the operation. In a setting of almost unprecedented secrecy within the U.S. government, John B. Connally, the former Treasury Secretary, about to assume a major role in the President's re-election campaign, personally advised the head of state that the U.S. would cooperate.[461]

The recipients of U.S. arms and cash were an insurgent ethnic group fighting for autonomy in a country bordering our ally. The bordering country and our ally had long been bitter enemies. They differed substantially in ideological orientation and in their relations with the U.S.

Evidence collected by the Committee suggests that the project was initiated primarily as a favor to our ally, who had cooperated with U.S. intelligence agencies, and who had come to feel menaced by his neighbor.

As our ally's aid dwarfed the U.S. aid package, our assistance can be seen as largely symbolic. Documents made available to the Committee indicate that the U.S. acted in effect as a guarantor that the insurgent group would not be summarily dropped by the foreign head of state.[462] Notwithstanding these implicit assurances, the insurgents were abruptly cut off by our ally, three years, thousands of deaths, and 16 million U.S. dollars later.[463]

It appears that, had the U.S. not reinforced our ally's prodding, the insurgents may have reached an accommodation with the central government, thus gaining at least a measure of autonomy while avoiding further bloodshed. Instead, our clients fought on, sustaining thousands of casualties and 200,000 refugees.

There is little doubt that the highly unusual security precautions and the circumvention of the Forty Committee were the product of fears by the President and Dr. Kissinger that details of the project would otherwise leak—a result which by all accounts would have mightily displeased our ally. It is also clear that the secrecy was motivated by a desire that the Department of State, which had consistently opposed such ventures in the region, be kept in the dark.[464]

Perhaps more than the President's disregard of the Forty Committee, the apparent "no win" policy of the U.S. and its ally deeply disturbed this Committee. Documents in the Committee's possession clearly show that the President, Dr. Kissinger and the foreign head of state hoped that our clients would not prevail.[465]. They preferred instead that the insurgents simply continue a level of hostilities sufficient to sap the resources of our ally's neighboring country.[466] This policy was not imparted to our clients, who were encouraged to continue fighting. Even in the context of covert action, ours was a cynical enterprise.

It is particularly ironic that, despite President Nixon's and Dr. Kissinger's encouragement of hostilities to keep the target country off-balance, the United States personally restrained the insurgents from an all-out offensive on one occasion when such an attack might have been successful because other events were occupying the neighboring country.[467]

All U.S. aid was channeled through our collaborator, without whose logistical help direct assist-

197

ance would have been impossible. Our national interest had thus become effectively meshed with his. Accordingly, when our ally reached an agreement with the target country and abruptly ended his own aid to the insurgents, the U.S. had no choice but to acquiesce. The extent of our ally's leverage over U.S. policy was such that he apparently made no effort to notify his junior American partners that the program's end was near.

The insurgents were clearly taken by surprise as well. Their adversaries, knowing of the impending aid cut-off, launched an all-out search-and-destroy campaign the day after the agreement was signed.[469] The autonomy movement was over and our former clients scattered before the central government's superior forces.[470]

The cynicism of the U.S. and its ally had not yet completely run its course, however. Despite direct pleas from the insurgent leader and the CIA station chief in the area to the President and Dr. Kissinger, the U.S. refused to extend humanitarian asistance to the thousands of refugees created by the abrupt termination of military aid. As the Committee staff was reminded by a high U.S. official, "covert action should not be confused with missionary work."[471]

Case 3: Angola

For reasons not altogether clear, and despite the opposition of senior government officials, the U.S. has been heavily involved in the current civil war in Angola.

The CIA has informed the Committee that since January 1975, it had expended over $31 million in military hardware, transportation costs, and cash payments by the end of 1975. The Committee has reason to believe that the actual U.S. investment is much higher. Information supplied to the Committee also suggests that the military intervention of the Soviet Union and Cuba is in large part a reaction to U.S. efforts to break a political stalemate, in favor of its clients.

The beneficiaries of U.S. aid are two of the three contesting factions: the National Front for the Independence of Angola (FNLA) and the National Union for the Total Independence of Angola (UNITA). The third faction contesting for control of the government, following independence on November 11, 1975, is the Soviet-backed Popular Movement for the Liberation of Angola (MPLA). CIA estimates that the fighting had claimed several thousand casualties by the end of 1975.

The main U.S. client is the National Front, headed by Holden Roberto, a longtime associate and relative of President Mobutu Sese Seko of neighboring Zaire. Subsequent to President Mobutu's request last winter to Dr. Kissinger, as independence for Angola became a certainty and liberation groups began to jockey for position, the Forty Committee approved furnishing Roberto $300,000 for various political action activities,[474] restricted to non-military objectives.

Later events have suggested that this infusion of U.S. aid, unprecedented[475] and massive in the underdeveloped colony, may have panicked the Soviets into arming their MPLA clients, whom they had backed for over a decade and who were now in danger of being eclipsed by the National Front. Events in Angola took a bellicose turn as the U.S. was requested by President Mobutu to make a serious military investment.

In early June, 1975, CIA prepared a proposal paper for military aid to pro-U.S. elements in Angola, the cost of which was set at $6 million. A revised program, costing $14 million, was approved by the Forty Committee and by President Ford in July. This was increased to $25 million in August, and to about $32 million in November. By mid-summer, it was decided that U.S. aid should not be given solely to Roberto, but instead, divided between him and UNITA's Jonas Savimbi.

The Committee has learned that a task force composed of high U.S. experts on Africa[477] strongly opposed military intervention; instead, last April they called for diplomatic efforts to encourage a political settlement among the three factions to avert bloodshed. Apparently at the direction of National Security Council aides, the task force recommendation was removed from the report and presented to NSC members as merely one policy option. The other two alternatives were a hands-off policy or substantial military intervention.

Of CIA's $31 million figure, said to represent expenditures to the end of 1975, about half is attributed to supply of light arms, mortars, ammunition, vehicles, boats, and communication equipment. The balance includes shipping expenses and cash payments. The Committee has reason to question the accuracy of CIA's valuation of military equipment sent to Angola.

A staff accountant on loan from the General Accounting Office has determined that CIA "costing" procedures and the use of surplus equipment have resulted in a substantial understatement of the value of U.S. aid. Examples include .45 caliber automatic weapons "valued" by CIA at $5.00 each and .30 caliber semi-automatic carbines at $7.55. Based on a sampling of ordnance cost figures and a comparison with Department of Defense procedures, staff advises that the CIA's ordnance figure should at least be doubled.

Dr. Kissinger has indicated that U.S. military intervention in Angola is based on three factors: Soviet support of the MPLA and the USSR's increased presence in Africa, U.S. policy to encourage moderate independence groups in southern Africa, and the U.S. interest in promoting the stability of Mobutu and other leadership figures in the area. Past support to Mobutu, along with his responsiveness to some of the United States recent diplomatic needs for Third World support, make it equally likely that the paramount factor in the U.S. involvement is Dr. Kissinger's desire to reward and protect African leaders in the area. The U.S.'s expressed opposition to the MPLA is puzzling in view of Director's Colby's statement to the Committee that there are scant ideological differences among the three factions, all of whom are nationalists above all else.[481]

Control of resources may be a factor. Angola has significant oil deposits and two American multinationals, Gulf and Texaco, operate in the off-shore area. Gulf had deposited some $100 million in concession fees in a national bank now under MPLA control. At the suggestion of the U.S. government, the company suspended further payments.

Until recently, the U.S.-backed National Front was supported by the People's Republic of China, which had provided about 100 military advisors. Moboutu has provided a staging area for U.S. arms shipments and has periodically sent Zairois troops, trained by the Republic of North Korea, into Angola to support Roberto's operations. Small numbers of South African forces have been in the country and are known to have been in contact with Savimbi's UNITA troops.

Pursuant to Section 662 of the Foreign Assistance Act of 1974, the President has found that the Angola action program is "important to the national security." As directed by the Act, CIA has briefed the Congressional oversight committees as to the Forty Committee approvals of increased amounts of military aid.

CIA officials have testified to the Committee that there appears to be little hope of an outright MPLA military defeat. Instead, U.S. efforts are now aimed at promoting a stalemate, and in turn, the ceasefire and the coalition government urged by the long-forgotten NSC task force.

Footnotes:

[431]Section 102 (d) (5) calls on CIA, under National Security Council direction, "to perform such other functions and duties related to intelligence affecting the national security as the National Security Council may from time to time direct."

[432]Mitchell Rogovin, Counsel to the DCI, argued that "before there was a 1947 Act there was a United States and a United States with a President with the authority to conduct foreign affairs and he conducted such affairs over the history of the nation which involved activity which we now know as covert activity. Now the 1947 Act did not give the President a power he did not have before. The 1947 Act merely came upon the scene as it was and it set up the National Security Council. The Council itself subsequently took its authority and devised a 40 Committee as an implementing system for getting information with respect to covert activity. So that the activity in 1972 grew from two seperate legal authorities for the President to pursue."

[434]Section 32 of Public Law 93-559 (The Foreign Assistance Act Amendments of 1974) states in part: "No funds appropriated under the authority of this or any other Act may be expended by or on behalf of the Central Intelligence Agency for operations in foreign countries, other than activities intended solely for obtaining necessary intelligence, unless and until the President of the United States finds that each such operation is important to the national security of the United States and reports, in a timely fashion,

a description and scope of such operation to the appropriate committees of the Congress, including the Committee on Foreign Relations of the United States Senate and the Committee on Foreign Affairs of the United States House of Representatives." The remaining four committees are the Armed Services and Appropriations Committees of the House of Representatives and the Senate.

[435]Subsequent to a subpoena issued by the Committee on Nov. 6, 1975, two staff members reviewed all records of the Forty Committee reflecting approvals for Covert Action from 1965 to 1975. All information and statistics used in the section entitled "Ten Year Survey" are drawn from the staff review of those documents. The staff presented their findings to the full Committee in Executive Session testimony on Dec. 9, 1975. During that session, Mr. Colby had an opportunity to express his views on the staff report and while he had reservations about the conclusions, he raised no substantial disagreement with the facts.

[447]It appears clear that this expenditure was made despite the fact that money was "not the problem." Cable from Chief of Station

To Headquarters in Washington   3 March "Ambassador continues to cogitate on nature, amount and channel for financial assistance an dtelling Station very little. He is aware of Station view that *money is not the problem*, [deleted] has plenty and any amount we contribue to [deleted] will have insignificant effect on electoral showing. If we could reduce the pernicious effect of interparty squabbling and get party to pull in unison this would be worth financial support. We do not exclude possibility Ambasador [deleted] will want to give some money strictly as a demonstration of 'solidarity,' and a case might be made for this, but not two million dollars worth." (Emphasis supplied)

MEMORANDUM FOR: Director of Central Intelli-
VIA: Deputy Director of Plans
SUBJECT: Forty Committee Approval
For Political Action Pro-
gram   18 February

"Costs

This program will cost $1,050,000 the first year and
$2,465,000 the second . . ."

MEMORANDUM FOR: Director of Central Intelligence
SUBJECT: Ambassador [deleted]
Proposed [deleted] Elec-
tion Program   7 March

"Costs

Of the $10,000,000, the $1,790,000 for the [deleted]
is to come from the budget approved on March 10 by
the 40 Committee . . .$8,300,000 in new funds will
be required."

[448]MEMORANDUM FOR: The Forty Commitee
SUBJECT: Political Action Pro-
gram for [deleted] to
Arrest the Growing
Power of the Commu-
nists   10 March

"1. History of CIA Supported Political Action in [de-
leted]. The United States government was concerned
in 1948 that the Communists would emerge from the
national elections sufficiently strong to enter the government as a major if not dominant force. As a counter, it was decided that CIA should give $1,000,000
to the center parties for this election with the bulk
going to [deleted].

"Between 1948 and 1964 funds provided to [de-
leted] totaled approximately $5,450, 000. Between
1948 and 1963 additional support to [deleted] in
eight national and regional elections amounted to
$11,800,000. Between 1958 and 1968, the [deleted]
received about $26,000,000 to support its opposition

to the Communist dominated labor confederation. [deleted] received some $11,350,000 during this period.

"Between 1948 and 1968 other organizations received about $10,550,000 of CIA assistance. This support was given to the following political parties associated with center or center-left governments . . .

"In sum, excluding the initial $1,000,000 spent in the 1948 campaign, CIA gave [deleted] and its related organizations $54,600,000 as well as $10,550,000 to the other non-Communist parties and affiliates for a grand total of $65,150,000 over approximately twenty years, starting in 1948 . . ."

449The Ambassador had decided during the first months of the project that he would go directly to the President for his approval, and that he would exclude the CIA from whatever plans he would propose.

Cable from Chief of Station
   To Headquarters   13 March
"Ambassador [deleted] case (which he hopes present to President [deleted] and [National Security Advisor]), and not to State Department or 40 Committee . . . Imperative keep these observations as privileged within CIA owing Ambassador [deleted] explicit admonitions to Chief of Station to effect he does not repeat not wish inform anyone in Washington his views until he personally sees President [deleted]."

Cable from Chief of Station
   To Headquarters   14 October
"Concur that Ambassador [deleted] will raise the need for political action in [deleted] in the future . . . A key to his thinking is his strong conviction that any political action program in [deleted] which requires 'interagency approval' is not likely to get off the ground."

Cable from Headquarters
    To Chief of Station   15 October

". . . . Keep in mind that Ambassador [deleted] previous proposal re support of [projects in other countries] . . . floundered in large measure because it was not submitted through proper channels and thus was not injected into interagency mechanism until too late."

Nonetheless, the Ambassador stated to the Committee that he had not really attempted to bypass the Forty Committee.

Comm. Hearings

"CHAIRMAN PIKE. But was not an effort made to have your plan approved by the President without going through the Forty Committee route?
AMBASSADOR [deleted]. No sir, it would never have occurred to me that this was even possible."

[450]The initial Forty Committee approval paper which was drafted by the CIA stated,
"4. Coordination.

"At the request of [National Security Advisor], this program has not yet been coordinated with Ambassador or with the Bureau of [deleted] of the Department of State."

The CIA, while waiting for the President to respond to the Ambassador's proposal, did not believe that the CIA could wait indefinitely for that answer.

Cable from Headquarters
    To CIA Chief of Station   7 January

"At this juncture, Ambassador [deleted] should not repeat not be apprised of this draft paper's preparation. CIA is preparing this draft paper . . . for internal purposes and it will not repeat not be discussed with State at this time."

[451]The CIA alluded to other approaches to the President by private individuals.

Cable from Chief of Station
  To Headquarters   10 February

"2. An important factor in Ambassador [deleted] desire to present an action program is his problem of how to cope with the many American and [deleted] channels to President [deleted] office which now exist. Ambassador [deleted] has become aware of this special character of [deleted]-U.S. relations and is trying to get a handle on this problem rather than having to react to the advice and influence offered by others."

Cable from Chief of Station
  To Headquarters   11 February

"B. Ambassador [deleted] insists that unless he proceeds quickly 'certain people' will push the White House into a 'disastrous program.' The name of [an international businessman who contacted the White House] finally emerged. 'If you think the [right-wing foreign intelligence officer's] program is bad, you should see the kind of stuff [international businessman] is trying to sell.' In the Ambassador's view '[international businessman] is further to the right than [right-wing politician].' "

State Department officials in talks with the Agency also expressed reservations in dealing with these channels to the White House.

MEMORANDUM
  FOR THE RECORD   14 JULY

"2. [State Department official] said that one of the problems that he had in dealing with [deleted] affairs is that people like [international businessman] had excellent access to higher echelons of our government, and there was no way of knowing their information input. He said that [international businessman] had very good relations with [deleted] of the White House. (The international businessman conducted foreign fund-raising activities for a U.S. political party.)"

[452]Testimony given to the Committee by the CIA Deputy Director for Operations states that ". . . The Forty Committee approval stated that Ambassador [deleted] would 'control the mix and implementation . . .' of the program and would be expected to 'forward recommendations' for additional overt activities which might be undertaken in support of U.S. objectives in [deleted]." Comm. Hearings . . .

The Agency was uncomfortable with this unaccustomed turn of events. In cables from the Station, it was reiterated that the Ambassador was to be the one calling the shots.

Cable from Chief of Station
    To Headquarters   June

"1. Morning 4 June I delivered to Ambassador, a sterile copy of your message. After reading it he commented that 'They still do not understand that the program as approved by 40 Committee and the President is only an illustrative one leaving to Ambassador [deleted] the authority to decide what should be done.'
"4. Headquarters is in error if it really believes friction with Ambassador [deleted] can be avoided if Ambassador understands CIA views better. He understands them only too well. It is this 'understanding' that causes the friction and it will continue. . ."

The Agency and the Ambassador had frequent dis-

208

agreements over the "mix and implementation" of the project and its developments.

Comm. Hearings at

"AMBASSADOR. One of the people who was here this morning, the Acting Chief of Station, couldn't get away from the fact that the Agency had traditionally run all this and [thought that] the Agency knew better what needed to be done and [couldn't accept] what the 40 Committee had said and the President had approved, that the authority and the mix and implementation would be mine. He felt that if he disagreed with something, that therefore they could veto it and send it back, you see, for whatever. Yes, I did object to this."

The Ambassador felt so strongly about his differences of opinion with the Acting Chief of Station that he mentioned their disagreements nine times during his testimony before the Committee.

The Ambassador reacted vigorously even when his authority was questioned by [the National Security adviser] and reviewed by the Forty Committee. When [the National Security adviser] decided that the CIA should submit a separate progress report of the project to the Forty Committee, the Ambassador was aroused.

Cable from Chief of Station
    To Headquarters   28 February

"1. You should be aware that Ambassador [deleted] reaction to (memo) was negative in the extreme. He considers it offensive to him personally that the CIA would submit annual report. Says it is not true that [National Security adviser] 'ruled' that CIA submit report. It was CIA that suggested that idea to him..."

At the annual 40 Committee review of the project,

reservations were expressed by the members on portions of the operation, particularly the funding of a moribund [political action group]. The Ambassador was annoyed at this interference from Washington and he apparently resorted to subterfuge.

Cable from Chief of Station
    To Headquarters   16 March

"1. Ambassador intensely annoyed by outcome of 40 Committee meeting.
"2. You will note that Ambassador's message states he has committed additional [amount of money] to [affiliated political action group] effort. This is not repeat repeat not true. He was urged not to make this statement because it: (A) not accurate and (B) still not determined that [affiliated political action group] could effectively use or absorb this additional amount Ambassador said he insisted on reporting that funds 'committed for tactical reasons . . .'"

456The Ambassador and the CIA had sharp disagreements about the funding of this [right-wing, senior intelligence officer] and his propaganda program. Initially, the Chief of Station expressed his reservations about the project to the Ambassador.

Cable from Chief of Station
    To Headquarters   10 February
"...3. In response to Chief of Station's question, 'Do you really care if [foreign intelligence officer] propaganda efforts are successful or not,' Ambassador [deleted] replied, 'Yes, I do, but not a helluva lot. Important thing is to demonstrate solidarity for the long pull.'"

When the Chief of Station continued to resist further on the funding, the Ambassador became very annoyed .

Cable from Chief of Station
   To Headquarters   11 February
"3. Ambassador [deleted] said Headquarters absolutely wrong. Said he had discussed in Washington (did not say with whom) and all agreed this was legitimate . . . Chief of Station expressed the view that Ambassador [deleted] should first clarify this point in personal exchange with CIA . . . He [Ambassador] thereupon accused·Chief of Station of dragging his feet in contacting [foreign intelligence officer], and said if this continued beyond today he would 'Instruct Marine guards not to let you in this building and put you on the airplane.' "Chief of Station said he thought this a bit extreme and expressed view that Ambassador [deleted] could hardly object to what appeared legitimate Headquarters question. He did object and with vigor."

The CIA headquarters shared the same concerns as the Station Chief and warned the Ambassador in conciliatory terms against funding, especially on a no-strings-attached. . . .

457. . . Control over funding was so loose that there was no way of checking to see if funds were being expended for the purposes for which they said the were to be used. The Ambassador said before the Committee, ". . . I think as it turned out that we did get our full money's worth.

"Now on the question of the possibility of a rip-off, that is quite true. The possibility exists . . ."

459[The beginning of this footnote was not available —*editor's note.*] . . . we do not wish to become involved, even indirectly, in operations which would have the effect of prolonging the insurgency, thereby encouraging separatist aspirations and possibly providing to the Soviet Union an opportunity to create difficulties for [two other U.S. allies]." A CIA cable from the COS in the area to the DCI contains the U.S. Ambassador's views on the proposal: "My reaction is against giving financial support to this operation unless there are important policy considerations to the contrary of which I am not aware . . . Furthermore, the road is open-ended and if we begin and then decide to withdraw there might be unfortunate misinterpretations of our reasons which could adversely affect our relations with [our ally]." A second proposal was turned down in August of 1971 and again in March of 1972. On the latter occasion, Dr. Kissinger conferred with a high State Department official in-depth on the proposal and agreed that it should be disapproved. . . .

[461]The Secretary of the 40 Committee hand-carried a brief one paragraph synopsis of the project to the members for them to initial. The conclusion that the procedure was simply pro-forma is indicated by the fact that John Connally had already informed our ally that the U.S. would provide support to the insurgents. In addition, even the pros and cons contained in the CIA proposal paper prepared for Dr. Kissinger were foregone conclusions. Responding to a question by staff concerning why CIA's negative views of the project were not put more forcefully, a CIA official responded that "the Committee must realize that CIA was told to prepare a paper on 'how' the project could be done, not 'whether' the project should be done." . . .

[462]On numerous occasions the leader of the ethnic group expressed his distrust of our allies' intentions. He did, however, trust the United States as indicated by his frequent statements that "he trusted no other major power" and asserted that if his cause were successful he was "ready to become the 51st state." (See COS cable to DCI of January 16, 1975, for one example.) In addition, his admiration for Dr. Kissinger was expressed on two occasions when he sent a gift of three rugs and later on the occasion of Dr. Kissinger's marriage, a gold and pearl necklace. A May 20, 1974, Memorandum to Brent Scowcroft explains the neces-

sity of keeping the gifts secret: "As you are aware, the relationship between the United States Government and the (ethnic group) remains extremely sensitive. Knowledge of its existence has been severely restricted; therefore, the fact that Dr. Kissinger has received this gift should be similarly restricted."

463The cut-off of aid to the ethnic group came as a severe shock to its leadership. A CIA cable from the COS to the DCI on March 15, 1975, describes the method used by our ally to inform the ethnic group's leadership. On March 5, a representative of our ally's intelligence service visited the headquarters of the ethnic group and "told [them] in bluntest imaginable terms that a) the border was being closed to all repeat all movement, b) . . . could expect no more assistance from [our ally], c) . . . should settle with our [ally's enemy] on whatever terms he could get, and d) his military units would be allowed to take refuge in [our ally's country] only in small groups "and only if they surrendered their arms to [our ally's] army."

464Elaborate measures were taken to insure that the Department of State did not gain knowledge of the project. Documents suggest that it may have originally been planned to keep the project so severely restricted that not even the Ambassador to the country involved was to be told. . . .

In addition, evidence in the Committee files is conflicting on whether Secretary of State William P. Rogers was ever informed of the project. Officials of Kissinger's staff and CIA officials assumed that he had been briefed since U. Alexis Johnson was a member of the Forty Committee. And, in an interview with staff, Mr. Rogers stated that he felt certain that he had been informed. Nevertheless, a cable from Secretary Rogers almost a year after the project began suggests that he did not have knowledge, as of June 22, 1973. The cable states that "in view of continued U.S.

policy not repeat not give encouragement to the [ethnic group's] hopes for U.S. assistance or recognition, we would intend keep contacts at country directorate level." Interview with William P. Rogers, by Aaron Donner, Oct. 20, 1975, copy on file with Sel. Comm. on Intell.

[465]The progressively deteriorating position of the ethnic group reflected the fact that none of the nations who were aiding them seriously desired that they realize their objective of an autonomous state. A CIA memo of March 22, 1974 states our ally's and the United States' position clearly: "We would think that [our ally] would not look with favor on the establishment of a formalized autonomous government. [Our ally] like ourselves, has seen benefit in a stalemate situation . . . in which [our ally's enemy] is intrinsically weakened by [the ethnic group's] refusal to relinquish its semi-autonomy. Neither [our ally] nor ourselves wish to see the matter resolved one way or the other."

[466]The CIA had early information which suggested that our ally would abandon the ethnic group the minute he came to an agreement with his enemy over border disputes. Two months after initiating the project a CIA memo of Oct. 17, 1972 states: "[Our ally] has apparently used [another government's] Foreign Minister to pass word to [his enemy] that he would be willing to allow peace to prevail [in the area] if [his enemy] would publicly agree to abrogate [a previous treaty concerning their respective borders]." In addition, CIA memos and cables characterize our ally's views of the ethnic group as "a card to play" in this dispute with his neighbor. And a CIA memo of March 22. 1974 characterizes the ethnic group as "a uniquely useful tool for weakening [our ally's enemy's] potential for international adventurism "

[467]A White House memorandum of October 16 1973, from Dr. Kissinger to the DCI states: "The

President concurs in your judgment in paragraph 3 of your memorandum of October 15 on the above subject. You should therefore send the following reply immediately to [the ethnic group]—We do not repeat not consider it advisable for you to undertake the offensive military action that [another government] has suggested to you.—For your information, we have consulted with [our ally] through the Ambassador and they have both made the same recommendation."

469The attack launched the day after the agreement was signed caught the ethnic group by surprise. A message from their headquarters to CIA on 10 March, 1975 read as follows: "Tnere is confusion and dismay among our people and forces. Our people's fate in unprecedented danger. Complete destruction hanging over our head. No explanation for all this. We appeal you and USG intervene according to your promises and not letting down ally, to save [ethnic leader's] life and dignity of our families, to find honorable solution to [our] problem." On that same day the Chief of Station sent the following cable to the DCI: "Is headquarters in touch with Kissinger's office on this; if USG does not handle this situation deftly in a way which will avoid giving the [ethnic group] the impression that we are abandoning them they are likely to go public. [Our ally's] action has not only shattered their political hopes; it endangers lives of thousands." The COS proceeded to make suggestions for what the USG could do to help and ended with the remark "it would be the decent thing for USG to do."

470Also on March 10, 1975 the following letter arrived from the leader of the ethnic group to Secretary of State, Henry Kissinger: "Your Excellency, Having always believed in the peaceful solution of disputes including those between [your ally and his enemy] we are pleased to see that their two countries have come to some agreement . . . However, our hearts bleed to see that an immediate by product of their

215

agreement is the destruction of our defenseless people in an unprecedented manner as [your ally] closed its border and stopped help to us completely and while [his enemy] began the biggest offensive they have ever launched and which is now being continued. Our movement and people are being destroyed in an unbelievable way with silence from everyone. We feel your Excellency that the United States has a moral and political responsibility towards our people who have committed themselves to your country's policy. In consideration of this situation we beg your Excellency to take action as immediately as possible on the following issues: 1) Stopping the . . . offensive and opening the way for talks between us . . . to arrive at a solution for our people which will at least be face saving. 2) Using whatever influence you have with [your ally] to help our people in this historically tragic and sad moment and at least in such a way that our people and [army] could maintain some livelihood and perform at least partisan activity in [our area] until our problem is also solved within the framework of an [overall] agreement. Mr. Secretary, we are anxiously awaiting your quick response and action and we are certain that the United States will not remain indifferent during these critical and trying times . . ."

A CIA cable from the COS to the Director on 22 March 1975 states: "No reply has been received from Secretary of State Henry Kissinger to the message from [the ethnic leader] . . . The two additional messages received by radio from [his] headquarters are forwarded this morning . . . and underscore the seriousness of [their] situation, the acute anxiety of their leaders and their emotional appeal that the USG use its influence with [our ally] to get an extension of the cease fire. This would permit the peaceful passage of . . . refugees to asylum . . . Hence, if the USG intends to take steps to avert a massacre it must intercede with [our ally] promptly." Interview with CIA official, by J. Boos, Oct. 18, 1975, copy on file with Sel. Comm. on Intell.

471Over 200,000 refugees managed to escape into our ally's country. Once there, however, neither the United States nor our ally extended adequate humanitarian assistance. In fact, our ally was later to forcibly return over 40,000 of the refugees and the United States government refused to admit even one refugee into the United States by way of political asylum even though they qualified for such admittance. . . .

474The political action program included the distribution of 50,000 campaign-type buttons identifying the wearer as a supporter of Roberto's FNLA.

475The United States has found itself in similar situations on other occasions. Having supported colonial power policies in previous years, they are constrained from developing a rapport with indigenous independence movements. The Soviets, however, are not similarly inhibited. Once the colonial power relinquishes control, the well-organized, well-financed, Soviet backed group is ready to step into the breach. The United States is forced at that point to scurry around looking for a rival faction or leader to support. The U.S. has often chosen leaders who had a prior relationship with the colonial power and whose nationalist credentials are thus somewhat suspect, or leaders who have spent most of their time outside the country waiting for the colonial power to depart. The point is that many of the U.S.-backed groups begin with a variety of factors working to their disadvantage.

477The task force was composed of African experts within the Department of State, DoD officials, CIA officials, and others. Officials from the Department of State have told this Committee that the majority of that task force recommended diplomatic efforts to encourage a political settlement rather than intervention. After they had prepared their report for the Secretary of State containing this recommendation, they were informed by National Security Council aides that it was improper for them to make a recommendation on policy. Instead, they were instructed to simply list diplomatic efforts as one option among many in their final report. Thus, the African experts who made up the task force were not allowed to place their recommendations on paper to be reviewed by the Forty Committee.

[481]The Committee attempted to determine the difference between the three contesting factions in Angola. Mr. Colby responded to questions of that nature: "They are all independents. They are all for black Africa. They are all for some fuzzy kind of social system, you know, without really much articulation, but some sort of let's not be exploited by the capitalist nations." The Committee also attempted to discern why certain nations were supporting different groups if they were all similar in outlook:

"MR. ASPIN. And why are the Chinese backing the moderate group?

"MR. COLBY. Because the Soviets are backing the MPLA is the simplest answer.

"MR. ASPIN. It sounds like that is why we are doing it.

"MR. COLBY. It is."

2. Intelligence Collection

Human and diplomatic risks are not confined to covert action. Certain methods of intelligence-gathering invite the same danger of war and infringement of the Constitutional rights of Americans.

The Committee has examined both technical and non-technical intelligence-gathering programs and has concluded that the risks accompanying them are often unacceptably great; that information obtained often does not justify the risk; the policy-makers have been insensitive to dangers, especially of the violation of U.S. citizens' rights; and, that there are inadequate policy-level mechanisms for the regular review of risk assessment.

a. Submarines

A highly technical U.S. Navy submarine reconnaissance program, often operating within unfriendly waters, has experienced at least 9 collisions with hostile vessels in the last ten years, over 110 possible detections, and at least three press exposures. Most of the submarines carry nuclear weapons.

The program clearly produces useful information on our adversaries' training exercises, weapons testing, and general naval capabilities. It is also clear, however, that the program is inherently risky. Committee staff's review of the program suggests if both Congress and the Department of the Navy were sufficiently motivated to provide the funds, technical capabilities could be developed which would make possible the acquisition of the same data through less hazardous means.

The Navy's own justification of the program as a "low risk" venture is inaccurate, and has, therefore, not met or resolved the Committee's misgivings.[487]

Documents provided the Committee by the Defense Department indicate that, while risk assessments are made prior to operations, they are ritualistic and pro forma. In fact, their mission risk assessments do not vary despite constant changes in political conditions, information sought, distance from enemy shores and hostile forces, and our adversaries' ability to detect the presence of U.S. submarines. During the hundreds of missions these submarines have conducted, the Navy has never assessed military risk as anything but "low." The Committee is, therefore, troubled by the completely pro forma nature of the mission risk assessment as it is presently accomplished.

Just as the Navy's assurances that the program is secure are inconsistent with the collisions, apparent detections, and press stories, their claims that the sensitive missions are closely monitored are belied by the scant tactical guidance given commanders and regular communications gaps. Once a U.S. submarine enters the 12-mile limit of another nation, communications security and the lack of certain technical capabilities make it impossible to independently verify the location of a submarine at any given moment. Many of these difficulties result from factors which are inherent in the nature of this covert operation.

Naval inquiries into collisions and other "untoward incidents," if held at all, are almost always conducted at a low level, effectively keeping policy-makers in the dark on changing operational conditions. Thus, it took a field-initiated, low-level investigation, conducted after three collisions in 1970, to determine that pre-mission training and operational guidelines for U.S. submarines on this type of sensitive mission needed revision and up-grading. If Washington-based review had been adequate, it would not have taken this field investigation to determine that U.S. submarines were following other submarines too closely. In addition, staff found no evidence which would

220

indicate that commanders of submarines colliding with hostile vessels have ever received disciplinary action of any kind. At times, commanders have escaped censure despite recommendations to that effect by a review panel.

Despite these faults, the Committee noted the procedures implemented by the Navy to insure the safety of the mission and the crew in situations which are inherently risky. Washington-based control, review, and coordination of this program has been an evolutionary matter over the years. At present it appears to be extremely well managed, with the exception of the risk assessment area and the failure to forward the results of low-level investigations for Washington-based review.

In reviewing past investigations and formal reviews, the Committee noted the Navy's implementation of previous suggestions for change. There is, however, one unfortunate exception. A previous review of this program suggested that the Department of the Navy make a firm commitment to the necessity of maintaining an intelligence capability with U.S. submarines by allocating funds to research and development efforts designed to increase both the capabilities and the security of their missions. The Navy has paid only lip service to this commitment.

Given these factors, the Committee urges a thorough review of the program's product and hazards, to avert another *Pueblo*, or worse, and to insure that important intelligence collection continues with significantly less risk than presently exists.

b. Interception of International Communications

The National Security Agency (NSA) systematically intercepts international communications, both voice and cable. NSA officials and the Director of Central

Intelligence concede that messages to and from American citizens and businesses have been picked up in the course of gathering foreign communications intelligence. They maintain, however, that these messages are small in number and usually discarded in any case.[493]

Earlier NSA programs of questionable legality focused on international narcotics traffic and radicalism, and even targeted Americans. The Committee's preliminary investigation reveals at least one new area of non-political and non-military emphasis in international intercept—economic intelligence. Communications interception in this area has rapidly developed since 1972, partly in reaction to the Arab oil embargo and the failure to obtain good information on Russian grain production and negotiations for the purchase with American corporations.

The Committee is not convinced that the current commercial intercept program has yielded sufficiently valuable data to justify its high cost and intrusion, however inadvertent, into the privacy of international communications of U.S. citizens and organizations. Inasmuch as the technical complexity of the program defies easy or quick evaluation, the Committee is hopeful that a permanent oversight mechanism will closely and comprehensively scrutinize the operation to determine whether the risks are necessary and acceptable.

c. Manipulation of the Media

The free flow of information, vital to a responsible and credible press, has been threatened as a result of CIA's use of the world media for cover and for clandestine information-gathering.

There are disturbing indications that the accuracy of many news stories has been undermined as well. Information supplied to the Committee suggests that some planted, falsified articles have reached readers in the U.S.[495]

Intelligence agencies have long prized journalists as informants and identity-covers. Newsmen generally enjoy great mobility, and are often admitted to areas denied to ordinary businessmen or to suspected intelligence types. Not expected to work in one fixed location, both bona fide journalists and masquerading intelligence officers can move about without arousing suspicions. They also have extraordinary access to important foreign leaders and diplomats.

CIA, as no doubt every other major intelligence agency in the world, has manipulated the media. Full-time foreign corrspondents for major U.S. publications have worked concurrently for CIA, passing along information received in the normal course of their regular jobs and even, on occasion, travelling to otherwise non-newsworthy areas to acquire data. Far more prevalent is the Agency's practice of retaining free-lancers and "stringers" as informants. A stringer working in a less-newsworthy country could supply stories to a newspaper, radio, and a weekly magazine, none of whom can justify a full-time correspondent. This may make the use of stringers even more insidious than exploitation of full-time journalists.

The Committee has learned that the employment of newsmen by CIA is usually without the knowledge or agreement of the employers back in the U.S. Publishers have been unable, despite strenuous effort, to learn from the Agency which, if any, of their employees have had a clandestine intelligence function.[498] Newsmen-informants apparently do not often disclose this relationship to their editors. The Committee has learned of cases in which informants moved from one bona fide press position to another, without ever making employers aware of their past or present CIA status.

CIA acknowledges that "stringers" and others with whom the Agency has a relationship are often directed to insert Agency-composed "news" articles into foreign publications and wire services. U.S. intelligence officials do not rule out the possibility that these planted stories may find their way into American newspapers from time to time, but insist that CIA does not intentionally propagandize in this country. CIA insensitivity to the possibility of its adultering news digested by Americans is indicated by its frequent manipulation of Reuters wire service dispatches—which regularly appear in U.S. media. Because Reuters is British, it is considered fair game.[499]

A number of CIA officers employed by U.S. and foreign publications write nothing at all. Their journalistic affiliation is a "cover"—a sham arrangement making possible full-time clandestine work for the Agency. With these arrangements, the employer's cooperation has been obtained.[500]

After the Washington *Star-News* discovered a CIA-media relationship in 1973, Director Colby ordered a review of these practices. Subsequently, the Agency terminated the informant relationships of five full-time employees of American periodicals. Stringers and free-lancers are still on the payroll, despite their periodic reporting for a U.S. media usually unaware of the writer's CIA connection.[501]

The use of American press enterprises as a cover has been tightened somewhat. No longer, for example, can a CIA officer in the field arrange for cover without headquarters approval.

Director Colby, citing the Agency's continuing need for reliable information and the increasing reluctance of private firms and the government to provide cover, has maintained that the recent reforms have reduced risks to an acceptable level.

d: CIA Presence in the Executive Branch

CIA personnel may be found in a host of U.S. departments and agencies, in the National Security Council, and in the White House itself.

Typically, their Agency affiliations are unknown to colleagues and to all others, except one or two leadership figures.[503] They sit on interagency panels whose members are unwitting.[504] In some cases these panels already include another, official, CIA representative, giving CIA undue representation.[505] Some of them work in positions involving evaluation of CIA's work product and proposals.[506]

These individuals are "detailees"—CIA employees on loan to the Executive, usually at the latter's request. They include all types, from gardeners and typists, to intelligence analysts and practitioners of covert action.[507]

Detailees are requested for a variety of reasons—because the White House wants to circumvent Congressional budget ceilings, because there are no other available secretaries with security clearances, because CIA professional expertise is highly regarded, or because the position had always been staffed by an Agency officer.[508]

The Committee has found no indications that CIA detailees are instructed to make clandestine reports to headquarters on the inner workings of the host-employer. Nor is there credible evidence that they are asked by CIA to perform in any manner which is inconsistent with the best interests of the host. Nonetheless, the Committee believes that detailing as presently practiced reflects an unwise policy.

At best, intelligence personnel such as electrical help are diverted from CIA duties thus frustrating the budget allocating intent of Congress. A far worse spectre is that of CIA officers assigned to such posts as the National Security Council where they are susceptible, despite all good intentions, to substantial conflicts of interest on the most sensitive issues. The latter problem is compounded by the fact that the detailee's background often is unknown to NSC colleagues who are also charged with CIA-related responsibilities. [509]

The Committee discovered detailees, whose Agency ties were closely held secrets, making recommendations on CIA covert action proposals to unwitting senior NSC officials. Such individuals also help conduct the NSC's evaluation of the intelligence product, and in that capacity regularly compare CIA's performance with that of rival agencies.

These individuals have impressed staff as highly motivated professionals, acutely aware of the problems resulting from divided loyalties. Their integrity is not at issue. But neither the White House nor the CIA is well served by an unnecessary policy which invites cynicism and compromises the quality of Executive Branch oversight of the intelligence community.

e. CIA Relationship with U.S. and Foreign Police

In creating the CIA, Congress clearly intended to deny it any domestic police functions. Their fear that a super-secret, bureaucratically powerful spy agency might evolve into a domestic secret police, has not been realized, respite shortcomings in control and oversight.

Evidence in Committee files, however, indicates that during the late 1960's and early 1970's, CIA allowed itself to become involved in domestic police activity. In addition, the Agency undertook other police assistance activities which jeopardized the integrity of an otherwise legitimate and useful U.S. foreign aid program.

Association and Collaboration with U.S. Police

Notwithstanding its charter's clear prohibition against internal security functions, CIA has maintained relationships—many entirely appropriate—with various Federal, state and local law enforcement agencies. Questionable activities prior to the Holtzman Amendment to the Omnibus Crime Control and Safe Streets Acts of 1968, included the training by CIA of domestic police and loans of Agency equipment for domestic use. In return, local police departments cooperate with CIA on matters of concern to the Agency's Office of Security. Both activities appear to have been improper. The first violated the charter's ban on domestic police functions, and the latter tended to circumvent jurisdiction of the FBI and the Department of Justice.

Of those activities, CIA's role as a source of ordinary as well as exotic equipment is perhaps the most troubling and publicized. The Agency has loaned such traditional gear as body protectors, billy clubs, mace, and similar civil disturbance paraphernalia. Most of the equipment was provided during the height of the Vietnam War movement and may have been used by local police during the May 1971 demonstrations in Washington.

More exotic loans consisted of decoders, clandestine transmitters, analyzers, and other wiretrapping devices.

A staff examination of these practices reveals that CIA officials usually provided equipment on a no-questions-asked basis, did not require the production of court orders for eavesdropping gear, and exercised virtually no control over the loaned items.

The record suggests that on one occasion, CIA-loaned equipment was used in an illegal wiretap. In June, 1971, Mr. Kenyon F. Ballew was severely wounded during a raid on his apartment by agents of the Division of Alcohol, Tobacco and Firearms, supported by police from Montgomery and Prince Georges Counties in Maryland.

The raid was conducted pursuant to a Federal search warrant for possession of suspected firearms and hand grenades. Plainclothes agents and police officers broke down the door to the apartment when Mr. Ballew failed to answer their knock. Mr. Ballew, a gun collector, picked up a pistol, was shot, and is now permanently disabled. He is partially paralyzed, walks only with the aid of a brace and cane, speaks with difficulty, and still has the police bullet lodged in his brain.

Mr. Ballew was never prosecuted for any gun control violations. The case received a large amount of publicity and was the subject of a number of investigations of alleged police misconduct. Mr. Ballew brought suit pursuant to the Federal Torts Claim Act and received an adverse judgment from the courts in February, 1975.

A CIA Office of Security employee assigned to liaison with the Montgomery County Police Department told staff that, in a conversation with a police inspector on the Ballew case, the possible use of CIA-loaned bugging equipment was revealed. He was advised that police intercepted a telephone conversation in which plans were outlined to "kill a cop." However, neither the affidavit in support of the search warrant, the subsequent investigations, nor the transcript of the civil suit reflected the existence of any wiretap. Mr. Ballew's case is now on appeal, and if there had been an illegal wiretap, he may be entitled to a new trial. While the Department of Justice's CIA Task Force has been made aware of this possible wiretap for months, it has apparently refused, both to act upon it,[517] and to notify the attorneys in the case.

CIA Involvement with Foreign Police

From the early 1950's until late 1973, CIA operated

a proprietary, International Police Services (IPS), in the Washington, D.C. area. It had the dual purpose of improving allies' internal security, and evaluating foreign cadets for pro-U.S. orientation, which might later enable CIA to recruit them as intelligence assets.

In the early 1960's the Agency for International Development's Office of Public Safety (AID-OPS) became actively involved in foreign police training. OPS' 14 week course was augmented by an additional four weeks of training at IPS, pursuant to a contractual arrangement with AID. Students were not made aware that they were being trained at a CIA facility, and only a handful of AID officials, including the Director of OPS, knew of IPS' CIA status.

Instructors were asked to record names of students who demonstrated a pro-American attitude. It does not appear, however, that the CIA attempted to recruit students while in the United States, although CIA documents indicate that with the cooperation of OPS, lists of OPS and IPS students were made available, along with biographical information, to CIA components for operational use.

As many as 5,000 foreign police officers from over 100 countries, many of whom have become high officials, unwittingly received training from the CIA. The position of these foreign police officers may have been damaged when, in 1973, IPS was revealed as a CIA front.

In addition to damaging the credibility of these foreign police officers, CIA's apparently unnecessary involvement with a legitimate foreign aid program could have seriously undermined that program from a propaganda standpoint.[523] Despite these realities, AID-OPS continued its relationship with IPS until late 1973. Department of State and AID officials should review these practices and develop alternative methods of administering foreign aid programs without CIA involvement, and support.

Footnotes:

[487]Each monthly mission schedule forwarded to the Joint Chiefs of Staff and the Forty Committee for approval has an alpha-numeric designator attached for mission risk assessment. By far the most frequently assigned is "4 A 4"; the first digit, "4", stands for "low military risk"; the second alpha character, "A", stands for "high intelligence value" and the third digit, "4", stands for "low political risk." No mission has ever been assessed a military risk factor other than "low." This evaluation is belied not only by the nine collisions, 110 possible detections, constantly fluctuating factors which should impact on the calculations of military risk such as presence of enemy forces in the area, distance from enemy shores, political conditions, etc., but also by a variety of statements by Navy personnel who have conducted studies on this program. . . .

[493]Comm. Hearings. . . .

"MR. ASPIN. . . . Does the National Security Agency monitor telephone calls between American citizens and foreigners abroad?

"MR. COLBY. The Agency does monitor foreign communications.

*   *   *

"MR. ASPIN. Does it involve a U.S. citizen at one end?

"MR. COLBY. On some occasions, that cannot be separated from the traffic that is being monitored. It is technologically impossible to separate them.

"MR. GIAIMO. Obviously, we know that in other countries you undoubtedly perform all kinds of intercepts.

"MR. COLBY. Incidentally we pick up material about Americans abroad; yes.

"MR. GIAIMO. That is the point I am trying to get at. Did you say that incidentally you are also intercepting American citizens?

"MR. COLBY. I did not want to say that we never, never covered any American citizens abroad. If I have made a mistake in what I said, that we were not—that we incidentally cover Americans in our foreign intelligence activities.

"MR. GIAIMO. You incidentally cover Americans where?

"MR. COLBY. I say we do incidentally cover Americans. I would like to get into a further description of this in executive session."

Ibid. . . .

"Chairman PIKE. Does your system intercept the telephone calls of American citizens?

"Gen. ALLEN. I believe that I can give a satisfactory answer to that question which will relieve the Committee's concern on that matter in closed session."

Although the Committee met for some four hours in Executive Session to take testimony from NSA Director Allen and Deputy Director Benson K. Buffham, primarily concerning the interception of international commercial communications, Gen. Allen apparently felt it necessary to clarify and elucidate that testimony in a follow-up letter to Chairman Pike on August 25, 1975:

"Dear Mr. Chairman:

"I am writing to provide additional clarification to the testimony I gave before your Committee on 8 August.

"At the present time, the telephone calls of U.S. citizens in the United States to a foreign location are not being monitored. The monitoring of telephone conversations of United States citizens in the United States to a location in the United States has never been authorized by NSA. Currently, we are not now monitoring any telephone circuits terminating in the United States.

"For several years prior to mid-1973, a few international radio-telephone circuits were monitored between the United States and foreign countries. This monitoring did include the calls of U.S. citizens as well as foreign nationals, and calls were sometimes selected for monitoring based on the name (or phone number) of a U.S. citizen provided us by another government agency. In the summer of 1973, the use of the names of U.S. citizens to select telephone calls was terminated and remains so.

"From mid 1973 until recently a search of our records reveals there were occasions where radio-telephone circuits between a foreign terminal and a U.S. terminal were monitored. On some occasions the monitoring was for the purpose of developing patterns of foreign communications use and, on yet other occasions, the monitoring was based on the foreign subscriber and the substance of the conversation was obtained. Our records indicate that in all of 1974, reports were made involving the substance of only eight telephone conversations, wherein a U.S. citizen might be presumed to have been conversing, and in these instances, only the foreign intelligence aspects of the conversation were reported, and the names of U.S. citizens were never used in these NSA reports. This number may be compared with reports involving [a vast number of] other foreign communications carried on international circuits.

"The executive directives applying to these efforts state: a. The purpose of the signals intelligence activities of the National Security Agency is to obtain foreign intelligence from foreign communications or foreign electronic signals. b. Foreign communications exclude communications between or among American citizens or entities.

"I hope this letter will help clarify the matter."

/s/ Lew Allen, Jr., Lieutenant General, USAF, Director, NSA/Chief, CSS.

[495]William E. Colby, Director of Central Intelli-

gence, told members of the Committee staff at an October 25, 1975 meeting, that the Agency plants propaganda in the foreign press, including English-language newspapers, and can not be inhibited by the possibility that these planted stories may be picked up by American news services, etc.

[498]The Deputy Director of Operations at the CIA explained that the Agency wants as few people as possible to know the Agency's sources. Therefore, the CIA considers "stringers" and free-lancers to be free agents, working for many employers and so there is no necessity for the CIA to inform a "stringer's" or free-lancer's publisher of his other employer (CIA). Committee staff meeting on October 25, 1975. . . .

[499]An ex-CIA Chief of Station explained that ". . . our American media assets . . . are given neither Agency guidance nor information which might influence a piece written for an American audience. These people are used entirely for intelligence gathering purposes, and are left free to write what they would have written had there been no connection with the Agency . . . This method is quite different from our handling of foreign media assets, writing for foreign audiences, where Agency influence over the content of certain articles is selectively applied." He further states, "CIA will undertake no activity in which there is a risk of influencing domestic public opinion either directly or indirectly." But he turns around in the next sentence to say: "The Agency does have a responsibility for undertaking certain propaganda activities in foreign countries." Director Colby emphatically stated on October 25, 1975 to members of the Committee staff and Congressman Johnson that he "differentiates between AP and Reuters. I consider AP to be an American wire service and therefore off limits . . . but Reuters is a foreign wire service." It was pointed out to Director Colby that Reuters, a British wire service, was frequently used by American media, but

this fact did not change his mind. In an effort to assure that official Washington is not deceived by planted articles in the foreign press, CIA maintains high-level liaison with the Department of State and the U.S. Information Agency to identify spurious stories.

500The CIA's Cover and Commercial staff files show that in 1975 11 CIA employees used media cover with 15 news field companies — TV, radio, newspapers, and magazines. Five of these are of major general news impact, nine of no major general news influence, and one a proprietary.

501When the CIA had fiduciary relations with five full-time correspondents of major American news organizations, three of their employers were unwitting, according to William E. Colby. . . .

503At the National Security Council, there are four CIA employees working as professional staff. Three of them are overt employees of the CIA, open employees. The fourth is an undercover employee, one who does not acknowledge the CIA as his true employer. Ironically, through committee staff interviews, the undercover employee was the only CIA detailee readily identified by his colleagues or subordinates.

504[Name deleted] sits on the Interagency Classification Review Committee (ICRC), representing the National Security Council staff, although he is actually detailed to the NSC staff from the CIA. The CIA also has a representative on the ICRC. [Name deleted] told the Committee staff that he does not tell other ICRC members of his true affiliation. The man who preceded [Name deleted] at the NSC was [Name deleted]. He also sat on the ICRC representing the NSC. And he was also a CIA detailee. Further, he was a key NSC staffer, but the only people at the NSC who knew that he was from the CIA were Dr. Kissinger and Alexander Haig.

505This Interagency Classification Review Committee rules on questions of declassification from the Executive branch agencies. These questions come up as a result of Freedom of Information Act (FOI) requests. If an FOI request is initially denied, the requester may appeal to the head of the Agency; and if that appeal is denied, he may appeal to the ICRC. Many of these declassification cases involve the CIA.

[506]The man who directed Operations CHAOS at the CIA is now detailed to the NSC staff as Director for Intelligence Coordination of the NSC staff. His task is to evaluate the quality of intelligence sent to the NSC, including intelligence from his regular employer, the CIA. He maintains close contact with the CIA as part of his job.

[507]There are, or have been, CIA detailees working at the White House (including the Federal Executive Institute, Cabinet Committee on Price Stability, White House Joint Committee on Science, Office of Emergency Preparedness, Council on International Economic Policy and President's Foreign Intelligence Advisory Board), the Department of Justice and the Bureau of Narcotics and Dangerous Drugs, the State Department and the Agency for International Development, the Treasury Department, the Defense Department and the Defense Intelligence Agency, the Federal Aviation Administration, the Federal Energy Administration, the Vice President's Office, the National Security Council and the Commerce Department.

The CIA details cover: communications technicians, biographic analysts, general illustrators, secretaries, clerks, couriers, laborers, telephone operators, graphic analysts, personal assistants, physical scientist, intelligence officers, operations officers, economists, administrators assistants, program analysts, chauffeurs, sky marshals, and stenographers.

[508]The White House used CIA detailees to keep the

total number of staff down, in contravention of Congressional appropriation staff ceilings. The NSC staff "borrows" secretaries initially from the CIA, until their secretaries get clearances, but in many cases, the CIA secretaries stay at the NSC for years. Many executive branches, such as the Department of the Treasury, use CIA professionals as advisors to Secretaries, etc. And finally, the NSC staffer responsible for covert action proposals and approvals is almost always from the CIA's Directorate of Operations, which requests the covert actions. He has sole custody of all the Forty Committee's records.

[509]See previous note on a key staffer at the NSC who made recommendations on policy options. He, therefore, was called upon to make these recommendations on CIA policies to people who did not know of his current CIA affiliation.

[517]The Agency's position in this case is that the Agency was not involved beyond the loan of audio equipment, which may have been used against Mr Ballew . . . .

[523]For example, the AID-OPS program was damaged considerably by allegations linking foreign police training to the CIA. In 1970, Dan Mitrione, a law enforcement officer of impeccable credentials and reputation, employed by AID as a Public Safety Advisor in Uruguay, was kidnapped and murdered by Tupamaro guerrillas. The Tupamaros alleged that Mitrione was a CIA "agent" and that Public Safety Advisors including Mitrione taught torture tactics to police. CIA documents indicate that although Mitrione may have had some contact with CIA officers stationed in Uruguay, he was not a CIA employee or informant. . . . Allegations of AID-OPS sponsored torture training, depicted in various press reports and the film "State of Siege," appear factually unsupportable. However, this type of allegation had a tremendous propaganda impact which contributed substantially to the termination of AID-OPS in 1975.

3. Domestic Intelligence Investigations

Domestic intelligence carries with it two distinct types of risks. There are programs that by their very nature and method offend individual liberties and statutory rights. Then there are legitimate intelligence methods that are improperly applied, turning the law-enforcers into law-breakers.

a. Programs as Abuses

COINTELPRO was a series of covert counterintelligence programs aimed at identifying, penetrating, and neutralizing subversive elements in the United States. The program itself consisted of myriad clandestine dirty tricks carried out by FBI agents against persons and organizations considered subversive by the FBI.[525] Careers were ruined, friendships severed, reputations sullied, businesses bankrupted and, in some cases, lives endangered.[526]

The FBI justified this aberration from traditional law enforcement programs by stating that it was dictated by the mood of the times. The FBI, as implementors of the program, thereby became the barometer of the country's mood, instead of fulfilling their statutory function of enforcing Federal laws.[527] Evidence received by the Committee of FBI racism,[527a] bias, and strong conservative ideology hardly qualifies it to review people's politics. Moreover, the Constitution prohibits such a role and protects the very things FBI was attempting to punish.

COINTELPRO is only one example. Another would be programs grouped under "anticipatory" intelligence.

FBI states: "Because the FBI's investigative responsibilities follow the contours of those entrusted to the Attorney General, the Bureau's domestic intelligence investigations are, of necessity, broader than investigations strictly designed to collect evidence for criminal proceedings. The FBI's domestic intelligence responsibilities have a distinct anticipatory, or preventive, purpose, requiring continuing investigative activity in cases wherein criminal conduct remains a future possibility. Whereas the evidence required to initiate an investigation under such a standard would obviously be something less than probable cause of a crime,[529] it would nevertheless be more than mere suspicion. The FBI itself states that advocacy of an ideology alone is not sufficient grounds for classifying a group as subversive.

Anticipatory domestic intelligence projects, however, do create serious problems on occasion. A few examples illustrate the point.

Lori Paton testified before the Committee on November 18, 1975. In 1974, Miss Paton, then a high school student, inadvertently wrote the Socialist Workers Party as an academic assignment. She intended to write to the Socialist *Labor* Party.

The FBI was conducting a "mail cover"[532] on the SWP and intercepted Miss Paton's misdirected letter. They immediately began an investigation of her, and the attendant publicity in Miss Paton's small town caused her great mental anguish.

The Bureau's response was that the "FBI did not publicize the fact" of Lori Paton's investigation, although they had interviewed her school principal and the local police chief.

Assume, however, that Miss Paton had correctly written to the SWP, as many people undoubtedly have. That fact alone would apparently have been grounds for an anticipatory investigation, even though it is hard to imagine what crimes could be anticipated by writing a letter. In addition, the chilling effect such investigations have on First Amendment rights, including freedom of association, is painfully clear.[534]

238

For those who do join SWP, the chill is likely to spread to employers. The Committee heard from one witness who termed FBI's inquiries about his employee, Bruce Bloy, who was an SWP member, as "presumptive, mysterious, and . . . aggressive."

Trash covers are another odious form of anticipatory investigations. The IPS trash cover has already been discussed, save for a comment on command and control. When FBI personnel were originally asked about trash covers by Committee staff, they stated: "we have not engaged in [trash covers] since July 1966 . . . We had no trash covers on the IPS." Two weeks later, at a Committee hearing, they corrected themselves. They stated that, while there was an FBI policy of not conducting trash covers, that policy was not always followed.

Two memoranda show that the Bureau knew of the trash covers and recognized the risks in such a method. The concerns? The "potential harm to the FBI and the Federal Government, per se, far outweigh the potential information that could be expected."[539] It was not risks to an individual's right of privacy that concerned the FBI.

b. Law Enforcement Turned Law-Breaking

The use of informants, albeit an effective law enforcement tool, is a method of investigation which is particularly subject to abuses of Constitutional rights and rights of privacy.

The Committee heard testimony from a former FBI informant named Robert Hardy. Mr. Hardy chronicled for the Committee his role in a 1971 Camden Draft Board break-in. Pursuant to FBI instructions, he infiltrated a peaceful anti-war group in Camden, New Jersey.[540] He instigated the burglary and supplied the would-be burglars with tools, money, technical assistance and encouragement.[541]

In sum, Mr. Hardy acted as an "agent-provocateur." At one point, he attempted to halt the actual burglary, because a conspiracy had been established. His FBI handling-agents insisted that the burglary be committed.[542]

The disturbing lesson is that in the FBI system there is virtually no mechanism to control agents in charge of informants. The FBI Manual of Instructions on Informants sets forth specific guidelines for the handling of informants, yet the uniqueness and secrecy surrounding each informant's relationship with the handling-agent impairs the effectiveness of those instructions.

In the Hardy case, the informant-agent relationship was further complicated by political considerations. The defendants in a celebrated case in nearby Harrisburg, Pennsylvania, had recently been acquitted of all conspiracy counts. The FBI apparently felt that an overt act such as an actual break-in would be required to insure a conviction, even though the alleged crime of conspiracy, which was the basis of later prosecution, appears to have been completed far in advance of the actual break-in.

It should be noted that Department of Justice attorneys were advised of this situation long before the break-in and did nothing to avert the course of events.

The Commitee investigated another example of lack of control over informants. The FBI used Robert Merritt as an informant on New Left activities during the early 1970's. His duties included reporting on activities at the Institute of Policy Studies. Merritt told the Committee that his FBI handling-agents instructed him to conduct break-ins, deliver unopened mail acquired illegally, and solicit and provide information to the FBI regarding homosexual proclivities of politically prominent people and individuals of the New Left.

The FBI agents who handled Merritt denied these

allegations under oath. They stated that Merritt acted on his own.

The handling-agents stated that they terminated Merritt because they ascertained that he had provided false information on one occasion and had reason to believe he provided false information at other times in the past. If this was true, it does not fit with other facts. During the seven months that Merritt was an FBI informant, he provided over 100 reports on at least 25 people. He had, in fact, been categorized as "reliable" in FBI records.

No effort was ever made to "correct" the Merritt reports, by indicating that the information contained therein might be unreliable. No prosecutive actions were ever recommended as a result of Merritt's allegedly wrong actions. His efforts apparently fit well with intelligence operations.

Furthermore, Merritt told staff that he had committed numerous illegal acts at the direction of District of Columbus Metropolitan Police.

His FBI handling-agents stated that although they acquired Merritt from the Metropolitan Police Department, they never inquired as to the nature of his prior activities as a police informant. This attitude of "see no evil, hear no evil" appears to violate the seemingly rigid regulations of the FBI Manual, designed to effect the recruitment of responsible and reliable informants.

Conflicting testimony in the Merritt matter reveals the problem itself. Since FBI agents' instructions to their informants are, by necessity, given orally and without witnesses, it is difficult, if not impossible, to accurately fix responsibility for an informant's actions.

If the FBI agent is at fault, the problem becomes one of administrative command and control. If, however, the informant has gone bad, the problem is more difficult. For example, if an informant successfully instigates others to commit a crime, as in the Hardy matter, his FBI contact agent may overlook the informant's improper actions, because the informant is important to a case for which the FBI agent is likely to receive credit.

The risk that informants may use illegal methods is heightened when one considers the kind of person needed to infiltrate suspected criminal elements. Understating the problem, James Adams, Assistant to the Director of FBI, testified before the Committee on November 18, 1975: "[T]he informants you develop are not recruited from Sunday Schools." The dubious character of most informants is compounded by the fact that informants are paid cash, and their payment is commensurate with the information they furnish. The more incriminating the information, the more lucrative the reward.

Electronic Surveillance—The Kissinger Wiretaps

In the last half-century, electronic technology has revolutionized the science of investigations. These developments also mean that "Big Brother" may be watching.

Improper application of electronic surveillance poses obvious risks because of its enormous potential for invading privacy and the difficulty of detecting intrusion.

Some examples follow.

In the spring of 1969, the Nixon White House was disturbed that extremely sensitive information regarding diplomatic relations and national security was leaking to the press on a fairly regular basis.

On May 9, 1969, William Beecher of the New York Times wrote an article on Cambodia which triggered a strong reaction from the White House. That day, a series of telephone calls to ascertain the source of the leaks took place. The calls were between Dr. Kissinger and J. Edgar Hoover, and between Colonel Alexander Haig and FBI personnel.

The apparent result of these consultations was the installation of a wiretap on the residence of a National Security Council staff on May 9, 1969. Significantly, approval for this "national security" wiretap was not requested until May 10, 1969. The wiretap was requested by Col. Haig "on the highest authority," and was not approved by Attorney General John Mitchell until May 12, 1969.

Seventeen persons were eventually wiretapped pursuant to this program.

Although the FBI never overheard information indicating any breach of national security, the taps continued for lengthy periods of time.

No approval was ever sought for extensions of the wiretaps as they continued unabated and unsupervised. In addition, the FBI continued to report information which can only be characterized as political or personal.

William C. Sullivan, former Chief of Intelligence for the FBI, told staff that FBI Director J. Edgar Hoover did not regard these taps as FBI operations, but as executive requests. According to Mr. Sullivan, Hoover insisted on sending copies of the transcripts directly to the White House, so the President would be apprised of the "service" FBI was providing.

Several risks were inherent in the FBI's national security wiretaps installed for Dr. Kissinger.

The first involved wiretapping United States citizens without prior judicial approval. These dangers were recognized by the Supreme Court in 1972. The Court held that electronic surveillance of domestic organizations or citizens was forbidden unless prior judicial approval was obtained.

Secondly, wiretapping State Department officials and members of the press, tends to stifle voices of criticism and dissenting views, and infringes upon freedom of the press.

Finally, the Kissinger wiretaps posed a risk that

the FBI could become the tool by which an Administration in power obtains political information.

The Houston Episode

On October 9, 1975, Anthony Zavala, a former narcotics officer with the Houston Police Department who had been sentenced to three years' imprisonment on wiretap convictions, told the Committee of widespread illegal police wiretapping in Houston, Texas, from 1969 through 1972.

Mr. Zavala recounted that wiretapping had become "second nature to us all," and "that it was all discussed freely, and that everyone knew what was going on."

In 1973, Anthony J. P. Farris, United States Attorney for the Southern District of Texas, learned of allegations of wiretapping. He brought this information to the attention of the FBI in the fall of 1973, and requested that the Bureau investigate.

They did not. His requests continued. Finally, in April 1974, the FBI assigned one special agent to investigate the case. He filed reports, which according to Farris were ". . . notable only in their lack of substance, consisting largely of Xeroxed newspaper articles."[572]

Footnotes:

[525]The primary programs were the Communist Party, U.S.A. program (commenced in 1956), the Socialist Workers Party program (commenced in 1961), the White Extremist program (commenced in 1964), the Black Extremist program (commenced in 1967), and the New Left Domestic program (commenced in 1968). Lesser programs were the Puerto Rican Bomber program (1966), Operation Hoodwink

(1966) (a program pitting the Mafia against the Communist Party), Operation Border Coverage (1961), the Cuban program (1961) and the Yugoslav program (1969). All COINTELPRO programs terminated after their existence was discovered following the burglary of the FBI office in Media, Pa. on April 27, 1971. Staff COINTELPRO briefing between W. Raymond Wannall, Assistant Director of the FBI in charge of the Intelligence Division and J.B.F. Oliphant and R. Vermeire, at FBI headquarters, Aug. 22, 1975, copy on file with Sel. Comm. on Intell.

526The following are but a few examples of specific COINTELPRO programs, of which there were a total of 3,247 proposed and 2,370 carried out:

In 1969, the FBI authorized an agent to send anonymous letters to the superior of Father Augustus Taylor, Jr., a Catholic priest, complaining of Father Taylor's speaking out on his television show against the war in Vietnam and of his public support of certain black organizations. Father Taylor's television show was subsequently cancelled and he was transferred. FBI COINTELPRO memoranda. . . .

In 1968, the FBI authorized interfering with a Mellon Foundation's decision of whether to give Unity Corporation, a black organization in Pittsburgh, Pennsylvania, a $150,000 grant. The FBI contacted a confidential source within the Mellon Foundation, the grant was denied, and the Unity Corporation subsequently went bankrupt. FBI COINTELPRO Memoranda. . . .

In 1969, the FBI approved furnishing information to a responsible Harvard University official that a student who was employed by the University was involved in Students for a Democratic Society (SDS) activities. Shortly thereafter, the student lost his job. FBI COINTELPRO Memoranda. . . .

More seriously, one program was carried out wherein an anonymous letter was set to the Black

245

Panther Party accusing one of their members of being a police informant. FBI COINTELPRO Memoranda 100-448006-2308. Another program authorized sending a threatening letter to Huey Newton purporting to be from a follower of Eldridge Cleaver. FBI COINTELPRO Memoranda. . . .

[527]"MR. VERMEIRE. Why was there such a significant break in investigative techniques in 1973?

"MR. WANNALL. Principally because an analysis was made by a predecessor and a determination, I think, that we should be aware, I think as we always have been, of the climate of the times and restructure on a strict statutory basis.

"I think the history of the Bureau, and I would not bore you with details, has been one of responsiveness, an awareness of the climate of the times, and restructuring." Staff Interview with W. Raymond Wannall, FBI Assistant Director in charge of Intelligence Division; Robert L. Shackelford, Section Chief, FBI Intelligence Division, and David Ryan, Supervisor, FBI Intelligence Division, by J.B.F. Oliphant, R. Vermeire, J. Atkisson and E. Miller, Nov. 5, 1975, copy on file with Sel. Comm. on Intell. •

[527a]A case in point was the FBI's alleged targeting of Congressman Andrew Young, of Georgia, wherein the FBI requested Arthur Murtagh, a Special Agent, to surreptitiously obtain Congressman Young's personal stationery and handwriting sample. At the time, Congressman Young was a candidate for Congress. Comm. Hearings, testimony of Arthur Murtagh, Nov. 18, 1975.

The FBI denies the aforementioned allegation. Furthermore, Black agents presently comprise approximately 1.2 percent of FBI agent personnel. Comm. Hearings, testimony of W. Raymond Wannall, Nov. 18, 1975.

[529]The Committee staff attempted to find out what triggered domestic intelligence investigations. The best answer appeared to be:

"MR. VERMEIRE. Investigation with respect to a particular crime?

"MR. SHACKELFORD. Potential crime.

"MR. VERMEIRE. Potential; is there probable cause?

"MR. SHACKELFORD. Of course not."

Probable cause, of course, has been the traditional test for arrest. . . .

[532]A mail cover is observing only what appears on the *outside* of an envelope or parcel, a practice which is carried out, of course, with the cooperation of postal authorities. The technique is perfectly legal.

[534]The risk may even be intended. As Dean Louis Pollak put it: "When the official investigation long outlives its initially professed justification—that is to say, reasoned suspicion or criminal activity imminent or actually carried out—at that point it is inescapable . . . that an important consequence, if not necessarily a purpose, of the continuing investigation will be the imposition of an official stigma on the political or research activity being carried out by the 'subject.' "

[539]"[The Washington Field Office] feels it would be most unwise at this point in time to seriously consider instituting a similar operation as encompassed by the utilization of this source [the trash cover]. Potential harm to the FBI and the Federal Government, per se, far outweigh the potential information that could be expected from such a reinstated operation." FBI Washington Field Office Memorandum to Headquarters, August 4, 1973.

[540]None of the group's members was known by the FBI to be violence-prone.

[541]All of which were paid for with FBI funds.

[542]The FBI's denial of this allegation appears in their Memorandum of Nov. 28, 1975. . . .

[572]The complete ineptitude of the FBI investigation of the Houston matter was brought out by Congressman Johnson's questioning of Mr. Farris:

"MR. JOHNSON. Can you tell me why in this case, when you requested information with respect to investigation of other law enforcement agencies—in this case the Houston Police Department—you didn't get any response from anybody who was of real significance?

"MR. FARRIS. . . . In all other cases they always responded; they always performed admirably; but in this case—the investigation of the allegations of illegal electronic surveillance by the police department in Houston—there was not only reluctance but obvious foot dragging.

"MR. JOHNSON. . . . What was the result of your contacts with Saxbe and Kelley and the others?

"MR. FARRIS. To quote myself in other hearings, zip; nothing. Saxbe didn't answer; the Deputy Attorney General of the United States didn't answer; the Assistant Attorney General Crime Section didn't answer. No one answered. I don't think they were listening.

*   *   *

"MR. JOHNSON. But you can characterize cooperation they received prior to that time as "zip."

"MR. FARRIS. It is not worthy of the name investigation; yes, sir.

"MR. JOHNSON. Once again, this is inconsistent with their response to other requests that you might make for other investigations?

"MR. FARRIS. That is correct."

4. SALT—Political Control of Intelligence

Nowhere is the risk of corrupting intelligence greater than in recent efforts to restrict and shape important data on Soviet compliance with strategic arms agreements.

Staff investigation and examination of key documents reveal that these SALT treaties, which are of grave strategic significance, were consummated without full intelligence input, that the prime U.S. official who sponsored the accords also effectively controls the verification of their feasibility, and that day-to-day intelligence analysis of compliance is hindered by arbitrary and inconsistent attempts to prevent leaks of SALT data.

The prime factor in this situation is Dr. Kissinger, with his passion for secrecy and his efforts to concentrate power and to consolidate ultimate control of important intelligence functions, through his various bureaucratic roles.

It is clear that, in the final stages of the SALT talks, U.S. negotiators did not fully consult or inform intelligence experts, who had been key figures in previous treaty sessions. Only Russian technical experts were on hand. Dr. Kissinger's private talks with Soviet leaders in this period were not disseminated. Some officials assert that "ambiguities" which plague the accords may have been the result of U.S. policy-makers' self-imposed intelligence blackout at the critical moment.[575]

The record indicates that Dr. Kissinger, U.S. architect of the accords, has attempted to control the dissemination and analysis of data on apparent Soviet violations of the SALT pact.

Although CIA, as the government's principal ana-

249

lytical arm, has both general and specific responsibility for the monitoring of SALT compliance, the Assistant to the President for National Security Affairs has advised the Agency to avoid any written judgments that the Soviets are in violation of SALT agreements. Such findings were to be privately communicated to the National Security Council, which, coincidentally, was headed by Dr. Kissinger.

When sensitive intelligence reports on Soviet compliance began to turn up with regularity, the National Security Council initiated the procedure of severely restricting dissemination of the information, by causing it to be placed in a "hold" status. Typically, the CIA Deputy Director for Intelligence would, in consultation with NSC staff, place an item on "hold" until Dr. Kissinger or his representative agreed to release it.

Two principal reasons have been given for access restrictions: fear of leaks by officials seeking to influence U.S. SALT policy;[578] and the need for adequate time to determine a report's real significance, thus avoiding rash judgments on complicated technical issues.

This unusual procedure, invoked previously in such momentous situations as the 1962 Cuban missile crisis, has been strangely implemented this time. At times, the Secretary of State, the Director of the Arms Control and Disarmament Agency, and key U.S. officials in SALT compliance meetings with the Soviets have not been aware of the existence of sensitive data suggesting Soviet cheating. Dissemination within several intelligence components has been haphazard and uncontrolled.[589]

Two other problems with the "hold" process detract from the integrity of the intelligence product. NSC staff, for example, has influenced the timing and content of intelligence community publications.[590]

Worse, both high officials and working level analysts have been cut off from information for periods of time ranging from days to six months.[591]

Dr. Kissinger's comments on this situation are at variance with the facts.[592]

The spectre of important information, suggesting Soviet violation of strategic arms limitations, purposefully withheld for extended periods of time from analysts, decision-makers and Members of Congress, has caused great controversy within the Intelligence Community.[593] In addition, it has raised questions as to the President's own knowledge of, and concurrence with, the "hold" procedure.[594]

The problem continues, as official fears of leaks and policymakers' penchant for a unified view on SALT goes on. Former State Department Bureau of Intelligence and Research Director Ray S. Cline, in testimony before the Committee, framed the issue: "I do think the Congress should be sure that the procedures for handling of strategic intelligence . . . should have certain checks and balances in them so that there is no possibility of suppression of information that is unattractive to policy makers." Cline concluded, "As I was leaving government, I found these procedures breaking down, and that is why I feel that the problem does deserve attention from the Congress."

Footnotes:

[575] Interview with U.S. intelligence officials. J. Boos Dec. 4, 1975, copy on file with Sel. Comm. on Intell. Admiral Elmo Zumwalt agreed in testimony to the Committee. . . .

[578] Testimony by William Hyland, Dec. 17, 1975: "I think the whole SALT process has been plagued by

leaks. Not only have negotating positions and fall-back positions appeared in the press before they could ever be put to the Russians, but the whole issue of compliance has been clouded by a considerable amount of misinformation which has appeared in journals such as *Aviation Week* and the newspapers on what the Soviets have or have not done."

[589]The Assistant Chiefs of Staff for Intelligence told staff they had not received SALT hold items. Interview by E. Sheketoff with Director of Naval Intelligence, and the Assistant Chief of Staff for In-, telligence of the Air Force, Dec. 15 & 16, 1975. On the other hand, one "hold" item was given to at least 75 people in CIA alone. Testimony by William Hyland and Edward Proctor, Dec. 17, 1975. DIA informed the Committee that it kept no records on "hold" dissemination and, consequently could not determine just who was authorized to see these sensitive items. Letter to the Committee, Dec. 16, 1975, from office of Thomas Latimer, Department of Defense; testimony by Edward Proctor, Dec. 17, 1975.

Key U.S. officials, like Sidney Graybeal and U. Alexis Johnson of the SALT compliance team, were kept away from some data. Deputy CIA Director Proctor noted: "After talking with General Walters around noon yesterday I called Ray Cline to tell him about the status outlined above. Cline was of course disappointed. He said that he had talked to Rush about the situation. Although Rush recalled being briefed by Duckett on [deleted] shortly after they were discovered, his recollection was very vague. Rush had not realized that Secretary Rogers had not been briefed. Ray reported that Rush was very concerned that Alex Johnson and Sid Graybeal had not been told. Rush is to talk to Rogers and urge that Rogers talk to Kissinger to get permission to tell Johnson and Graybeal." Edward Proctor, Note for the Record, July 13, 1973.

[590]. . . Col. Merritt of the NSC staff told the CIA official that "Dr. Kissinger wanted to avoid any written judgments to the effect that the Soviets have violated any of the SALT agreements. If the Director believes the Soviets may be in violation, this should be the subject of a memorandum from him to Dr. Kissinger. The judgment that a violation is considered to have occurred is one that will be made at the NSC level."

[591]. . . In one case, the head of the U.S. SALT team in Geneva, U. Alexis Johnston, was not told of a secret understanding made a year earlier on an agreed interpretation of the treaty. Johnson first learned of this from his Soviet counterparts. His cable to Washington is as follows:

"To: The White House for General Scowcroft Only

"From: U. Alexis Johnson SALT Geneva

"I. You will note that statement by Ustinov at yesterday's SCC meeting contained reftel [sic—*editor's note*] refers to 'the agreed interpretive statements of May 26 and July 29, 1972, . . .' We have no record here, and no one in the delegation has any recollection of latter statement. Presume it was a result of Henry's exchanges with Dobrynin following Moscow summit. Would appreciate text or summary of contents, so that we will be in position to handle when Soviets again raise matter in present negotiations on destruction, dismantling and replacement procedures. Presumably Phil Odeen or Bill Hyland are familiar with subject. Warm regards, Johnson." June 7, 1973.

Admiral Zumwalt testified to the same effect. Comm. Hearings . . . Dec. 2, 1975.

[592]Dr. Kissinger: "Whatever compliance issues existed at the time were brought to the attention of the Verification Panel." Kissinger press conference, Wash., D.C., Dec. 9, 1975.

From documentary evidence: The Verification Panel consists of the Assistant to the President for National Security Affairs, Deputy Secretary of State,

Chairman of Joint Chiefs of Staff, Director of ACDA, and the Director of Central Intelligence. Intelligence on SALT compliance with is put on hold routinely goes to only the Secretary of Defense, Director of DIA, and Kissinger.

Dr. Kissinger: "All the decisions of the Verification Panel with respect to compliance have been unanimous."

From documentary evidence: One member wrote a memo on Jan. 14, 1975: "Upon further consideration following the recent Verification Panel meeting on SALT which addressed compliance issues, I am concerned about the decision not to raise the issue of Air Defense Testing . . . This testing could have major strategic implications and its impact, in my opinion, was not sufficiently assessed at this recent session of the Verification Panel."

The Panel also does not vote or make formal decisions.

Dr. Kissinger: "There is nobody who has claimed that the issue of compliance was not being adequately pursued. There is nobody who has objected to the handling of the information."

Documentary evidence: Proctor memo of 13 July, 1973 . . . Colby letter to Richard Kennedy, Nov. 14, 1974 . . .

Dr. Kissinger: "All intelligence concerning alleged noncompliance was immediately distributed to all the members of the Verification Panel . . ."

* * *

Dr. Kissinger: "The longest time an item was on 'hold' was two months."

From documentary evidence: Some items were on "hold": 19 June 1973-8 Aug. 1973; 28 June 1974-17 Dec. 1974; 26 July 1974-17 Dec. 1974; 11 Sept. 1974-17 Dec. 1974; 23 Sept. 1974-17 Dec. 1974.

Dr. Kissinger: "No Soviet interference actions have interfered with our national means of detection."

From documentary evidence: Some important concealment activities, as well as Soviets interfering with national means of verification.

[593]On January 13, 1973 Dr. Edward Proctor, Deputy Director of the CIA for Intelligence and a member of the SALT Steering Group, informed Acting Director of Central Intelligence Walters that "It is now 24 days since we reported to Dr. Kissinger on the detection of several" alleged Soviet SALT violations. Proctor noted that the "hold" items had been restricted for so long as to raise suspicions "that important information is being withheld" from the many people in the intelligence community who had related responsibilities. Proctor advised that "there is little likelihood that it [the hold item] will be lifted soon," and that Mr. Odeen of Dr. Kissinger's staff 'would like to see a draft of the Monitoring Report with the item in it to recommend to Kissinger whether the Report should be published and whether it should have the item in it." Note for the Record, July 13, 1973, Edward W. Proctor.

[594]Proctor wrote on July 13 that "Earlier this morning, I had discussed with General Walters and Mr. Colby the DCI's obligation—a la Watergate—to make sure that the President knew of the withholding of intelligence, was aware of the consequences of prolonged delay in informing others in the Executive and Legislative Branches, and nonetheless had approved the continuation of the restrictions." *Ibid*. The President was never personally approached. ☐

Section Three:

Committee Recommendations

A. A HOUSE COMMITTEE ON INTELLIGENCE

1. The select committee recommends that there be formed a standing Committee on Intelligence of the House of Representatives.

a. The committee membership should reflect a broad representation of political and philosophical views.

b. The committee should consist of not more than 13 or less than nine members, designated by the Speaker in consultation with the minority leader, representing approximately the same political ratio as the House of Representatives.

c. No member of the committee may serve more than 3 consecutive terms on the committee, and no member of the staff may serve more than 6 years.

d. Any past or current member of the committee staff who shall release, without authorization of the committee, materials or information obtained by the committee shall be immediately terminated from employment and shall be fully subject to criminal and civil action, notwithstanding legislative immunity.

e. The committee shall be vested with subpoena power and shall have the right to enforce by a proceeding for civil contempt its subpoenas in the U.S. District Court for the District of Columbia or any other court of competent jurisdiction, without authorization from the House, provided the committee has so designated by resolution. The committee staff shall be given statutory standing to represent the committee in any proceeding arising from the issuance of a subpoena.

f. The committee's jurisdiction shall include all legislative and oversight functions relating to all U.S. agencies and departments engaged in foreign or domestic intelligence. The committee shall have exclusive jurisdiction for budget authorization for all intelligence activities and exclusive jurisdiction for all covert action operations. All remaining oversight functions may be concurrent with other committees of the House.

1. The select committee recommends that rule XI.2 (e)(2) of the House Rules is amended to read as follows:

"Each committee shall keep a complete record of all committee action which shall include a copy of all reports, statements, and testimony of witnesses whether received in open or in executive session."

2. The committee shall have the right to release any information or documents in its possession or control by a vote of a majority of the members of the committee under such terms and conditions as the committee shall deem advisable. The committee, in making the decision whether or not to release such information, shall have the right, but not the duty, to consult with other agencies of the Government within the intelligence community or executive branch with regard to any decision relating to the release of such heretofore secret information.

3. In the event of a negative vote by the committee on the release of certain classified information, a member of the committee may apprise the other Members of the House that the committee possesses information which he believes ought to be made public. Other Members of the House would then be authorized to have access to that information, provided they sign an agreement not to divulge the information. If these other Members agree that this information ought to be made public, they will sign a petition attesting to that. Upon obtaining the signatures of one-fifth of the House, the House shall convene in secret session for the purpose of advising the entire membership of the House of that information. The House may then vote to release the information to the public.

4. The select committee recommends that the rules of the House be revised to provide that any Member who reveals any classified information which jeopardizes the national security of the United States may be censured or expelled by a two-thirds vote of the House.

C. COVERT ACTION

1. The select committee recommends that all activities involving direct or indirect attempts to assassinate any individual and all paramilitary activities shall be prohibited except in time of war.

2. The select committee recommends that as to other covert action by any U.S. intelligence component, the following shall be required within 48 hours of initial approval.

a. The Director of Central Intelligence shall notify the committee in writing, stating in detail the nature, extent, purpose, risks, likelihood of success, and costs of the operation.

b. The President shall certify in writing to the committee that such covert action operation is required to protect the national security of the United States.

c. The committee shall be provided with duplicate originals of the written recommendations of each member of the 40 committee or its successor.

3. All covert action operations shall be terminated no later than 12 months from the date of affirmative recommendation by the 40 committee or its successor.

D. NSA AS AN INDEPENDENT AGENCY

1. The select committee recommends that the existence of the Na-

tional Security Agency should be recognized by specific legislation and that such legislation provide for civilian control of NSA. Further, it is recommended that such legislation specifically define the role of NSA with reference to the monitoring of communications of Americans.

E. DISCLOSURE OF BUDGET TOTALS

1. The select committee recommends that all intelligence related items be included as intelligence expenditures in the President's budget, and that there be disclosure of the total single sum budgeted for each agency involved in intelligence, or if such an item is a part or portion of the budget of another agency or department that it be separately identified as a single item.

F. PROHIBITION OF FUND TRANSFERS

1. The select committee recommends there be appropriate legislation to prohibit any significant transfer of funds between agencies or departments in connection with intelligence activities.

2. The select committee recommends there be appropriate legislation to prohibit any significant reprograming of funds within agencies or departments in connection with intelligence activities without the specific approval of the Intelligence Committee and appropriate committees of Congress.

3. The select committee recommends there be appropriate legislation to prohibit any significant expenditures of reserve or contingency funds in connection with intelligence activities without specific approval of the Intelligence Committee and appropriate committees of Congress.

G. DIRECTOR OF CENTRAL INTELLIGENCE

1. The select committee recommends that a Director of Central Intelligence shall be created, separate, from any of the operating or analytic intelligence agencies for the purpose of coordinating and overseeing the entire foreign intelligence community with a view to eliminating duplication in collection and promoting competition in analysis. The DCI shall be nominated by the President with the advice and consent of the Senate. This office shall have the following powers and duties:

(a) The DCI shall be the chief foreign intelligence officer of the United States, and shall be responsible for the supervision and control of all agencies of the United States engaged in foreign intelligence.

(b) The DCI shall be a Member of the National Security Council.

(c) the DCI may not hold a position or title with respect to any other agencies of Government.

(d) The DCI shall, along with such other duties, constitute an Office of Inspector General for all of the foreign intelligence agencies, including other agencies of government or branches of the military which have foreign intelligence functions. Such agencies shall have the obligation to report all instances of misconduct or allegations of misconduct to the DCI. This shall not constitute a limitation upon the respective agencies reporting to the DCI from maintaining their own Inspector General staff or similar body.

259

(e) The DCI shall have an adequate staff for the purposes expressed herein and be responsible for the national intelligence estimates and daily briefings of the President.

(f) The DCI shall be responsible for the preparation of the national intelligence estimates and such reports shall be immediately supplied to the appropriate committees of Congress on request.

(g) All budget requests shall be prepared by the agencies under the jurisdiction of the DCI. As those parts of budget of the military services or components of Department of Defense, they shall be submitted as an independent part of such budgets to the DCI.

(h) The DCI shall be charged with the functions of coordinating foreign intelligence agencies under its jurisdiction, the elimination of duplication, the periodic evaluation of the performance and efficiency of the agencies in question, and shall report to Congress on the foregoing at least annually.

(i) The DCI shall conduct a comprehensive inquiry into the causes of intelligence failures, including: inadequate collection tasking; analytical bias; duplication; unusable technical output; excessive compartmentation; and withholding of information by senior officials, and report to the Committee on Intelligence within 1 year.

H. FULL GAO AUDIT AUTHORITY

1. The select committee recommends that the General Accounting Office be empowered to conduct a full and complete management as well as financial audit of all intelligence agencies. There shall be no limitation on the GAO in the performance of these functions by any executive classification system, and the audit function of GAO shall specifically apply to those funds which presently may be expended on certification of a Director of an Agency alone.

I. INTERNAL FINANCIAL MANAGEMENT

1. The select committee recommends that the CIA internal audit staff be increased and given complete access to CIA financial records, and that overseas stations be audited at least annually. It is further recommended that all proprietary and procurement mechanisms be subjected to annual comprehensive review, by the CIA's internal audit staff.

J. FULL DISCLOSURE TO CONGRESS

1. The select committee recommends that existing legislation (National Security Act of 1947, Sec. 102 (d)(3)) restricting the Directors and heads of foreign intelligence agencies from providing full information to Congress should be amended to exclude committees of Congress having appropriate jurisdiction.

K. NEW FOREIGN OPERATIONS SUBCOMMITTEE OF NSC

1. The select committee recommends that the National Security Act of 1947 be amended to provide for the establishment of a permanent Foreign Operations Subcommittee of the National Security Council. The subcommittee's jurisdiction, function and composition shall be as follows:

(*a*) The subcommittee shall have jurisdiction over all authorized activities of U.S. foreign intelligence agencies except those solely related to the gathering of intelligence.

(*b*) The subcommittee shall advise the President on all proposed covert or clandestine activities and on hazardous collecting activities.

(*c*) Each member of the subcommittee shall be required by law to submit his individual assessments of each proposal to the President in writing. The assessment should cover such matters as the likelihood of success, the benefits of success, the damage resulting from failure or exposure, the risks against the potential benefits and alternate ways of accomplishing the goal.

(*d*) The subcommittee shall be chaired by the Assistant to the President for National Security Affairs and shall be composed of:

> Assistant to the President for National Security Affairs;
> Director of Central Intelligence;
> Secretary of State;
> Secretary of Defense;
> Deputy Director for Intelligence of CIA;
> Chairman of the Joint Chiefs of Staff;
> The ambassador(s), if there is one, and assistant secretaries of state for the affected countries and areas.

L. DEFENSE INTELLIGENCE AGENCY

1. The select committee recommends that the Defense Intelligence Agency be abolished and that its functions be transferred to the Assistant Secretary of Defense for Intelligence and the CIA.

M. DETAILEES

1. The select committee recommends that intelligence agencies disclose the affiliation of employees on detail to other Government agencies or departments to all immediate colleagues and superiors.

N. ASSISTANT FOR NATIONAL SECURITY AFFAIRS

1. The select committee recommends that the Assistant to the President for National Security Affairs be prohibited from holding any cabinet-level position.

O. RESTRICTIONS ON POLICE TRAINING AND RELATIONSHIPS

1. The select committee recommends that no agency of the United States engaged principally in foreign or military intelligence, directly or indirectly engage in the training or the supplying of domestic police agencies of the United States, and that contacts between police agencies of the United States and U.S. foreign or military intelligence agencies be limited to those circumstances which shall be required on account of internal security or the normal requirements and functions of such police agencies.

P. MEDIA, RELIGION, AND EDUCATION

1. The select committee recommends that U.S. intelligence agencies not covertly provide money or other valuable consideration to persons

associated with religious or educational institutions, or to employees or representatives of any journal or electronic media with general circulation in the United States or use such institutions or individuals for purposes of cover. The foregoing prohibitions are intended to apply to American citizens and institutions.

2. The select committee further recommends that U.S. intelligence agencies not covertly publish books, or plant or suppress stories in any journals or electronic media with general circulation in the United States.

Q. RESTRICTIONS ON MILITARY INTELLIGENCE

1. The select committee recommends that the intelligence components of the armed services of the United States be prohibited from engaging in covert action within the United States. It is further recommended that clandestine activities against nonmilitary U.S. citizens abroad be proscribed.

R. CLASSIFICATION

1. The select committee recommends that the classification of information be the subject of the enactment of specific legislation; and further, as an adjunct to such legislation there be provided a method of regular declassification.

S. INSPECTOR GENERAL FOR INTELLIGENCE

1. The select committee recommends the establishment of an independent Office of the Inspector General for Intelligence, who shall have full authority to investigate any possible or potential misconduct on the part of the various intelligence agencies or the personnel therein. The IGI shall be appointed by the President, with the approval of the Senate, for a term of 10 years and shall not be permitted to succeed himself. The IGI shall have full access on demand to all records and personnel of the intelligence agencies for the purpose of pursuing his investigations. He shall make an annual report to the Congress of his activities and make such additional reports to the intelligence committees or other appropriate oversight committees as he may choose or the committees may direct.

T. DOMESTIC

1. The select committee recommends that judicial warrant must issue, on probable cause, before an informant or any other agent of the FBI may infiltrate any domestic group or association, when investigation of such group or association or its members is based solely on title 18 U.S.C. §§ 2383, 2384, 2385.

2. The select committee recommends that the Director of the FBI have a term of office no longer than 2 presidential terms.

3. The select committee recommends that the Internal Security Branch of the Intelligence Division be abolished and that the counterintelligence branch be reorganized to constitute a full division named the Counter-Intelligence Division; that the mission of this Division be limited to investigating and countering the efforts of foreign directed groups and individuals against the United States.

4. The select committee recommends the transfer of all investigations of alleged criminal activity by domestic groups or individual members thereof to the General Investigative Division.

5. The select committee recommends that regulations be promulgated that tie the investigation of activities of terrorist groups closely to specific violations of criminal law within the investigative jurisdiction of the FBI and that charge the Department of Justice with determining when a domestic political action group may be appropriately targeted for investigation of terrorist activities.

ADDITIONAL RECOMMENDATIONS OF HON. LES ASPIN

All the hearings, all the hassles and all the headlines should have underscored the fact that the Select Committee really faced three challenges:

how to banish abuses from the intelligence system;

how to control covert operations; and

how to improve the intelligence product, the analyses for which we spend so much money.

The committee has approved a number of recommendations which go to the heart of these problems.

The establishment of an Independent Inspector General for Intelligence will provide an office designed exclusively to hawkeye the intelligence community and see that it is adhering to the law.

The institutionalization of a successor to the 40 Committee will provide systematic direction of covert operations by the executive branch for the first time.

And creation of a more powerful director of central intelligence will for the first time give one man the authority to whip the many intelligence fiefdoms into line and eliminate the duplication and waste that the committee found to be rife.

I think that there is more that we could have done and I have two additional proposals.

The select committee suggested that a standing committee be informed of an approved covert operation within 48 hours after its approval. I have proposed that a standing committee be informed of covert operations before they are approved by the President. The standing committee or committees should not have veto power, but the committees, or their members individually, should have the opportunity to make their views known to the President.

No doubt a number of members would simply write out a list of reservations to cover themselves in case an operation went wrong. But is that bad? It is a good idea to have advice reaching the President from a few people who have a bias for negativism. There is too much me-tooism in the executive branch already.

Furthermore, if the members of the new 40 Committee knew that Congress was part of the consultative process, they would be likely to move with greater care and discretion than has been true in the past. Prior notification of Congress is one more governor on the intelligence vehicle which could inhibit the kind of reckless driving the committee uncovered in its investigations.

The committee, in a number of its recommendations, has sought to provide a framework for improvement. But we have left the CIA high and dry organizationally. I believe that the CIA should be divided into two separate agencies—one devoted only to analysis and the other responsible for clandestine collection and covert operations.

Splitting the CIA is the key to attracting the kinds of young men and women we need in intelligence analysis. The hostility the CIA has aroused is bound to discourage many good people from applying. Furthermore, the analysts need interchanges with academia, and these ties have been strained by the public perceptions that anyone connected with the CIA has blood on his hands.

We have also seen, as in the Bay of Pigs, that proximity breeds bias. One side of the CIA planned the Bay of Pigs. The other side of the CIA was not in a position to analyze it independently and critically.

Critics say it is impossible to separate covert collection from covert operations, that many of the same people are used for the two purposes. This is quite true. However, my proposal leaves covert collection and covert operations in the same organization and simply splits them off from the analytical function.

No improvements will result if proposals for reform are consigned to the archives like the report of this committee. Our intelligence services have been ignored by Congress in the past—and we have seen the consequences of that inattention. Congress now has a second chance to decide if it wishes to play Pontius Pilate and wash its hands of an unpleasant business or confront the issue headon. I hope the Congress will not abdicate its responsibilities any more.

LES ASPIN.

———

ADDITIONAL RECOMMENDATIONS OF HON. RONALD V. DELLUMS

I supported the committee majority in bringing to the House of Representatives those recommendations finally adopted by the committee. However, this should not indicate my approval of all the adopted recommendations; several are not strong enough and several additional recommendations should have been adopted.

These recommendations should stimulate extremely important and timely discussion, debate and consensus about such vital and basic questions as:

(1) Is secrecy compatible with principles of democracy ostensibly embodied in our constitutional form of government?

(2) If and where is secrecy necessary?

(3) How much secrecy is required and what forms should it take?

(4) What safeguards against abuse are required?

(5) What, if any, are our legitimate and necessary intelligence needs?

(6) How much change, restructuring, and/or elimination of organizations are required to meet on the one hand the "legitimate" intelligence needs of our Nation, and on the other hand safeguard against abuse of people, power, and the Constitution?

(7) As our world continues its rapid changes and shifts, what level of our already limited resources do we perceive as necessary to meet our intelligence needs?

These and other questions must be discussed and debated within an atmosphere of reason. To resolve these questions and reach some consensus, it will demand the best within each of us as representatives of the people. The issues both implicitly and explicitly raised by the committee recommendations are of extreme importance and must be addressed within that context.

I oppose the committee's recommendation regarding: (A) A House Committee on Intelligence, insofar as, ". . . The committee shall have exclusive jurisdiction . . . for all covert action operations." I believe that this information should be more widely shared. Discerning oversight is facilitated by involving several relevant committees, and I think jurisdiction over covert action operations should be shared with those committees presently involved.

I am opposed to that part of the recommendation regarding: (B) Release of information (4) "The select committee recommends that the rules of the House be revised to provide that any member who reveals any classified information which jeopardizes the national security of the United States may be censored or expelled by a two-thirds vote of the House."

"National security" is now an infamous phrase, one open to mischievous interpretation. There is a great danger in constructing a chilling system which allows demagogues the easy opportunity of injuring a member by making reckless charges.

The committee's recommendation on covert action is not satisfactory. The committee recommendations say, "1. The select committee recommends that all activities involving direct or indirect attempts to assassinate any individual and all paramilitary activities shall be prohibited except in time of war."

We should prohibit all covert action.

We live in a world becoming increasingly smaller and interdependent, a world in which secrecy and cloak and dagger methods, in my estimation, are anachronisms from the past. They should have no place today in the world we will continue to live in.

It seems to me that whatever action this country takes in a world that is becoming this small and this interdependent ought to be overt action. The United States ought to begin to play an aggressive role as an advocate of peace in the world, as an advocate of humanitarian concerns, and frankly I believe that the level of secrecy that we have been exposed to as members of this committee flies in the face of democratic principle.

Many people conveniently wrap themselves quite fully in the flag, but when pressed to the wall on whether or not they are willing seriously to support democratic principles, I find that they are willing to sidestep principle.

Democracy is based on a notion of the development of a consensus. In my estimation covert action does not provide for that consensus. It does not provide for debate needed to achieve consensus. Instead, covert actions are recommended and approved by a small select group of people. The actions can at some point be extremely expensive, at some point extraordinarily risky and at some point fly in the face of open debate on any given question. I think that detrimental to the democratic process.

I am willing to try democracy. My concern is that our democracy has been, for the most part, a charade or merely symbolic, and I am not sure that many of us truly believe in the concept of majority rule.

I am concerned about secretly providing arms and aid to other countries, presidents able to sit down with other presidents and making deals. Yet these things are issues we found that are part of the range of covert actions utilized by this country.

I think our world is much too complicated to continue to function effectively in this manner. The more we get involved in covert action, the more we become accused of covert actions in places where we may not be involved at all.

So. the question is. does it really assist this country's role in the world to continue these kind of activities. My answer is no. Indeed, I think we do much more harm continuing to function covertly.

Many of these operations are well-known except to the people of the States and/or their representatives. So where does the covert rationale apply? It keeps people who are part of this society out of the decision. and it comes at a level which keeps representatives of the people out of those decisions.

I see no justification for covert operations. If we want to assist, then why not do it in the open and let the debate deal with the question of what our role "ought" to be somewhere in the world. On the basis of a consensus publicly made. then we can assist. But why do we have to play games? Why do we have to get involved?

Another related question is where have covert operations taken us? Are the nations that we have been involved with free democratic societies where the masses of people have benefits of democracy, or are those nations for the most part, military dictators, right-wing juntas, or regimes with extraordinary wealth and power in the hands of a few elitists?

If the latter holds, it totally contradicts stated principles of this country. If we have been involved in covert actions which generated democracy, freedom and justice around the world, maybe we might arrive at some different conclusion. But I don't think anyone can justify continued covert action on grounds that we foster and develop democracy around the world.

If covert action isn't banned, the committee's recommendations on covert action should be strengthened and it should be required that the Oversight Committee have preknowledge of all major covert activities.

The nature of covert actions and espionage subtract from the main responsibility of the CIA—to serve as an independent central research and analysis facility. Since active involvement in clandestine operations can force analysis to be silenced for policy needs. certain present functions of the CIA should be divided and a separate espionage (human intelligence)/clandestine operations agency be formed.

In his testimony, Dr. Ray S. Cline called for a central research and analysis facility to provide objective assessments of national security data to Congress and the National Security Council. I agree. and I believe this ought to be a separate organization. not linked to any policymaker other than the President and as free from other institutional bias as possible. Actually, research and analysis are the original functions of the CIA and are functions that the Central Intelligence Agency apparently does better than any other agency in the intelligence community. Its research and analysis functions should be facilitated.

I recommend that the Central Intelligence Agency be split into two agencies—an intelligence research and analysis agency and a second agency to conduct whatever espionage and covert action functions are authorized.

In addition, I recommend that both the new intelligence research and analysis agency and the new espionage and covert agency be independent agencies subject to all controls recommended by this Committee.

Possible violations of law by intelligence agency employees or agents should be investigated and, if required, prosecuted by the Department of Justice. No agency should have the right or capability to bar investigation or prosecution. In addition to criminal penalties there must be provision for civil liability for abuses of authority. Legislation should provide for jurisdiction, justiciability and standing, discovery, and relief.

Several other recommendations are included in my supplemental views to the report of the House Select Committee on Intelligence. Every member and the public must have access to that report.

It is imperative that the House of Representatives now consider these issues and pass legislation based on these recommendations.

RONALD V. DELLUMS.

ADDITIONAL RECOMMENDATIONS OF HON. WILLIAM LEHMAN

There is no question in my mind that the United States must have a strong, effective, professional intelligence service. Our national security depends on it.

Yet that intelligence service is but part of our Government. And, like all parts, it must be balanced against a continuing need for and our tradition of an open society, as well as this Nation's moral position throughout the world. For, if this Nation does not maintain that moral position, there is now no other country in the world who can take our place.

If I were CIA Director, I would be happy to see a strong congressional oversight committee, because it would be the most effective safeguard against wrongly conceived and wrongly motivated covert actions originating in the executive branch.

Despite allegations to the contrary, congressional investigations have not prevented the Agency from doing an effective job. Past performance bears this out; in fact, the failure of the CIA and other intelligence agencies to give adequate warning of several international crises may simply indicate the limited ability of intelligence to safeguard our national security.

There was, for example, the October 1973, Mideast war, where there was more than enough information available to warn of the impending Arab attack. There were other failures as well: the 1974 coup in Cyprus and the subsequent Turkish invasion; the Indian nuclear explosion; the Soviet invasion of Czechoslovakia; the Tet offensive in Vietnam; and the leftist coup in Portugal. All of these "failures" occurred long before any congressional committee was directed to investigate the intelligence community.

The intelligence community has operated in the past with a virtual blank check budget. This not only removes any incentive to curtail wasteful programs, but, through the very availability of funds, leads to both foolish and dangerous covert operations.

Yet, I am concerned by the committee's recommendation that a line-item figure for the CIA appear in the budget. Is it really possible to get a true and accurate figure? In the event that one of the branches of the armed services details a vessel to the CIA, is the cost of that vessel a part of the costs of intelligence? In my view, a line-item figure for the Agency must conform to principles of sound accounting practice. Only then will it have any meaning at all.

The committee hearings on the FBI documented the problem of informants turned agents-provocateur. Informants are necessary; the use of provocateurs is totally contrary to principles of decency and honesty.

One of these agents-provocateur was William Lemmer, who worked in Florida as an informant for the Bureau. Lemmer infiltrated the Vietnam Veterans Against the War and became one of the most active members of the chapter. As such, he allegedly suggested violent means of expressing VVAW disagreement with the country's Vietnam war policy. This kind of activity, directed by the Nation's foremost law enforcement agency, is plainly and starkly wrong.

THE IRS

IRS projects such as "Operation Leprechaun", "Operation Trade Winds", and "Operation Haven", clearly demonstrate that the IRS has gone far beyond its prescribed role in tax enforcement. Each of these projects involved illegalities and abuses by the intelligence division of IRS in my own State of Florida.

I would only comment here that our system is grossly misused when Federal agencies violate the law in their attempts to enforce it. To adopt the methods of criminals is to become indistinguishable from them.

RECOMMENDATIONS

I strongly support the committee's recommendation that no member of the House serve on the new oversight committee we propose for more than 6 years. Such a limitation will help to ensure that the committee's members retain their objectivity and not come to look on the intelligence community as their own private preserve.

A similar limitation should be imposed on the Directors of the CIA and FBI, so that neither is allowed to serve for so many years that he can no longer distinguish between himself and his job.

One of the committee's recommendations would require the FBI agents or informants have a judicial warrant before attempting to infiltrate any domestic group or association. I agree that this requirement is necessary to protect the rights of American citizens, but, in light of recent tragedies perpetrated by international terrorists groups, I feel that such a restriction should not be imposed when the group or association is wholly or partly made up of aliens.

SUMMARY

In comparison with other intelligence agencies, and, indeed, with Government agencies in general, I find the CIA to be highly professional and very dedicated. Despite past lack of accountability, the CIA is doing a high level, cost effective job, particularly in its intelligence gathering function.

However, there are serious deficiencies in the operation of the CIA. Much constructive rebuilding must be done if American intelligence activities are to be conducted with responsibility and integrity—and without undermining the spirit of our democratic society.

BILL LEHMAN.

A. A HOUSE COMMITTEE ON INTELLIGENCE

1. I recommend that there be formed a standing Committee on Intelligence of the House of Representatives, and that committee shall consist of members who hold the respect and confidence of the general membership of the House.

a. The membership of the standing Committee on Intelligence shall be selected from sitting members of the following House committees:

2 Members from Armed Services.
2 Members from Internal Relations.
1 Member from Science and Technology.
1 Member from Banking and Currency.
1 Member from Judiciary.
1 Member from Public Works and Transportation.
1 Member from Government Operations.
1 Member from Interstate and Foreign Commerce.
A Chairman to be nominated by the Speaker.

b. The candidates for membership on the standing Committee on Intelligence shall be nominated by resolution from the above listed committees, supplying the number of members designated above. Nominees shall then be confirmed by the Democratic caucus or the Republican conference by means of a secret ballot. Vacancies shall be filled by like action.

c. Candidate selection for service on the standing Committee on Intelligence shall be based on individual qualifications and technical expertise, rather than party affiliation, except that, the total membership of the standing Committee on Intelligence must always have no less than one-third of its total members from each of the major parties. Should the occasion arise when a Major Party does not have one-third of its members represented on the committee, the Speaker shall designate to the nominating committee or committees the necessary number of partisan candidates to be selected.

B. RELEASE OF INFORMATION

1. I recommend that the standing Committee on Intelligence, or any member of the committee, shall not directly or indirectly release any information, documents or data bearing a security classification unless and until the following sequential procedures have been completed:

(a) The committee passes a resolution expressing the need and reason for declassification.

(b) The appropriate administrative agency has been allowed reasonable time to agree with the declassification or to present reasons for opposition.

(c) A House Leadership Committee, consisting of the Speaker, the Majority Leader, the Minority Leader, the Majority and Minority Whips and the chairmen of the committees from which the Intelligence Committee Membership has been selected (a majority of the total being present), shall approve or disapprove of the declassification and release.

(d) Notwithstanding the committee's approval or disapproval, any committee member who disagrees shall have a right to petition individual members of the Leadership Committee. If three or more members of the Leadership Committee shall concur, said member shall have a right to be heard by the full Leadership Committee.

(e) Any Intelligence Committee member who shall release any materials, documents, or data bearing a security classification, without complying with the above provisions shall be subject to expulsion from the House of Representatives and shall be subject to appropriate criminal or civil action, notwithstanding legislative immunity.

2. a. Any member of the House having knowledge of classified materials, documents or data who shall release such material, documents or data without obtaining the approval of a majority of the members of the Leadership Committee shall be subject to expulsion from the House of Representatives and shall be subject to any appropriate criminal or civil actions, notwithstanding legislative immunity.

C. PENALTIES FOR IMPROPER RELEASE OF CLASSIFIED INFORMATION

I recommend that the United States Code be amended to provide criminal sanctions against any person who shall disclose or reveal properly classified information, documents, data, or plans concerning the national security of the United States, such sanctions to apply regardless of intent to harm the United States or to aid a foreign nation, notwithstanding legislative immunity.

DALE MILFORD.

RECOMMENDATION OF HON. MORGAN F. MURPHY

In light of the investigation by the House Select Committee on Intelligence, I recommend that Congress enact legislation or amend existing legislation to protect the confidentiality of tax records of American citizens.

Section 6103 of the Internal Revenue Code refers to tax returns as "public records" but specifies that they be "open to inspection only upon order of the President and under rules and regulations prescribed by the Secretary or his delegate and approved by the President."

Public use and abuse of the records, however, have been more the rule than the exception in the recent past. There has been little emphasis on the need for protecting the confidentiality of tax records.

I recommend a shift in emphasis back to the basic right of taxpayers to privacy regarding their tax affairs. We must do more than limit disclosures to certain agencies, individuals, congressional committees, and States. We must require the entity seeking tax information to prove that such information is essential to the entity's function and further, that the tax information cannot otherwise be acquired. I suggest that House and Senate committees with jurisdiction act with all deliberate speed to finalize their work on legislation to better ensure the privacy of tax records.

MORGAN F. MURPHY.

ADDITIONAL RECOMMENDATION OF HON. JAMES V. STANTON

I would go beyond recommendation N of the select committee, which proposes that the Assistant to the President for National Security Affairs be prohibited from holding any Cabinet-level position, by recommending the enactment of legislation which (1) states that the individual who holds this position cannot hold any other office in the Federal Government, nor may he be a member of the Armed Forces, (2) requires Senate confirmation of this position, and (3) in order to achieve these purposes, establishes statutorily the position of Special Assistant to the President for National Security Affairs. I have introduced a bill, H.R. 10754, which embodies these provisions.

JAMES V. STANTON.

ALTERNATIVE RECOMMENDATIONS OF HON. ROBERT McCLORY

I support the recommendations contained in the majority report under headings: D, F, G, I, J, L, N, O, Q, R, and S (with the exception of section 1). I do not approve of the other recommendations and I offer the following alternative recommendations in those areas in which I believe reform is necessary and appropriate.

ALTERNATIVE RECOMMENDATIONS OF HON. ROBERT McCORY

I recommend that there be established a permanent standing Committee on Intelligence of the House of Representatives.

1. The committee shall consist of five members composed of one member from each of the following committees: (a) Appropriations, (b) Armed Services, (c) International Relations, (d) Judiciary, and (e) Government Operations; no more than three of whom shall be members of the same political party. The committee membership should reflect a broad representation of political and philosophical views.

2. No member of the committee may serve more than 3 consecutive terms on the committee, and no member of the staff may serve more than 6 consecutive years.

3. Any past or current member of the committee staff who shall release, without authorization of the committee, materials or information obtained by the committee shall be immediately terminated from employment and shall be fully subject to criminal and civil liability, notwithstanding legislative immunity.

4. The committee's jurisdiction shall include all legislative and oversight functions relating to all U.S. agencies and departments engaged in foreign or domestic intelligence activities. The committee shall have exclusive jurisdiction for budget authorization for all intelligence activities and exclusive jurisdiction for all covert action operations. All remaining oversight functions may be concurrent with other committees of the House.

5. The committee shall be vested with subpoena power, and the rules of the House should be amended to give the committee the right to enforce its subpoenas through a civil contempt proceeding in the U.S. District Court for the District of Columbia without specific authorization from the full House.

B. RELEASE OF INFORMATION

1. I recommend that the House Committee on Intelligence have the right to release any classified information or documents in its possession or control only if the following procedures are adhered to:

(a) the committee shall have the duty to consult with other agencies of the Government within the intelligence community or the executive branch with respect to the public disclosure of any classified information before any formal committee vote on release.

(*b*) After such consultation, the committee may, by an affirmative vote of a majority of the members, submit the material proposed to be released to the President.

(*c*) If within a reasonable period of time the President certifies in writing that the disclosure of the material would be detrimental to the national security of the United States, the material would not be disclosed or released. Failing any such Presidential certification, the committee would be able to release the material.

(*d*) In the event of such a certification by the President, the committee shall be given standing to sue and the U.S. District Court for the District of Columbia shall be given jurisdiction over such disputes, so that the matter can be submitted to the courts for judicial determination.

C. COVERT ACTION

1. I recommend that all activities involving direct or indirect attempts to assassinate any individual be prohibited by law except in time of war.

2. I recommend that appropriate legislation be enacted to require prior approval by the House Committee on Intelligence for all military and paramilitary covert actions proposed by the U.S. Government, including those actions in which arms or funds for arms would be provided covertly.

3. I recommend that, as to all other covert actions of a significant size or involving significant risk, the Director of Central Intelligence be required, within 48 hours of initial implementation, to notify the committee in writing and in detail of the nature, extent, purpose, risk and costs of the operation.

D. IMPROVED SECURITY FOR CLASSIFIED INFORMATION IN THE HOUSE

1. I recommend that the Rules of the House be revised to provide that any member who violates the confidentiality of any executive session of any House committee may be censured or expelled by a two-thirds vote of the House.

2. I recommend that the rules of the House be amended to provide that any committee of the House which has access to classified information has the authority to discipline any member which it reasonably believes has disclosed or publicized such information in violation of the rules of confidentiality duly adopted by such committee. These committees ought to be delegated authority by the full House to take appropriate disciplinary action against such a member to ensure compliance with the rules of confidentiality. Appropriate disciplinary action could be taken only after a vote of a majority of the majority members and a majority of the minority members of the committee; and any member against whom such disciplinary action is taken shall have a right of appeal to the full House.

E. GAO AUDIT AUTHORITY

I recommend that the General Accounting Office be empowered to conduct full and complete financial audits of all intelligence agencies. There should not be any limitation on GAO access in the performance of these functions by any classification system, and the financial audit function of GAO should specifically apply to those funds which currently may be expended on certification of a Director of an agency alone.

F. DETAILEES

I recommend that intelligence agencies disclose the affiliation of their employees on detail to other Government agencies or departments to the heads of such agencies; and that detailees not be placed in any position in which an actual or apparent conflict of interest might exist.

ROBERT McCLORY.

———

DISSENTING AND ADDITIONAL RECOMMENDATIONS OF HON. DAVID C. TREEN

(To the Recommendations of the House Select Committee on Intelligence)

The following are my specific recommendations (on the subjects which they concern) which may differ, vary or coincide with recommendations on similar subjects by the majority. The absence of any recommendation on a subject covered by the majority is not to be construed as concurrence or nonconcurrence with the majority recommendation.

Recommendation No. 1: Joint Oversight Committee

I recommend that there be established a Joint Congressional Committee on Foreign Intelligence which committee shall have oversight and legislative authority with respect to all foreign intelligence activities.

(a) The joint committee shall consist of no more than 14 members, equally divided between the House and Senate. The committees of the House and Senate having jurisdiction over international affairs, armed services, and defense appropriations shall each be entitled to representation on the joint committee by at least one member of those committees.

(b) Membership on the joint committee shall be limited to a period of 6 years and, beginning with the fifth year, at least one-third of the committee membership shall consist of new members.

(c) Any past or current member of the joint committee staff who shall release, without proper authorization, materials or information obtained by the joint committee shall be immediately terminated from employment and shall be fully subject to criminal and civil action, not withstanding any plea of legislative immunity.

(d) The joint committee shall be vested with subpoena power, and the rules of the House shall be amended to give the joint committee the right to enforce its subpoenas through a civil contempt proceeding in the U.S. District Court for the District of Columbia without specific authorization from the full House.

Recommendation No. 2: Obligations of the Executive Branch

I recommend that the executive branch be required to keep the joint committee promptly and fully informed as to all intelligence activities, including covert actions, and including full disclosure of allocations wherever they may be in the budget with regard to foreign intelligence and all expenditures of funds by all departments and agencies of the executive branch for foreign intelligence and covert activities.

Recommendation No. 3: Access to and Release of Classified Information

I recommend that the rules of the House and Senate, where necessary, be conformed to accommodate the following recommendations, and that, where necessary, legislation be enacted in aid thereof:

(*a*) Access to information and materials furnished to the joint committee in executive session or classified secret by the executive branch shall not be accessible to other members of Congress except upon a resolution permitting such access adopted by a two-thirds vote of the membership of both the House and Senate Members, voting in person and not by proxy.

(*b*) Prior to any action to permit access of such information to other Members of Congress, the executive branch shall be given reasonable opportunity to testify and present evidence in executive session regarding the proposed action.

(*c*) Materials and information received from the executive branch in executive session of the joint committee or otherwise classified secret by the executive branch may be publicly released only upon adoption of the resolution specified in subparagraph (a) above and upon the adoption of a resolution permitting public disclosure adopted by a two-thirds vote of the membership of both the House and Senate, the debate on which shall be conducted in secret session, and the vote on which shall be in open session by recorded vote.

(*d*) Any Member of Congress who reveals any information in violation of the foregoing procedures may be censured or expelled by a two-third vote of the House or the Senate, as the case may be.

Recommendation No. 4: Agreements for the Handling of Classified Information

I recommend that any information furnished to the joint committee by the executive branch under an agreement with the joint committee for the handling of such information shall be binding in accordance with the terms of that agreement on the joint committee, on the House and Senate, and on each Member of Congress. Violation of the terms of the agreement shall be grounds for censure or expulsion by a two-thirds vote of the House or Senate, as the case may be.

Recommendation No. 5: Director of Central Intelligence

I recommend that a Director of Central Intelligence shall be established, separate from any of the operating intelligence agencies, for the purpose of coordinating and overseeing the foreign intelligence community. His purpose shall be to eliminate duplication in collection and promote competition in analysis.

(a) The DCI shall be appointed by the President with the advice and consent of the Senate.

(b) The DCI shall be the chief foreign intelligence officer of the United States, and shall be responsible for the supervision and control of all agencies of the United States engaged in foreign intelligence.

(c) The DCI shall be a member of the National Security Council.

274

(d) The DCI may not hold any other position, office or title in the U.S. Government.

(e) The DCI shall, along with such other duties, constitute an office of Inspector General for all of the foreign intelligence agencies, including all agencies of Government which have foreign intelligence functions. Such agency shall have the obligation to report all allegations of misconduct and/or unlawful activities to the DCI.

(f) The DCI shall be responsible for the national intelligence estimates and daily briefings of the President.

(g) The DCI shall be responsible for reporting to the Joint Committee on Intelligence and other appropriate committees of Congress.

(h) All budget requests which include funds for foreign intelligence or covert activities shall, insofar as such funds are concerned, be prepared in consultation with the DCI. Although the funds for foreign intelligence activities will continue to be budgeted in the respective agency budgets, the DCI shall be responsible to the joint committee for full reporting on the foreign intelligence and covert activities funding set forth in all agency budgets.

(i) The DCI shall coordinate the functions of all foreign intelligence agencies under his jurisdiction, shall eliminate unnecessary duplication, conduct periodic evaluation of the performance and efficiency of the agencies, and report to Congress on the foregoing at least annually.

Recommendation No. 6: Disclosures to Congress

I recommend that existing law (Sec. 102(d)3 of the National Security Act of 1947) which restricts officials of the executive branch from providing information be amended to specifically exclude from any such prohibition all committees of Congress having appropriate jurisdiction.

Recommendation No. 7: Assistant for National Security Affairs

I recommend that the Assistant to the President for National Security Affairs be prohibited from holding any other position, office or title in the U.S. Government.

Recommendation No. 8: News Media and Publications

(1) I recommend that U.S. foreign intelligence agencies be prohibited from covertly providing money or other valuable consideration to employees or full-time representatives of any journal or electronic media with general circulation in the United States, and prohibited from utilizing such individuals for purposes of cover; except that such prohibition shall not apply to the occasional or casual furnisher of news stories or articles to the news media.

(2) I recommend that the U.S. intelligence agencies be prohibited from the covert publication of books, articles or stories in any journals or electronic media with general circulation in the United States.

Recommendation No. 9: Classification

I recommend that the classification and declassification of information be the subject of specific legislation by the Congress.

Recommendation No. 10: Director of the FBI

I recommend that the Director of the FBI have a term of office of 5 years and that no director serve more than two 5-year terms.

Recommendation No. 11: Infiltration of Groups or Associations

I recommend that judicial warrant must issue, on probable cause, before an informant or any other agent of the FBI may infiltrate any domestic group or association, when (1) investigation of such group or association or its members is based solely on title 18 U.S.C. sec. 2383, 2384, 2385, and (2) there is no credible evidence that such group or association, or any person connected therewith has encouraged, advocated or suggested the use of violence, terrorists activities or other unlawful activity.

Recommendation No. 12: Study of Intelligence Operations of Foreign Nations

I recommend that the Joint Congressional Committee on Intelligence (or, in the absence of the creation of such a committee, the appropriate congressional committee or committees) promptly commence a detailed investigation and study of the intelligence operations of foreign nations, including, but not limited to the intelligence operations of the U.S.S.R. and the Peoples Republic of China, which investigation and inquiry shall include, but not be limited to, the following:

(a) The means by which intelligence is gathered relating to activities of the United States and its allies, both within and outside of the United States.

(b) The extent of valuable and/or critical intelligence information gathered by foreign nations from publicly available journals and documents.

(c) The methods employed by and the extent of success of foreign nations in the recruitment of American or allied nationals in espionage activities, and the methods employed by and the extent of success of foreign nations in infiltrating the U.S. Government or U.S. organizations, corporations, associations and groups.

DAVID C. TREEN.

ALTERNATIVE RECOMMENDATIONS OF HON. ROBERT W. KASTEN, JR.

INTRODUCTION

Although I wholeheartedly support many of the recommendations proposed by the committee's majority, the majority proposals collectively do not accurately reflect my judgments concerning the reforms and improvements which should be made in the U.S. intelligence community.

To indicate specific points of agreement and disagreement, I have reproduced below the majority recommendations together with my own alternative or additional proposals. Language in the majority report with which I disagree has been stricken out; my alternative or additional language has been underscored.* In several instances, I have also added brief comments in brackets following the recommendation to which the comments refer.

A. A HOUSE COMMITTEE ON INTELLIGENCE

1. The select committee recommends that there be formed a [standing] *Joint* Committee on Intelligence of the House of Representatives *and the Senate.*

a. The committee membership should reflect a broad representation of political and philosophical views.

------

* GPO style, set in italic type.

276

b. The committee should consist of not more than 13 or less than nine members, designated by *the President pro tem of the Senate and* the Speaker of the House in consultation with the minority leader of *each House. The majority shall have one more than one-half of the members appointed from either House.*

c. No Member of the committee may serve more than 3 consecutive terms on the committee, and no member of the staff may serve more than 6 years.

d. Any past or current member of the committee staff who shall release, without authorization of the committee, materials or information obtained by the committee shall be immediately terminated from employment and shall be fully subject to criminal and civil action, notwithstanding legislative immunity.

e. The committee shall be vested with subpoena power and shall have the right to enforce by a proceeding for civil contempt its subpoenas in the U.S. District Court for the District of Columbia or any other court of competent jurisdiction, [without authorization] *if authorized* [from the House, provided the committee has so designated] by resolution. The committee staff shall be given statutory standing to represent the committee in any proceeding arising from the issuance of a subpoena.

f. The committee's jurisdiction shall include all legislative and oversight functions relating to all U.S. agencies and departments engaged in foreign or domestic intelligence. The committee shall have exclusive jurisdiction for budget authorization for all intelligence activities and exclusive jurisdiction for all covert action operations. All remaining oversight functions may be concurrent with other committees.

[NOTE: I am opposed to the creation of two oversight committees on intelligence: one in the House and one in the Senate. I favor instead the creation of a joint committee because it will reduce the burden on the DCI and intelligence officials of repeating testimony before committees with similar jurisdiction and also reduce the burden of Congress by having many members assigned to tasks which are duplicative. In addition, concentration of oversight in one joint committee would reduce the possibility of unauthorized disclosure of information and more importantly would help assure that problems would not "fall between two chairs" and be addressed by neither committee. The fact that each appropriations committee would have an oversight function reduces the possibility that one joint committee would be co-opted by the intelligency agency.]

B. RELEASE OF INFORMATION

1. The select committee recommends that rule XI.2 (e) (2) of the House Rules is amended to read as follows:

"Each committee shall keep a complete record of all committee action which shall include a copy of all reports, statements, and testimony of witnesses whether received in open or in executive session."

[2. The Committee shall have the right to release any information or documents in its possession or control by a vote of a majority of the Members of the Committee under such terms and conditions as the committee shall deem advisable. The Committee, in making the decision whether or not to release such information, shall have the right, but not the duty, to consult with other agencies of the government within the intelligence community or executive branch with regard to any decision relating to the release of such heretofore secret information.]

2. (a) *The Joint Committee on Intelligence may disclose any information upon the committee's determination that the national interest would be served by such disclosure. In any case in which such committee decides to disclose any information requested to be kept secret by the President, such committee shall notify the President to that effect. Such committee may not disclose such information until the expiration of 10 days following the day on which notice is transmitted to the President. If (1) prior to disclosure of such information the President submits a written certification to the Senate and the House through such committee stating his opinion, and the reasons therefor, that the threat to national security posed by such disclosure outweighs any public interest in disclosure and that the question of disclosure is of such importance to the vital interests of the United States that it requires a decision by the full Senate and the House of Representatives and (2) after receipt of a certification by the President made pursuant to this subsection, the Joint Committee on Intelligence decides to refer the question of disclosure of such information to the Senate and the House of Representatives, such information may not be disclosed unless the Senate and the House of Representatives agree to a resolution approving the disclosure of such information, or the Senate and the House of Representatives agree to a resolution referring the matter to the Joint Committee on Intelligence for final disposition and the Joint Committee on Intelligence thereafter approves the disclosure of such information.*

(b) *Any question referred to the Senate and the House of Representatives by the Joint Committee on Intelligence pursuant to subsection (a) shall be disposed by the Senate and the House of Representatives by a vote on such question within 3 calendar days following the day on which the question is reported to the Senate and the House of Representatives excluding days on which the Senate and the House of Representatives are not in session.*

[3. In the event of a negative vote by the Committee on the release of certain classified information, a Member of the Committee may apprise the other Members of the House that the Committee possesses information which he believes ought to be made public. Other Members of the House would then be authorized to have access to that information, provided they sign an agreement not to divulge the information. If these other Members agree that this information ought to be made public, they will sign a petition attesting to that. Upon obtaining the signatures of one-fifth of the House, the House shall convene in secret session for the purpose of advising the entire Membership of the House of that information. The House may then vote to release the information to the public.]

3. [4.] The select committee recommends that the rules of the House be revised to provide that any member who reveals any classified information which jeopardizes the national security of the United States may be censured or expelled by a two-thirds vote of the House.

C. COVERT ACTION

1. The select committee recommends that all activities involving direct or indirect attempts to assassinate any individual [and all

paramilitary activities] shall be prohibited except in time of war.

2. The select committee recommends that as to other covert action by any U.S. intelligence component, the following shall be required within 48 hours of [initial] approval *by the President.*

a. The Director of Central Intelligence shall notify the *joint* committee in writing, stating in detail the nature, extent, purpose, risks, likelihood of success, and costs of the operation.

[b. The President shall certify in writing to the Committee that such covert action operation is required to protect the national security of the United States.]

[c.] *b.* The committee shall be provided with duplicate originals of the written recommendations of each member of the 40 Committee or its successor.

3. *Reports on all* covert action operations shall be [terminated no later than 12 months from the date of affirmative recommendation by the 40 Committee or its successor.] *submitted every 6 months by the DCI, or as requested, to the joint committee.*

D. NSA

[1. The Select Committee recommends that the existence of the National Security Agency should be recognized by specific legislation and that such legislation provide for civilian control of NSA. Further, it is recommended that such legislation specifically define the role of NSA with reference to the monitoring of communications of Americans.]

1. The Director and the Deputy Director of the NSA shall be appointed by the President and confirmed by the Senate.

[E. DISCLOSURE OF BUDGET TOTALS]

[1. The Select Committee recommends that all intelligence related items be included as intelligence expenditures in the President's budget, and that there be disclosure of the total single sum budgeted for each agency involved in intelligence, or if such an item is a part or portion of the budget of another agency or department that it be separately identified as a single item.]

[F.] *F.* PROHIBITION OF FUND TRANSFERS

1. The select committee recommends there be appropriate legislation to prohibit any significant transfer of funds between agencies or departments in connection with intelligence activities.

2. The select committee recommends there be appropriate legislation to prohibit any significant reprogramming of funds within agencies or departments in connection with intelligence activities without the specific approval of the Intelligence Committee and appropriate committees of Congress.

3. The select committee recommends there be appropriate legislation to prohibit any significant expenditures of reserve or contingency funds in connection with intelligence activities without specific approval of the Inteligence Committee and appropriate committees of Congress.

1. The select committee recommends that a Director of Central Intelligence shall be created, separate from any of the operating or analytic intelligence agencies for the purpose of coordinating and overseeing the entire foreign intelligence community with a view to eliminating duplication in collection and promoting competition in analysis. The DCI shall be nominated by the President with the advice and consent of the Senate. This office shall have the following powers and duties:

a. The DCI shall be the chief foreign intelligence officer of the United States, and shall be responsible for the supervision and control of all agencies of the United States engaged in foreign intelligence, *including FBI counterintelligence.*

【b. The DCI shall be a Member of the National Security Council.】

【c.】 *b.* The DCI may not hold a position or title with respect to any other agencies of government.

【c. *d.* The DCI shall, along with such other duties, constitute an Office of Inspector General for all of the foreign intelligence agencies, including other agencies of government or branches of the military which have foreign intelligence functions. Such agencies shall have the obligation to report all instances of misconduct to the DCI. This shall not constitute a limitation upon the respective agencies reporting to the DCI from maintaining their own Inspector General staff or similar body.】

d. The DCI shall have an adequate staff for the purposes expressed herein and be responsible for the national intelligence estimates and daily briefings of the President.

e. The DCI shall be responsible for the preparation of the national intelligence estimates and such reports shall be immediately supplied to the appropriate committees of Congress on request.

f. All budget requests shall be prepared by the agencies under the jurisdiction of the DCI. As to those parts of budget of the military services or components of Department of Defense, they shall be submitted as an independent part of such budgets to the DCI.

g. The DCI shall be charged with the functions of coordinating foreign intelligence agencies under its jurisdiction, the elimination of duplication, the periodic evaluation of the performance and efficiency of the agencies in question, and shall report to Congress on the foregoing at least annually.

h. The DCI shall conduct a comprehensive inquiry into the causes of intelligence failures, including: inadequate collection tasking; analytical bias; duplication; unusable technical output; excessive compartmentation; and withholding of information by senior officials, and report to the Committee on Intelligence within 1 year.

i. The President's Foreign Intelligence Advisory Board (PFIAB) should be created by statute as an oversight and advisory board whose mission would be to oversee and advise on the direction, guidance and control of the intelligence community through the authority of the DCI who would also serve as chairman of the PFIAB.

The DCI would have overall authority and responsibility for making recommendations to the National Security Council on any intelligence related matter. 50 U.S.C. sec. 403(d)(1)(2) would be deleted from the statutory authority of the CIA and transferred to the DCI as chairman of the PFIAB:

(d) *For the purpose of coordinating the intelligence activities of the several Government departments and agencies in the interest of national security, it shall be the duty of the DCI under direction of the National Security Council—*

(1) to advise the National Security Council in matters concerning such intelligence activities of the Government departments and agencies as relate to national security;

(2) to make recommendations to the National Security Council for the coordination of such intelligence activities of the departments and agencies of the Government as related to the national security.

[NOTE: In essence, the PFIAB Chairman/DCI would become the Nation's principal foreign intelligence officer, with authority over intelligence community budgets and resources, with independence from CIA institutional affiliation, and with right of direct access to the President as well as being statutory advisor to the National Security Council.

The President's Foreign Intelligence Advisory Board—a prestigious board of private citizens acting in coordinated capacity with their chairman, the DCI, would enable the nation to benefit from the exceptional knowledge and experience of its private citizens who would exercise both an oversight and advisory role on sensitive intelligence matters.]

[H.] *G.* FULL GAO AUDIT AUTHORITY

1. The select committee recommends that the General Accounting Office be empowered to conduct a full and complete management as well as financial audit of all intelligence agencies. There shall be no limitation on the GAO in the performance of these functions by an executive classification system, and the audit function of GAO shall specifically apply to those funds which presently may be expended on certification of a Director of an agency alone.

[I. INTERNAL FINANCIAL MANAGEMENT]

[1. The Select Committee recommends that the CIA internal audit staff be increased and given complete access to CIA financial records, and that overseas stations be audited at least annually.] It is further recommended that all proprietary and procurement mechanisms be subjected to annual comprehensive review, by the [CIA's internal audit staff.] *GAO.*

[J.] *II.* FULL DISCLOSURE TO CONGRESS

1. The select committee recommends that existing legislation (National Security Act of 1947, sec. 102(d)(3)) restricting the Directors and heads of foreign intelligence agencies from providing full information to Congress should be amended to exclude [Committees of Congress having appropriate jurisdiction.] *the Joint Committee on intelligence; Provided that they, in accordance with the DCI's statutory duty to protect sources and methods, could withhold the names of agents, sources and methods of intelligence from such committee.*

281

1. The select committee recommends that the National Security Act of 1947 be amended to provide for the establishment of a permanent Foreign Operations Subcommittee of the National Security Council. The subcommittee's jurisdiction, function and composition shall be as follows:

[a. The Subcommittee shall have jurisdiction over all authorized activities of U.S. foreign intelligence agencies except those solely related to the gathering of intelligence.**]**

b. The subcommittee shall advise the President on all proposed covert or clandestine **[**activities**]** *operations* and on hazardous collecting activities.

c. Each member of the subcommittee shall be required **[**by law**]** to submit his individual assessments of each proposal to the President in writing. The assessment should cover such matters a the likelihood of success, the benefits of success, the damage resulting from failure or exposure, the risks against the potential benefits and alternate ways of accomplishing the goal.

d. The subcommittee shall be chaired by the Assistant to the President for National Security Affairs and shall be composed of:

> Assistant to the President for National Security Affairs;
> Director of Central Intelligence;
> Secretary of State;
> Secretary of Defense;
> Deputy Director for Intelligence of CIA;
> Chairman of the Joint Chiefs of Staff;
> **[**The ambassador(s), if there is one, and**]**
> *The* assistant secretaries of state for the **[**affected countries and areas.**]** *region affected.*

1. The select committee recommends that the Defense Intelligence Agency be abolished and that its functions be transferred to **[**the Assistant Secretary of Defense for Intelligence and the CIA.**]** *J–2 of the Joint Chiefs of Staff.*

1. The select committee recommends that intelligence agencies disclose the affiliation of employees on detail to other government agencies or departments to all immediate colleagues and superiors *and to the director of such department or agency.*

1. The select committee recommends that the Assistant to the President for National Security Affairs be prohibited from holding any cabinet-level position.

1. The select committee recommends that no agency of the United States engaged principally in foreign or military intelligence, directly

or indirectly engage in the training or the supplying of domestic police agencies of the United States, and that contacts between police agencies of the United States and U.S. foreign or military intelligence agencies be limited to those circumstances which shall be required on account of internal security or the normal requirements and functions of such police agencies.

[P.] *N.* MEDIA, [RELIGION, AND EDUCATION]

1. The select committee recommends that U.S. intelligence agencies not covertly provide money or other valuable consideration [to persons associated with religious or educational institutions, or] to employees or representatives of any journal or electronic media with general circulation in the United States or use such institutions or individuals for purposes of cover. The foregoing prohibitions are intended to apply to American citizens and institutions.

2. The select committee further recommends that U.S. intelligence agencies not covertly publish books *or articles* or plant [or suppress] stories in any journals or electronic media with general circulation in the United States.

3. In the event that an employee of an intelligence agency publishes a book or article he shall be identified in the publication as an employee of such agency.

[Q. RESTRICTIONS ON MILITARY INTELLIGENCE]

[1. The Select Committee recommends that the intellgence components of the Armed Services of the United States be prohibited from engaging in covert action within the United States. It is further recommended that clandestine activities against non-military United States citizens abroad be proscribed.]

[R.] *O.* CLASSIFICATION

1. The select committee recommends that the classification of information be the subject of the enactment of specific legislation; and further, as an adjunct to such legislation there by provided a method of regular declassification.

[S.] *P.* INSPECTOR GENERAL FOR INTELLIGENCE

1. The select committee recommends the establishment of an independent Office of the Inspector General for Intelligence, who shall have full authority to investigate any possible or potential misconduct on the part of the various intelligence agencies or the personnel therein. The IGI shall be appointed by the President, with the approval of the Senate, for a term of 10 years and shall not be permitted to succeed himself. The IGI shall have full access on demand to all records and personnel of the intelligence agencies for the purpose of pursuing his investigations. He shall make an annual report to the Congress of his activities and make such additional reports to the intelligence committees or other appropriate oversight committees as he may choose or the committees may direct.

[T. DOMESTIC]

[1. The Select Committee recommends that judicial warrant must issue, on probable cause, before an informant or any other agent of the FBI may infiltrate any domestic group or association, when investigation of such group or association or its members is based solely on title 18 U.S.C. § 2383, 2384, 2385.

[2. The select committee recommends that the Director of the FBI have a term of office no longer than 2 presidential terms.

[3. The select committee recommends that the Internal Security Branch of the Intelligence Division be abolished and that the Counter-Intelligence Branch be reorganized to constitute a full division named the Counter-Intelligence Division; that the mission of this division be limited to investigating and countering the efforts of foreign directed groups and individuals against the United States.

[4. The select committee recommends the transfer of all investigations of alleged criminal activity by domestic groups or individual members thereof to the General Investigative Division.

[5. The select committee recommends that regulations be promulgated that tie the investigation of activities of terrorist groups closely to specific violations of criminal law within the investigative jurisdiction of the FBI and that charge the Department of Justice with determining when a domestic political action group may be appropriately targeted for investigation of terrorist activities.]

CONCLUSION

As these recommendations indicate, my service on the select committee has convinced me that reforms are necessary to improve the organization, performance, and control of the U.S. intelligence community. At the same time, the experience of the past months has again confirmed my understanding of how important an effective intelligence capability is to the future security of the American people. Intelligence officials can and must operate in a manner consistent with the individual rights and liberties guaranteed by the Constitution. These protections must be guaranteed, but so must the right of the American people to live in security and peace. It is both possible and essential for the intelligence agencies to perform their responsibilities effectively, and by means which protect both individual rights and national security.

At a minimum, the intelligence community must regain the trust and confidence of the people whom it serves. It is tragic that it was necessary to establish this committee to inquire into the activities of agencies on which we depend so heavily for our security. But it would be even more tragic if the results of our investigation were now to be ignored. Implementing the recommendations I have proposed will contribute significantly to ensuring that there will be no need for another such committee to be established in the future. Both Congress and the American people must recognize the need to complete the task which we have only begun.

ROBERT W. KASTEN, Jr.

O